Manufacture in town and country
before the factory

Manufacture in town and country before the factory

Edited by

MAXINE BERG,

PAT HUDSON and MICHAEL SONENSCHER

CAMBRIDGE UNIV

Cambri

London   New York

Melbourne

Published by the Press Syndicate of the University of Cambridge
The Pitt Building, Trumpington Street, Cambridge CB2 1RP
32 East 57th Street, New York, NY 10022, USA
296 Beaconsfield Parade, Middle Park, Melbourne 3206, Australia

First published 1983

Printed in Great Britain at
the University Press, Cambridge

Library of Congress catalogue card number: 83–1842

British Library Cataloguing in Publication Data

Manufacture in town and country before the factory.
1. Europe – Industries – History
I. Berg, Maxine   II. Hudson, Pat
III. Sonenscher, Michael
338'.094   HC240.I52

ISBN   0 521 24820 5

TM

Contents

PART II 'WORK' AND 'WAGES'

Illustrations

Map

Acknowledgements

This collection of essays is based on the SSRC Conference on Manufacture in Town and Country before the Factory organised by Maxine Berg, Pat Hudson and Michael Sonenscher, held in Balliol College, Oxford, in September 1980. We would like to thank the SSRC Economic and Social History Committee for funding that conference, and we are particularly grateful to all who attended the conference for contributing to a very stimulating discussion. The revisions of some of the papers included in this collection, and some of the points made in the introduction, owe a great deal to the discussion at this conference. We are grateful to Peter Mathias for the encouragement and practical assistance he gave towards organising our project. We are indebted to the secretaries of the Warwick University Economics Department who carried the bulk of the paperwork and typing for the conference, and later for the book. Rachel Norman translated Jürgen Schlumbohm's contribution, and the Institut für Sozialgeschichte gave us permission to translate and print a revised version of his 'Der saisonale Rhythmus der Leinenproduktion im Osnabrücker Lande während des späten 18. und der ersten Hälfte des 19. Jahrhunderts', which was first published in *Archiv für Sozialgeschichte*. William Davies and his colleagues saw our book through the Press with great care and patience.

1

Manufacture in town and country before the factory

MAXINE BERG, PAT HUDSON AND
MICHAEL SONENSCHER

Well before the advent of the factory system, wealth in Europe was visible in the form of an immense accumulation of commodities. Richard Steele's engagingly exotic 'Fashionable Inventory', published in *The Tatler* in 1711, presented a range of items–from a 'musk coloured velvet mantle lined with squirrel skins' and a 'silver cheese toaster', to 'seven cakes of superfine Spanish wool, half a dozen of Portugal dishes and a quire of paper from thence' – whose rich detail testifies to the magnitude and diversity of the world of goods available for opulent consumption in metropolitan society in the age of manufacture. Defoe in 1726 described the immense extent of England's inland trade which 'extended in every part of the island'. Almost every manufacturing county of England was employed in making the various components of a suit of clothes consisting of a coat of woollen cloth that came from Yorkshire, a waistcoat of cullamancoe from Norwich, breeches of strong drugget from Devizes and Wiltshire, stockings of yarn from Westmorland, a hat of felt from Leicestershire, gloves of leather from Somerset, shoes from Northampton, buttons from Macclesfield or, if metal, from Birmingham, garters from Manchester, and a shirt of handmade linen from Lancashire or Scotland.[1] How was this wide range and quality of goods made? How was the work of those who produced them perceived and lived? What *was* manufacture without machines? Surprisingly, adequate answers to these questions are likely to be hesitant and tentative.

In many respects, current understanding of manufacture before the advent of factory production is not all that different from the excellent but brief characterisation produced nearly thirty years ago by T. S. Ashton.[2] With a few

1 L. E. Steele (ed.), *The Essays of Richard Steele* (London, 1945), pp. 183–6. The phrase 'the world of goods' is, of course, derived from Mary Douglas and B. Isherwood, *The World of Goods: Towards an Anthropology of Consumption* (London, 1979). Daniel Defoe, *The Complete English Tradesman* (London, 1726), I, 401.
2 T. S. Ashton, *An Economic History of England: The Eighteenth Century* (London, 1955), Ch. VII.

qualifications, his description of the organisation of work in the eighteenth-century English economy remains sufficiently familiar to stand as a model of the general features of manufacture before the advent of mechanised production. Underemployment was the 'normal' condition of labour in town and country; work was irregular and indebtedness the natural result. 'Casual' methods of earning naturally engendered 'casual' habits of living: leisure preference was almost universal. In many trades and branches of manufacture there was a tradition that workers would have a share in the product of their labour. Thus the line separating 'established rights' from 'barefaced robbery' was difficult to draw; there was a close connection between 'long pay' and the embezzlement of materials. The great diversity, both in form and in amount, of workers' payments reflected the fact that it was 'hardly possible to speak of a regional let alone a national market for labour'.

The combination of customary payments, perquisites, irregularity of employment and partially monetised wage systems which Ashton described was indicative of a society in which the medium of exchange was still closely bound to the nature of the direct product of labour and the direct needs of those engaged in production. Money, in other words, mediated many transactions to a limited extent. In this situation, where the social power of the medium of exchange was limited, the power of different kinds of community – trade, family, confraternity, regional or religious affiliation – which might have bound individuals together was the greater. This much is a truism.[3] The implications of that truism are very much more difficult to define.

It is easier to define the development of the system of production before the factory by itemising what was *not* to be found there than it is to understand how that system worked in its own terms. How did the power of the different kinds of 'community' function to ensure that work was carried out? How did these communities establish some degree of continuity in the relationships between those engaged in production – merchants and masters, masters and journeymen, men and women, apprentices and journeymen, adults and children? How, in

3   More recent studies of manufacture in eighteenth-century Britain have added little to the analytical framework outlined by Ashton, although they have added something to our understanding of the nature of custom and convention in certain trades. See, for example, J. G. Rule, *The Experience of Labour in 18th Century Industry* (London, 1981); R. Malcolmson, *Life and Labour in England 1700–1800* (London, 1981); C. R. Dobson, *Masters and Journeymen: A Pre-history of Industrial Relations 1717–1800* (London, 1980). The as yet unpublished work of P. Linebaugh, 'Tyburn: A Study of Crime and the Labouring Poor in 18th Century London', unpublished Ph.D. thesis (University of Warwick, 1975), promises to take matters very much further. With the exception of the work of Pierre Vilar, very few of the classics of recent French historical writing, particularly those associated with the *Annales*, have touched upon manufacture as a substantial analytical problem. See the remarks by M. Morineau in his long review of F. Braudel, *Civilisation materielle, économie et capitalisme*, in *Revue d'Histoire moderne et contemporaine*, XXVIII (1981), 635–6.

other words, did the forms of power implicitly present in the relationship between each and any one of the social partners listed above *work* in an only partially monetised world?[4] It is worth posing this type of question at the outset because it leaves the notion of the economy of the pre-industrial world relatively open.[5] While it would be absurd *not* to examine the economies of pre-industrial societies, it has been only too easy to assume that the word 'economy' has a self-evident meaning in this sort of context. This has happened because a great deal of the discussion of manufacture before the factory has been subordinated to another, traditionally more substantial, question.

For many years, historians have been concerned to explain how and why towards the late eighteenth century, 'mechanisation took command' of the business of producing commodities.[6] In different ways, the terms 'Industrial Revolution', 'industrial system' or 'industrial capitalism' have been used to suggest that a crucial turning-point in the history of production occurred in Britain at a specific time. This emphasis upon the discontinuity symbolised by the factory has ensured that much of the analysis of earlier material systems has centred upon two interrelated questions.

The first of these is a somewhat teleological one concerned with the problem of the origins of the industrial system and, whether presented in the form of 'the transition from feudalism to capitalism', 'the causes of the Industrial Revolution' or 'the origins of the modern world system', it takes a certain definition of the nature of the economy, the market and the factory as both its end and its beginning.[7] Very schematically the procedure adopted usually consists of examining and explaining those forces which contributed to the formation of 'modern' economies, markets and systems of production. The second question centres upon the problem of failures and abortions and, in its turn, follows a procedure designed to explain why in certain times and places the emergence of modern economic systems did not occur.

4 On non-monetised transactions and their analysis in a different context, see P. Bourdieu, *Esquisse d'une théorie de la pratique* (Geneva, 1972) and *Le Sens pratique* (Paris, 1980). More generally, see M. De Certeau (ed.), *L'Invention du quotidien*, 2 vols. (Paris, 1980).
5 On the dangers of anachronism in analysing non-market economies, see K. Tribe, *Genealogies of Capitalism* (London, 1981) and, in the context of the relationship between the seventeenth-century English economy and seventeenth-century theories of property, see J. Tully, 'The Framework of Natural Rights in Locke's Analysis of Property: A Contextual Reconstruction', in A. Parel and T. Flanagan (eds.), *Theories of Property: Aristotle to the Present* (Waterloo, 1979), and *idem, A Discourse on Property* (Cambridge, 1980). Both these inquiries reflect the substantial discussion of historicity and its modes which has taken place among historians of political thought and historians of science over the past fifteen years or so, with fruitful implications for mere historians.
6 The phrase is from S. Giedeion, *Mechanisation Takes Command* (New York and Oxford, 1948).
7 See, for example, R. Hilton (ed.), *The Transition from Feudalism to Capitalism* (London, 1976); R. M. Hartwell (ed.), *The Causes of the Industrial Revolution in England* (London, 1967); I. Wallerstein, *The Modern World System*, 2 vols. (London, 1974 and 1980).

In both cases, the starting-point for the examination of the society, period and material system in question is an assumption that the categories underpinning the analysis of modern economies can be transposed to other and different types of social relationship. Any accusation of simple-minded linearity can be met with the response that sophisticated analysis calls for comparison between successful and unsuccessful types of transition. Yet from this standpoint the fact remains that a greater or lesser quantity of the appropriate ingredients have been common to both successful and unsuccessful cases: home demand or foreign demand, fixed capital or variable capital, skilled labour or unskilled labour, labour surplus or labour deficit, low-quality commodities or high-quality commodities, high transactions costs or low transactions costs, capitalist classes or non-capitalist *rentiers*, integrated markets or regional markets, wage–price differentials or price–interest differentials. The litany is impressive and is a testimony to the variety of accounts which have been produced to explain the Industrial Revolution.[8] In the last analysis, however, the terms of the many conflicting interpretations of the Industrial Revolution have been defined by two key symbols: the machine and the market. The degree of productivity of the former and the size and extent of the latter mark the traditional analytical limits of the economic historians' approach to the phenomenon of 'Industrial Revolution'.[9]

The essays brought together in this volume are, to varying degrees, situated outside of this boundary. Their appearance owes itself to a number of changes in the way in which industry, industrialisation and the transition from feudalism to capitalism have come to be defined. Three of these changes are worth dwelling upon in detail because they have done much to erode the classical boundaries within which the question of industrialisation has been enclosed. They are, firstly, the shift to a slow evolutionary view of capital accumulation and technological change in the process of industrialisation, in which the emphasis is placed as much on changes in the culture and organisation of labour as on mechanical innovation; secondly, the progress of social history; and, thirdly, the theory of proto-industrialisation and the research which it has stimulated. A brief survey of these three areas will indicate the context of debate and inquiry which has provoked the writing of this book.

---

8 The literature and debates are summarised in D. McCloskey and R. Floud (eds.), *The Economic History of Britain Since 1700*, 2 vols. (Cambridge, 1981), I.

9 The formulation may be rather schematic; for one example, however, see F. Crouzet, 'Essai de construction d'un indice annuel de la production industrielle française au xixe siècle', *Annales, Economies, Sociétés, Civilisations*, 25 (1970), 56–99, where the revolution of 1848 and the war of 1870 are presented as 'facteurs exogènes' to the regular and continuous growth of French industry.

CAPITAL, LABOUR DISCIPLINE AND TECHNOLOGY

Recent research in economic history has questioned the extent of fixed capital formation during the early phases of British industrialisation. This challenge has imposed fundamental revisions upon the traditional image of rapid change, machinery and the factory at the end of the eighteenth century. At the macro-economic level theories of economic growth which stressed a direct relation between levels of capital formation and rates of growth in output have come under fire. English indices suggested, as François Crouzet concluded, that high investment ratios might accompany rapid growth in productivity and income, but this was no proof of any causal relation between the two.[10] Enormous variations in the indices themselves, all of which contain substantial margins of error, make it difficult to accept arguments based only on these.[11] Micro-economic studies indicate, however, that not only was capital formation relatively low during Britain's takeoff, but fixed capital formation was really rather insignificant. The individual experiences of firms and industries in the eighteenth century convey the overriding impression that it was circulating capital which mattered and this was tied up in raw materials, inventories, credit and debt, and wages.

It was short-term capital that was needed and which was indeed available in a whole series of customary, traditional and non-institutional arrangements, so that a primitive banking system and limited long-term finance imposed no brake on expansion. Eighteenth-century businesses existed within a web of credit which supported the complex interchanges of outwork, the purchase of materials and the sale of goods. Small productive units and simple technology as well as ingenuity in economising on capital, even in the advanced cotton industry, made fixed capital formation less than problematic. The original and painstaking research of Chapman[12] on the insurance valuations of cotton factories confirmed the earlier impression of Edwards[13] that the typical mill in the first phases of the factory system tied up less than half the total capital invested. Works by Jenkins and Hudson have indicated that the proportion was even lower in the wool textile sector around the turn of the eighteenth century – possibly as low as one sixth overall but varying greatly up

10 François Crouzet (ed.), *Capital Formation in the Industrial Revolution* (London, 1972), Editor's Introduction.
11 See Charles Feinstein, 'Capital', *Cambridge Economic History of Europe*, Vol. VII, Part I (Cambridge, 1978) for a discussion of the different indices.
12 S. D. Chapman, 'Fixed Capital Formation in the British Cotton Manufacturing Industry', in J. P. P. Higgins and S. Pollard (eds.), *Aspects of Capital Investment in Great Britain 1750–1850* (London, 1971).
13 M. M. Edwards, *The Growth of the British Cotton Trade 1780–1815* (Manchester, 1967).

to around 40% depending on the type of manufacturing concern.[14]

Early machinery was made of wood and constructed by workers themselves. A jenny in 1795 cost £6 and a mule £30; a hand loom in 1811 could be had for £5 and a stocking frame for £15. Even a small steam engine was available for £150 to £200, while large ones cost £500 to £800. And those who could not raise this fixed capital could rely on renting accommodation and/or power, and join a thriving market in second-hand machinery.[15]

Though fixed capital was more prominent in the metal extracting and processing industries, even here – in most of the industry – until the beginning of the nineteenth century fixed capital was comparable in size to annual turnover and was smaller than circulating capital. The birth of that classic symbol of Britain's Industrial Revolution, the steam engine, was, as the recent research of N. von Tunzelman has demonstrated, not nearly so eventful as its later development and application have led us to believe. British industry was still predominantly powered by water at the end of the eighteenth century, and even by 1850 14% of British industry and 9% of the textile industry were still run by water. Relatively cheap Savery and Newcomen engines used on their own or to supplement water power proved a viable alternative to the major fixed expense of a Watt engine until beyond the end of the eighteenth century.[16]

The emergence of a new mode of production with the Industrial Revolution now begs for renewed research into its complex relations with its past. Whence came those customs and traditions which spun the web of credit? What were those unspoken relations between the organisation of work and technological change – relations which made the break with the past so hesitant and yet ultimately so final?

Emphasis on circulating capital and the gradual nature of technological change which was embodied in fixed investment during the period of rapid growth in industrial productivity has shifted the focus of historical analysis to the composition, culture and power relationships of and between those engaged in manufacture, whether as capitalists or as workers. Even the evolution of that symbol of industrialisation, the factory, is increasingly viewed in the light of the changes which it wrought in labour discipline and control rather than in that of its strict association with technological advance. It is a story implying gradual metamorphosis and considerable elements of continuity with the past.

Many historians, ranging from Reinhard Bendix to Sidney Pollard and E. P.

14 D. T. Jenkins, *The West Riding Wool Textile Industry, 1770–1835: A Study in Fixed Capital Formation* (Eddington, 1975); Pat Hudson, 'The Genesis of Industrial Capital in the West Riding Wool Textile Industry 1770–1850', unpublished D. Phil. thesis (University of York, 1981), Ch. 2.
15 F. Crouzet, 'Capital Formation in Great Britain During the Industrial Revolution', in Crouzet (ed.), *Capital Formation*; Peter Mathias (ed.), *The Transformation of England* (London, 1979).
16 N. von Tunzelman, *Steam Power and Industrialisation to 1860* (Oxford, 1978).

Thompson, have looked to the relationship between the discipline of labour and the origins of the factory system.[17] The factory was regarded as the key means of quelling the impetuous and undisciplined work rhythms underlying pre-industrial modes of production. If the factory system has now been analysed in the light of the role it played in organising labour rather than in that of its associations with new technology, there is a sense in which historians have been over-impressed with the new departure it represented. They have too easily accepted the hopeful, but not altogether realistic, comment of contemporaries like Andrew Ure. His oft-cited praise of Richard Arkwright went far to identify the factory with labour discipline:

The main difficulty did not, to my apprehension, lie so much in the invention of a proper self-acting mechanism for drawing out and twisting cotton into a continuous thread, as in the distribution of the different members of the apparatus into one co-operative body . . . and above all in training human beings to renounce their desultory habits of work, and to identify themselves with the unvarying regularity of the complex automaton. To devise and administer a successful code of factory discipline, suited to the necessities of factory diligence, was the Herculean enterprise, the noble achievement of Arkwright.[18]

Marx himself drew on this in setting out the achievements of modern industry: 'Capital can appropriate to itself all the functions of specification, organisation and control, and perform them independently of labour. It can, therefore, impose its objectives on the labour process . . . Labour serves the machine and not the machine labour.'[19]

Landes, Pollard, Bendix and more recently Marglin and Braverman have all accepted the great superiority of the factory system and the machine as ways of organising labour.[20] But, as other historians have shown, the factory system did not end the sway of the family economy, for in many textile mills in England and in France, not just in the eighteenth century, but late in the nineteenth century, labour recruitment and discipline as well as workers' struggle were mediated through the needs and dynamic of the family-based workforce.[21] Neither did the

17 R. Bendix, *Work and Authority in Industry* (Berkeley, 1974); S. Pollard, 'Factory Discipline in the Industrial Revolution', *Economic History Review*, 2nd Series, 16 (1963–4); E. P. Thompson, 'Time, Work Discipline and Industrial Capitalism', *Past and Present*, 38 (1967), reprinted in M. W. Flinn and T. C. Smout, *Essays in Social History* (Oxford, 1974).

18 Andrew Ure, *The Philosophy of Manufactures* (London, 1835); passage reprinted in M. Berg, *Technology and Toil in Nineteenth Century Britain* (London, 1979), p. 65.

19 Karl Marx, *Capital*, cited in Berg, *Technology and Toil*, p. 5.

20 Stephen Marglin, 'What Bosses Do', in André Gorz, *The Division of Labour* (Atlantic Highlands, N. J., 1976); Harry Braverman, *Labour and Monopoly Capital* (London, 1974).

21 N. J. Smelser, *Social Change in the Industrial Revolution* (London, 1959); M. M. Edwards and R. Lloyd-Jones, 'N. J. Smelser and the Cotton Factory Family: A Reassessment', in N. B. Harte and K. G. Ponting, *Textile History and Economic History: Essays in Honour of Miss Julia de Lacy Mann* (Manchester, 1973); William Reddy, 'Skeins, Scales, Discounts, Steam and Other Objects of Crowd Justice in Early French Textile Mills', *Comparative Studies in Society and*

self-acting machinery which was meant to remove the need for highly skilled mule spinners in fact come anywhere near achieving this.[22] In many other industries, workers adapted their own culture and rhythms of work to new contexts so that the factory never became that capitalist-controlled and utterly rational form of work organisation which many historians and economists have claimed it to be.

Some historians have recognised that other forms of industrial organisation did indeed have their own advantages. Subcontracting, for instance, was, if not a method of management, at least a method of evading management. Under this form of organisation the gap between the raw materials and the finished product was filled not by paid employees arranged in a descending hierarchy, but by contractors to whom the production job was delegated. They hired their own employees, supervised the work process and received a piece-rate from the company. It was a system which not only reduced direct supervisory duties, but also enabled the entrepreneur to share risks, capital and technical knowledge with the subcontractor or his outworkers.[23]

The literature on the origins of labour discipline, anachronistic in its approach though some of it has been, has thus had to ask what motivated labour in the period to work in that desultory, intemperate manner which supposedly needed to be contained and disciplined. All those characteristics bound up in what economists put under the category of 'backward-sloping labour supply curve' need to be analysed in their own right. Some have been described, but few are understood.

If time and money were important to industrial capitalist methods and organisation, did they matter as much before the factory system? From the legions of complaints heard from manufacturers and economic commentators in the eighteenth century, we assume that they did. Time was capital, and profits in the pre-industrial economy were determined by the velocity of circulating capital. Capital was accumulated by reducing the duration that stocks of goods were tied up between stages of the production process and marketing. Yet workers and artisans appear to have failed to acquire a sense of the importance of this time keeping. Saving time might have saved capital, but it did not mean more returns for workers. From the workers' standpoint, time was not money. Hence the widely observed leisure preference. In Adam Smith's words: 'Our ancestors were idle for want of a sufficient encouragement to industry. It is better, says the

History, 21 (1979), 204–13; idem, 'Modes de paiement et contrôle du travail dans les filatures de coton en France,1750–1848', Revue du Nord, 63 (1981), 135–46; William Lazonick, 'The Subjection of Labour to Capital: The Rise of the Capitalist System', Review of Radical Political Economy, 10 (1978); idem, 'Industrial Relations and Technical Change: The Case of the Self-Acting Mule', Cambridge Journal of Economics, 3 (1979), 231–62.
22   Lazonick, 'Industrial Relations and Technical Change'.
23   Sidney Pollard, The Genesis of Modern Management (London, 1965).

proverb, to play for nothing than to work for nothing.'[24] In one sense the wage increases offered were too small to induce any significant increase in effort. But in another, equally important, sense money wages as such were not a dominant part of the pre-industrial workers' economy. Hoskins describes the domestic economy of Wigston manor before the enclosures as one in which most of the life of the peasantry was determined outside the market.[25] Sonenscher's essay reproduced below confirms this impression for the urban trades of Paris, and Hudson's research on the Yorkshire textile industry has shown that non-monetary transactions prevailed as late as the mid nineteenth century.

Working for a set time for a set market wage did not necessarily hold the kind of meaning for a pre-industrial workforce as it did for the masters. The economy of needs and the acquisition of social status within the local community were only partially related to participation in the market and to the accumulation of monetary wealth and commodities. The imposition of industrial discipline had therefore to go hand in hand with the imposition of new needs and definitions of subsistence mediated through the market-place. The wider social implications of the plutocracy which Adam Smith discusses in *The Theory of Moral Sentiments* were fundamental to the new responses required of an industrial workforce. It was thus that a revolution in production methods coincided with the creation of new consumption patterns and the much vaunted 'home market' of the eighteenth century.

There was, in addition, a long tradition of acquiring portions of income in ways other than the wage. The failure to keep time and to respond to wages was associated with the need to engage in a whole series of extra-curricular activities yielding up various forms of non-monetary and monetary income. Industrial discipline could only succeed as these other sources of income started to dry up. Thus the importance of the emergence of restrictions on gleaning, poaching and gathering wood.

A major difficulty with the literature on industrial discipline is that it has taken on the prejudices of contemporaries who complained about the casual licentious lives of the poor. Much of the literature has assumed that there was no pattern, time sense or discipline to the way artisans and agricultural labourers conducted their lives. Thompson compares their casual life-style to that of mothers and housewives.[26] It is true that the latter respond to different rhythms than those dictated by the clock and the working week. Theirs is not, however, a casual life-style; it is one orientated to care for others. The rhythm of life and work of housewives is not just task-orientated; it is governed by a strict day by day and

24 Cited in Peter Mathias, 'Leisure and Wages in Theory and Practice', in Mathias (ed.), *The Transformation of England.*
25 W. G. Hoskins, *The Midland Peasant* (London, 1957).
26 Thompson, 'Time, Work Discipline', p. 55.

week by week time discipline, and continuous thinking of the future. The time discipline of housewives is conditioned by children's demands for feeding, clothing and sleeping, and the maintenance of health and learning. Not only is time disciplined; it is spent on others in different ways, leaving virtually none of it for the housewife to 'waste' on herself. This time discipline of family life has very important implications for the time discipline of the pre-industrial artisan. The rhythms of life of the artisan intersected with the rhythms of domestic life because home was in most cases the place of work. In addition, the working patterns of artisans were confined within the constraints of set delivery times of raw materials, availability of assistants who might have had a different time economy, set dates for markets and fairs, and the time patterns of other social and income-earning activities. Time and discipline did matter before the factory system. They were not measured by minutes and hours, but they were measured all the same.

An understanding of the continuities in labour attitudes and culture during the Industrial Revolution also requires consideration of the extent and importance of technological change before the factory. As historians have played down the significance of the large-scale technological breakthroughs of the Industrial Revolution, we have become more aware that technological change was not confined to new power sources and mechanisation. Attention has been drawn to a whole series of 'intermediate' technical changes, to the new skills, adaptive know-how and innovations in hand technologies which prompted great increases in productivity in apparently craft-dominated spheres. The new significance given to this empirical technical change must now force a reconsideration of earlier technologies which provided the foundations for piecemeal progress.[27] First, however, historians have to dislodge a general assumption of static technologies before the eighteenth century. However primitive these early technologies and however limited their impact beside the great innovations of the late eighteenth and nineteenth centuries, it is still the case they may have had an important effect on the division of labour, the organisation of work and the nature and attitudes of the workforce. But we know virtually nothing of these.

An exemplary and detailed empirical study of the impact of technical change in a pre-industrial manufacture can be found in Myska's study of the Czech iron industry over several centuries.[28] This shows that technical change, however primitive, did lead to a transformation in the structure of ownership, to a change in the situation of the labour force and to new production relations. Myska details how a series of medieval technical changes clustered in the fourteenth

27   See Peter Mathias, 'Skills and the Diffusion of Innovations from Britain in the Eighteenth Century', in Mathias (ed.), *The Transformation of England*, pp. 21–44.
28   Milan Myska, 'Pre-industrial Iron Making in the Czech Lands: The Labour Force and Productive Relations c. 1350–1840', *Past and Present*, 82 (February 1979).

century – the shaft, machine hammer and water power – all changed the organisation of work by introducing a new division of labour between miners, charcoal suppliers and foundrymen. The widespread use of water power over the next centuries made for greater specialisation among iron workers as foundry operations were separated off from hammer operations. The spread of the charcoal blast-furnace between 1600 and 1840 intensified this division of labour, throwing up a series of new trades – smelters, foundrymen, and forge masters. This change in technology, furthermore, created a new scale of demand for fixed capital, and the introduction of continuous process production increased the scale of demand for circulating capital. With this development, ownership of the works shifted from non-aristocratic iron masters to large landowners.

Besides these rather striking technical changes must be placed a whole series of new hand tools and intermediate technologies. One such example is the technology of the hardware trades. Unlike the large-scale techniques of Myska's iron works, those of the hardware trades were known to be those which 'alone... require more force than the arm and tools of the workman could yield... still leaving his skill and experience of head, hand and eye in full exercise'.[29] The earliest working equipment of these trades comprised anvil, hammer, file and grindstone, followed by the lathe, then by rolling mill, stamp, press and drawbench. This was a kind of technology not adapted to continuous process or mass production. Its hallmark was flexibility and application, according to the dictates of artisan skill, to the production of a wide range of different articles. But these new tools also provided the opportunity for extensive subdivision of process and extreme specialisation of product. Stamping was separated from the further divided finishing processes. In eighteenth-century Birmingham there were not only button mould turners, button burnishers and button finishers, but gold and silver button makers, horn button makers and inlaid platina button makers. There was, in fact, an important path of artisan technical change which is often neglected by historians. Technical change took the form of small improvements and adaptations of basic machinery and hand tools. Innovation was often wrapped up in the workman's skill at adaptation.[30] Many such innovations went unpatented, and some were lost to the world when their product passed out of fashion. The Birmingham manufacturers were the archetypal carriers of such a path of technical change. Even in the nineteenth century:

The secret manufacturers who locked their doors and who led James Drake to complain in 1825 that the tourist trade was endangered by their behaviour were in all probability men who found it easier to withhold their innovations by keeping them dark rather than by the

---

29   W. Hawkes Smith, *Birmingham and its Vicinity as a Manufacturing and Commercial District* (London, 1836), p. 1.
30   See Mathias, 'Skills and the Diffusion of Innovations'.

enforcement of a patent with all the publicity for the specification that this method involved.[31]

A witness to the Select Committee on Arts and Manufactures in 1824 also pointed out:

Our Birmingham machines are rarely, if ever, mentioned in the scientific works of the day. The Birmingham machine is ephemeral . . . it has its existence only during the fashion of a certain article, and it is contained within the precincts of a single manufacture or a town.[32]

These technical advances in tools also reacted back on the organisation of production. The range of tools, and particularly of lathes, also underpinned the middle-sized workshop of some capital. In Birmingham this held its own with the garret room and conjugal family workshop.[33] The viability of these tools and machines, along with the artisans and small firms, was enhanced rather than reduced by new sources of power which were applied when the steam turbine was developed in the latter part of the nineteenth century.[34] The equation of technical change with the factory form of organisation therefore ignores this other equally significant path of technological change. Even in their own terms, as several historians have emphasised, the large-scale technological changes of the textile revolution had more humble beginnings which might have led elsewhere, but for key business decisions. The early spinning-jenny could be adapted to the small family production unit, but was more often built to specifications which demanded its use in large workshops.[35] Similarly Arkwright's waterframe was initially built on a small scale and was turned by hand. But Arkwright himself restricted it by licence to units of at least a thousand spindles, so that it became economic only when erected in water-powered units.[36]

Our limited knowledge of the impact of early technical changes such as these must stand beside our ignorance of an even more important source of gains in productivity before the factory – the market-place itself. Just as circulating capital dominated capital formation, so the greatest gains in productivity were to be had by cutting down the time of circulation, or, in other words, increasing the velocity of circulating capital. At a time when the bulk of capital was tied up in

31 See M. Berg, 'Technology and the Division of Labour in the Age of Manufactures: The case of the Birmingham Toy Trades', unpublished paper, British Society for the History of Science, Workshop on New Perspectives in the History of Technology, Manchester, March 1981.
32 Cited in J. H. Clapham, An Economic History of Modern Britain, 4 vols. (Cambridge, 1930), I, 156.
33 See Berg, 'Technology and the Division of Labour'.
34 See David S. Landes, The Unbound Prometheus (Cambridge, 1969), p. 279. This point was also illustrated by J. R. Harris and Marie Rowlands in their discussion of the Lancashire tool makers and the Black Country trades in the nineteenth and twentieth centuries at the SSRC Conference on Manufacture in Town and Country before the Factory, Oxford, September 1980.
35 Edwards and Lloyd-Jones, 'N. J. Smelser and the Cotton Factory Family', pp. 306–7.
36 R. L. Hills, 'Hargreaves, Arkwright and Crompton: Why Three Inventors?', Textile History, 10 (1979).

debts, wages, inventories and goods in transit, any innovation which speeded up the time it took for goods to pass through the various stages of production, to be transported and to come to market was crucial. Innovations in transport and communication, retailing and market institutions all reduced the costs of circulating capital, and these just as much as actual technical innovations increased profitability.

The dynamic of the domestic industries and urban trades was attuned to the vital economy of the market-place at least as much as to the economy of the workplace. Jürgen Schlumbohm's essay indicates how the varied fluctuations of three different types of market affected production schedules and organisational structures in the case of the German linen industry. And the essay by Michael Sonenscher indicates the significance of the web of credit and debt relations. But still we know far too little of the actual working of markets in the eighteenth century, and of the micro-economic impact of improvements in transport and the breakdown of monopolies which clogged the circulation of commodities.

Questions of fixed and circulating capital, of technology, labour discipline and markets which have been generated within the framework of economic history have had to call upon other sorts of question based on the much more relativistic approaches of social history. These are the subject of the next section.

SOCIAL HISTORY

The less dramatic way in which the early industrial system has come to be characterised has intersected with the development of what, over the past two decades, has come to be called social history. Although it has been easy to ridicule some of the more descriptively recondite achievements of some of its practitioners, the development of social history has been the second broad area of change in perspective which underlies, to a greater or lesser extent, the contributions to this collection.[37] For if technological change and the development of markets can be recognised as only partially adequate accounts of the process of industrialisation, then other areas of social activity also require analysis and explanation. The sense of historical relativity characteristic of social history has created an openness to the *otherness* of the institutions, forms of behaviour and patterns of belief found in different times and places.[38] The

---

37 The analytical content of 'social history' has given rise to some discussion: see T. Judt, 'A Clown in Regal Purple: Social History and the Historians', *History Workshop Journal*, 7 (1979), 66–94. For more considered discussion of the matter, see P. Vilar, *Une Histoire en construction* (Paris, 1982); G. Eley and K. Nield, 'Why Does Social History Ignore Politics?', *Social History*, 5 (1980), 249–71; P. Abrams, 'History, Sociology, Historical Sociology', *Past and Present*, 87 (1980), 3–16.

38 See, as ever, the work of Lucien Febvre, particularly his *Le Problème de l'incroyance au XVIe siècle* (Paris, 1942).

concern of social historians with questions of an anthropological sort – and with behaviour in which the opposition between 'culture' and 'practical reason' cannot be presupposed – has indicated the value of examining aspects of the apparently non-economic in order to understand the nature of production, distribution, exchange and consumption in terms which fall outside the market-derived preoccupations of classical economic history.[39] Markets, after all, have a history – and the transition from the notion of the market as a physical place to that of the market as an impersonal social mechanism has long been recognised as something which calls for more than a chronicle of the growing volume of goods and money in circulation.[40]

Thus it is now widely accepted that many of the forms of behaviour and patterns of belief found in rural societies in early modern Europe were governed by concerns which derived from the interplay between family resources and strategies on the one hand and a variety of non-monetary obligations, reciprocities and conventional practices on the other.[41] Despite a recent assertion to the contrary, it is difficult to sustain an argument which would have it that 'agrarian individualism' can be demonstrated to have existed in England well before the sixteenth century.[42] The fact that goods were bought and sold, that some agricultural labour was carried out for money wages and that some rural tenancies were of a contractual sort does not, in itself, call the equally well-documented context of custom and convention into question.[43]

The research of a generation of social historians has thus done a great deal to make more intelligible the idiom in which social relationships in rural communities were lived. It is now clear that there was more to a food riot, to a charivari or to many of the acts which led to criminal prosecution than price or market fluctuations are able to disclose.[44] It is also clear that many aspects of the organisation of production both before and after the development of the factory system were determined not just by the interaction between technology, wage

---

39 M. Sahlins, *Culture and Practical Reason* (Chicago, 1976).
40 The classic formulation of the matter was by K. Polanyi, *The Great Transformation* (London, 1945); see also A. O. Hirschmann, *The Passions and the Interests* (Princeton, 1977).
41 See, for example, J. Goody et al., *Family and Inheritance* (Cambridge, 1976); N. Z. Davis, 'Ghosts, Kin and Progeny: Some Features of Family Life in Early Modern France', *Daedalus*, 106 (1977), 87–114; G. Bouchard, 'L'Etude des structures familiales pré-industrielles: pour un renversement des perspectives', *Revue d'Histoire Moderne et Contemporaine*, 28 (1981), 545–71.
42 A. Macfarlane, *The Origins of English Individualism* (Oxford, 1978) and *idem, The Justice and the Mare's Ale* (Oxford, 1981).
43 For one example, see J. M. Neeson, 'Common Right and Enclosure in Eighteenth Century Northamptonshire', unpublished Ph.D. thesis (University of Warwick, 1977); and, in a different but equally 'monetised' context, P. de Saint-Jacob, *Les Paysans de la Bourgogne du nord* (Paris, 1960).
44 E. P. Thompson, 'The Moral Economy of the English Crowd in the 18th Century', *Past and Present*, 50 (1971), 76–136; *idem*, 'Rough Music: Le Charivari anglais', *Annales, Economies, Sociétés, Civilisations*, 27a (1972), 285–312; Linebaugh, 'Tyburn: Crime and the Labouring Poor'.

levels and the state of the labour market in different times and places but by a range of social and cultural customs and historical traditions. The notion of work itself has come to be divested of some of its timeless connotations and endowed with a degree of historical specificity.[45] A number of detailed studies of the organisation of work in a variety of different contexts have done much to indicate the close relationship between production and the broader configuration of social transactions of which it formed a part. As a result it is no longer possible to analyse the economy on the basis of an assumption that work and the details of particular labour processes can be taken for granted.

A series of fine studies by two North American historians have done much to reveal how much of the organisation of production in the cotton industry of nineteenth-century France on the one hand, and the Newfoundland fishing industry on the other, was bound up with the existence of relatively impermeable and unsocialised forms of task allocation, customary practice and conventional arrangement created by working people themselves. In the latter case, much of what related to the organisation of work was created through the social conventions bound up with mumming at Christmas.[46] In the case of the former, close examination of the forms of wage payment in the cotton mills of early-nineteenth-century Lille or Sainte-Marie-aux-Mines in Alsace has shown how erroneously simplistic an equation between the development of steam-powered factory production and the emergence of the characteristically modern form of working-class action – the strike – can be. The crowds of cotton workers who deserted their mills on one day but returned to them the next were not engaged in any embryonic or undeveloped form of strike activity. Instead they were bringing a well-established repertoire of tactical manoeuvre, centred upon the market-place and the price of corn, to systems of wage payment which replicated the meanings of the market within the arena of the factory.[47]

The preoccupation of historians with the interplay between the concrete detail of work and the manner in which it informed the texture of daily life has meant, of course, a renewal of interest in the notion of class as a lived relationship. As a result, it is now possible to envisage ways in which the various concerns of labour historians, social historians and historians of technology might be brought together within a broader framework of comparative analysis.[48] This sort of

45 See, for example, W. Sewell, *Work and Revolution in France: The Language of Labour from the Ancien Régime to 1848* (Cambridge, 1980), and the studies by Reddy, Sider and Price cited below.
46 G. M. Sider, 'Christmas Mumming and the New Year in Outport Newfoundland', *Past and Present*, 71 (1976), 102–25; and *idem*, 'The Ties that Bind: Culture and Agriculture, Property and Propriety in the Newfoundland Village Fishery', *Social History*, 5 (1980), 1–39.
47 Reddy, 'Skeins, Scales, Discounts', and *idem*, 'Modes de paiement'.
48 An invitation to such a project is implicit in E. J. Hobsbawm's note on the word 'strike' in *The Age of Revolution 1789–1848* (Mentor, 1965), p. 250.

concern has been voiced in several recent studies of different branches of production in the nineteenth century. In one of them it has been shown how much the organisation of the building trades in nineteenth-century Britain depended upon the ability of large contractors to measure work with any precision.[49] This was a capacity which they did not have until the imposition of an hourly wage rate after 1880. Until then, work organisation was largely a matter of direct negotiation between employers and workers within a framework of informal convention. Trade unionism and an institutionalised system of wage bargaining were the products of the imposition of an hourly rate, which served to change the character of work itself.

The results of this type of study have, it is clear, substantial implications for the traditional divisions between economic history, labour history and social history. They are, moreover, a timely reminder that work has only rarely been an individual activity. In most instances – whether it was carried out in mines, shipyards, building sites and the few centralised 'proto-factories' of the eighteenth century, or in the dispersed workshops of the urban trades – work involved a number of different kinds of co-operative (and hence potentially conflicting) relationship. The terms of the relationships between merchants and masters, between master and master, masters and men, journeymen and apprentices, men and women, adults and children – all, to varying degrees, involved in the organisation, allocation and execution of work – were not necessarily set in a monetary way. Thus a great deal of any comparative history of production before the development of the factory system is likely to be found in differences between the sorts of non-monetary transaction which allowed for co-operation between these various parties to be secured and maintained. This is likely to involve examination of the everyday world outside of work as well as of the details of manufacturing procedure itself.

PROTO-INDUSTRIALISATION

The third body of recent literature which has led to greater relativism in the study of early modern society is that concerning the concept of proto-industrialisation. This is to some extent an irony, as proto-industrialisation was initially conceived as a linear model of transition to the factory and was based on neo-classical economic assumptions and the theory of comparative advantage.[50] In spite of this, the concept has provoked more sophisticated analysis and research on a vast spectrum of socio-cultural experience at the level of the household unit of

---

49   R. Price, *Masters, Unions and Men* (Cambridge, 1980).
50   See F. F. Mendels, 'Proto-industrialization: The First Phase of the Industrialization Process', *Journal of Economic History*, 32 (1972).

production, reproduction and consumption.[51] Thus macro and micro research have been integrated in an unusual and stimulating manner. How did this come about?

It is a truism that a major feature of European change, particularly since the seventeenth century, was a vast increase in commercial manufacturing production in the countryside. In the last decade, however, F. F. Mendels and others have seen this development as sufficiently pervasive and dynamic to have provided the matrix of early modern economic and social change, paving the way for factory production and wage labour at a later date. Thus rural domestic industry developing apace in certain key regions constituted the 'first phase of the industrialisation process', which through its manifold implications created the conditions for 'industrialisation proper'.[52]

The so-called 'proto-industry phase' was marked by several distinct characteristics. It was, first of all, associated with the extension of the world market for mass-produced goods from the sixteenth century. This market grew at such a pace that traditional urban production could not efficiently respond, hampered as it was by guild restrictions and high labour costs. Secondly, the increasing specialisation of areas of proto-industrial production was accompanied by the complementary development of adjacent regions to supply agricultural products. A symbiotic relationship between regions, based on comparative advantage, thus ensued, so that agricultural change was viewed as an integral part of the proto-industrialisation process.

Manufacturing took place in the peasant household usually in combination with agricultural subsistence activity, but was generally organised by merchants residing in nearby urban centres. The inter-relationship between the peasant family economy and merchant capital was a major characteristic of the proto-industrial phase, isolating it from earlier and later periods. Circulating capital dominated production, and labour was still tied to the land, living in a world of traditional peasant culture and values. Furthermore, where labour, through access to the land, was able to secure part of its own reproduction needs and, at the same time, was largely incapable of corporate protest, the differential profit accruing to capital could be substantial and higher than in a centralised system employing full wage labour.

Mendels, who first conceptualised this process of proto-industrial specialisation, stressed the greater efficiency it brought to the use of labour, especially in

---

51   See for example, H. Medick, 'The Proto-industrial Family Economy: The Structural Function of Household and Family during the Transition from Peasant Society to Industrial Capitalism', *Social History*, 3 (Oct. 1976); D. Levine, *Family Formation in an Age of Nascent Capitalism* (London, 1976); L. K. Berkner, 'Family, Social Structure and Rural Industry: A Comparative Study of the Waldviertel and the Pays de Caux in the 18th Century', unpublished Ph.D. thesis (Harvard University, 1973).
52   Mendels, 'Proto-industrialization', p. 241.

areas of temperate agriculture characterised by great seasonal imbalances in labour demand.[53] Mendels argued that seasonal pools of unemployed and underemployed labour were the magnets which attracted putting-out production to a region. Once established, proto-industry became the spur to a process of regional transformation, stimulating capital formation, the growth of rural and urban market facilities and the build up of entrepreneurial skills and technical expertise.

Perhaps the most important implication of proto-industry was the effect which it is said to have had on demographic and cultural developments. Mendels has argued that income-earning opportunities outside of agriculture freed marriage from the traditional constraints of inheritance and patriarchal control. The result was earlier marriage and rapid rates of population increase in proto-industrial regions. In Flanders, for example, the number of marriages was closely related to the movement of linen prices.[54] Levine and others have offered supporting evidence of similar direct links between the income-earning possibilities of rural industry and population change.[55] But Jeannin has recently warned that demographic research has by no means reached a stage where the hypothesis that proto-industry caused population growth can be asserted as a generality.[56] High population density and early marriage could, conversely, just as easily have acted as the original factors attracting the growth of rural production in an area.

The same problems of causation may, to some extent, be applicable to the detailed work done by Medick, Braun and others on the relationship between rural production and changing social and familial values and practices.[57] Braun has supported Mendels's view of the effect of proto-industry on inheritance patterns. Greater subdivision and fragmentation, he argues, were the natural corollary to industrial by-employments. The process allowed a larger population to be supported on the same land area, and gradually resulted in the complete separation of labour from the land. Thus proto-industry created an industrial proletariat before the factory.

On the basis of work by Chayanov, and by various German authorities who analysed cottage industry as a system of production,[58] Medick has emphasised

53   F. F. Mendels, 'Seasons and Regions in Agriculture and Industry', in S. Pollard (ed.), *Region und Industrialisierung* (Göttingen, 1980).
54   Mendels, 'Industrialisation and Population Pressure in Eighteenth Century Flanders', unpublished Ph.D. thesis (University of Wisconsin, 1970).
55   Levine, *Family Formation*; R. Braun, *Industrialisierung und Volksleben* (Zurich, 1960); J. D. Chambers, 'The Vale of Trent 1660–1800', *Economic History Review*, Supplement No. 3 (1957).
56   P. Jeannin, 'La Proto-industrialisation: développement ou impasse?', *Annales, Economies, Sociétés, Civilisations*, 35a (1980), 52–65.
57   Braun, *Industrialisierung*.
58   A. V. Chayanov, *The Theory of Peasant Economy*, ed. D. Thamer, B. Kerblay, and R. E. K. Smith (Irwin, 1966). For a discussion of the German theorists from Sombart to Schmoller see P. Kriedte, H. Medick and J. Schlumbohm, *Industrialization Before Industrialization* (Cambridge, 1982), Introduction.

the tendency of peasants to self-exploitation in household units geared to the maximisation of gross product rather than to net profit. This same labour–consumer balance has also, however, to be set against the replacement of labour effort through consumption and leisure, through feasting, playing and drinking in exactly those situations of potential growth in which the capitalist putter-out could have obtained maximum profits.[59]

Thus recent work has begun to examine in detail the effects of proto-industry on the household and family: gender differentiation, sexual freedoms and awareness, demographic imperatives, attitudes to work and leisure, and consumption patterns and horizons. But this research has only underlined the great difficulty of generalising about these complex changes. Different branches of production, associated with different organisational structures and different labour processes, make it impossible to isolate any homogeneous socio-cultural response. It would seem wise, as Schlumbohm has suggested, to place proto-industrialisation within a wider context of societal transformation, which was polymorphic, varying greatly between regions, branches of industry and time.[60]

Even when the diversity of rural change and its implications is recognised, most of the proto-industry literature still tends to view the complexity of economic, social and familial relationships in the past in terms of their transitional qualities rather than in terms of their own internal characteristics. Much of the theory which has guided work on the history of the family, for example, has been in the structural functionalist mould. By transposing twentieth-century ideas of the continuous progress and dynamism of socio-economic structures one is in danger of losing sight of the nature of these phenomena placed in their own time. Elements of durability and continuity in economic and personal relationships and in ideas and beliefs may have complemented rather than conflicted with different paths of change. A true sense of the place of customary and traditional values and practices as well as of alternative types of industrial organisation and production process is lost in the search for impelling dynamics and the key to 'progress'.

The linear framework of theories of industrialisation, of which proto-industrialisation is only one example, has also prevented an adequate analysis of the place of different types of industrial organisation. Decentralised modes of organisation have been viewed only as precursors of factory mass production or as inferior remnants amid the more advanced centralised and mechanised types of production. In the same manner, different forms of proto-industry have been analysed as more or less progressive: the *Kaufsystem* and other artisan structures have been pushed into the shadow of the 'more advanced' *Verlagsystem*. Not

---

59   Medick, 'The Proto-industrial Family Economy', p. 301.
60   J. Schlumbohm, 'Productivity of Labour, Process of Production and Relations of Production', unpublished paper, 1980, p. 28.

only is the successful coexistence of several different forms of domestic industry a challenge to such ideas, but the long-continued complementarity between centralised and dispersed manufacturing raises its own questions. Centralised production processes before the late eighteenth century and dispersed production since the nineteenth century have been either ignored or their significance dismissed in the proto-industry framework. There has furthermore been little interest in exploring the reasons for and the connections between the many different structures of production which exist within all periods and phases of capitalist development.

Despite its linear paradigm, the proto-industry literature has brought issues of fundamental importance to the forefront of historical debate and has stimulated valuable research into the origins, nature and implications of pre-factory manufacture. Several aspects of proto-industry research have been influential in the writing of this volume and are worth dwelling upon here.

The agrarian and institutional setting

For many years historians have been interested in the prevalence of rural manufacture in certain types of farming region. Recent work has highlighted the importance of three elements of the agrarian environment which influenced the location and subsequent development of proto-industry. They are: the comparative advantage of other non-industrial or formerly industrial areas in commercial agriculture, the seasonality or intensity of rural labour demand and, finally, the institutional and historical features of a community.

Mendels and Jones have both emphasised the gradual specialisation of regions within the European continent and stressed the importance of the region as a unit of study:

Differences of topography, soil, and precipitation influenced the costs of crop production and gave rise in most European countries to one set of regions with comparative advantage in growing food crops and another where comparative advantage lay somewhere among the following options or combinations of options: pastoral husbandry, mining, lumbering, the export of labour as harvesters, domestic servants, construction workers, or mercenary troops and cottage industry... the early modern European countryside did gradually separate out into broad categories of regions with two sorts of ecosystem and economy, one agricultural, the other proto-industrial, linked by trade.[61]

Jones described the emergence of the north and west of England as the prime centre of manufacturing industry in the eighteenth century.[62] The characteristic improvements of the Agricultural Revolution gave comparative advantage in the

61   E. L. Jones, 'Environment, Agriculture and Industrialisation', *Agricultural History*, 51 (1977), 494.
62   E. L. Jones, 'Agricultural Origins of Industry', *Past and Present*, 40 (1968).

south and east to agriculture. The light soil areas of early enclosure for sheep rearing adapted most readily to rotational techniques of mixed farming and root crops. The Midlands and north could not compete in efficiency of cereal production with the south and thus specialised in pastoral farming. In the case of the Midland clay area this entailed a shift from arable to grass in the mid eighteenth century which generated a mass of underemployed and unemployed labour in the countryside. These areas became the major location of many rural industries, including lace making, hosiery, and metalwares.

The same pattern of regional specialisation has been traced on the continent as well as in Asia and North America. In Silesia, for example, there was a growth of the linen industry in the foothills of the Riesengeberge after the Thirty Years War; the number of rural workers increased whilst the number of town workers fell. This development was sustained by the importation of grain from the serf-farmed plains east of the Elbe.[63] In the Black Forest, clocks, light ironwork, musical instruments, gloves and lace were made as by-employments from the late seventeenth century, and cotton spinning was carried out in the mountains of the Alpine zone in Switzerland.[64] The densest rural industry in Germany arose in the Rhineland, whilst in Sweden much the same pattern emerged: agriculturally poor areas developed industrial by-employments on a considerable scale, while regions better suited to crop growing concentrated on producing surplus food for sale.[65]

The idea of development along the lines of comparative advantage has been complemented by the importance attached to seasonal labour surpluses in the industrial regions. These surpluses determined that rural production was most often associated with pastoralism rather than with arable farming. Mendels has argued that the temperate farming of north-west Europe, with its slack season, encouraged rural by-employment in putting-out systems. In the *petite culture* of southern Europe, where the vine predominated, labour demands were spread more evenly throughout the year and proto-industry was limited or non-existent.[66]

The major weakness of the comparative advantage model of regional specialisation is its assumption of individual and social rationality in the various farming regions, and the implication that production will always adjust to

63 W. O. Henderson, *Studies in the Economic Policy of Frederick the Great* (London, 1963), p. 140; quoted by Jones, 'Agricultural Origins', p. 65.
64 Jones, 'Agricultural Origins'; J. H. Clapham, *The Economic Development of France and Germany 1815–1914* (Cambridge, 1961), pp. 95–6.
65 H. Kisch, 'Growth Deterrents of a Medieval Heritage: The Aachen Area Woollen Trades before 1790', *Journal of Economic History*, 24 (1964); *idem*, 'The Textile Industries of Silesia and the Rhineland', *Journal of Economic History*, 19 (1959); E. Heckscher, *An Economic History of Sweden* (Harvard, 1954), pp. 172–3.
66 Mendels, 'Seasons and Regions'.

comparative advantage in the long run. In reality regional specialisation was fundamentally affected by custom and tradition, embodied in the motivations and practice of economic actors, and in the variety of institutional environments.

Schremmer has recently commented on these constraints in the case of Bavaria and Württemberg:

the underlying assumption is that rural industry followed the lines of markets with prices, wages, buying, selling, supply and demand, income utilisation; in short, the type of monetary market economy which exists today. But these modern markets were only partly established for rural industry. But what we do discover is the parallel existence of supplementary and non-monetary invisible local markets for proto-industrial goods, services and labour – quasi markets based upon barter exchange. There existed something approaching a mixed labour service and product rotation within the community... and [this] produced a relatively static economy with a remarkable stability.[67]

In the case of Bavaria and Württemberg the full workings of comparative advantage linking the progress of rural industry to 'industrialisation proper' was blocked by the fact that:

the way of life and consciousness of both individuals and the population as a whole was more influenced by the traditional concepts of sufficiency than by the thrusting attitudes of an achieving society.[68]

There are thus good reasons for the institutional environment in which rural industry existed to be a close concern of historians. The history of a region, particularly the degree of disintegration of feudal structures and the development of personal freedom and property rights, affected the emergence of rural industry and conditioned its development. Thirsk has argued that industries in the English countryside grew primarily in regions not only dominated by pastoral farming, but where there was also no strong framework of co-operative agriculture and where freeholders and customary tenants had firm property rights.[69] Chambers agreed that owners of circulating capital looked for labour in areas of weak manorialism which allowed immigration and the division of property among small cultivators.[70] Thus areas of new settlement, offering opportunities for squatters and associated with partible inheritance, were particularly attractive to employers in offering a source of cheap underemployed labour. In this way the Kentish Weald, north and west Wiltshire, central Suffolk, and parts of the West Riding of Yorkshire became major manufacturing areas. In the Dales of North

---

67   E. Schremmer, 'Proto-industrialisation: A Step Towards Industrialisation?', *Journal of Economic History*, forthcoming, p. 125.

68   *Ibid.*, p. 132.

69   J. Thirsk, 'Industries in the Countryside', in F. J. Fisher (ed.), *Essays in the Economic and Social History of Tudor and Stuart England* (Cambridge, 1961), pp. 70–2, 86–8.

70   J. D. Chambers, 'The Rural Domestic Industries', in *Second International Conference of Economic History* (Aix-en-Provence) (Paris, 1963), pp. 428–9.

Yorkshire equal partition between heirs had very forcibly driven the populace to hand stocking knitting: 'They knitted as they walked the village streets, they knitted in the dark because they were too poor to have a light, they knitted for dear life because life was so cheap.'[71] Hey has demonstrated that it was not so much partible inheritance or weak manorialism that was important in attracting rural industry but access to common rights which allowed squatters to settle.[72] This was a feature of areas of the north-west Midlands. Near West Bromwich, for example, settlements consisted of small groups of cottages or 'ends' around the heaths. Cottagers kept cows and sheep on the heath and made up their income by work in the metal trades.

In many areas of rural industry there is no doubt that historical developments encouraged the growth of a poor populace which was forced to seek a supplementary source of income. In other areas of rural manufacture it appears that this pressure 'from below' was not just an escape from starvation but what Hey has described as 'a vigorous response to additional opportunities for profit'.[73] This type of response would appear to have been associated with an agrarian environment populated by smallholders with some capital and/or by rural artisans. Hey, for example, described Staffordshire as 'not a poor district where families eked out a living through by-employments but one rich in industrial resources with expanding opportunities for profit'.[74]

It has also been argued that different trades adapted to or were encouraged by particular types of agricultural arrangements. Rowlands and Hey have both demonstrated the close association between the clustering of particular metal-ware trades and specific types of farming community.[75] The product type, the production processes and the organisation of production of nail making and scythe making were as distinct as their geographical location. Similarly, in the West Riding of Yorkshire, woollen and worsted production were separately located. As Hudson's essay in this volume shows, the putting-out system of worsted manufacture and the *Kaufsystem* of the woollen branch were each associated with different topographical and institutional features, in particular the nature and history of landholding and inheritance.

The proto-industry literature has tended to play down the vitality of rural *Kaufsystems*, despite Deyon's recent exhortations to the contrary.[76] Rural

71 *Ibid.*, p. 430.
72 D. G. Hey, *The Rural Metalworkers of the Sheffield Region*, Leicester University, Department of English Local History, Occasional Papers, 2nd Series, No. 5 (Leicester, 1972).
73 *Ibid.*, p. 21.
74 *Ibid.*
75 D. G. Hey, 'A Dual Economy in South Yorkshire', *Agricultural History Review*, 17 (1969); M. B. Rowlands, *Masters and Men in the West Midland Metalware Trades Before the Industrial Revolution* (Manchester, 1975).
76 P. Deyon, 'L'Enjeu des discussions autour du concept de proto-industrialisation', *Revue du Nord*, 240 (1979).

industry has largely been viewed in a Ricardian fashion as a response to population pressure and land scarcity which drove a community to take up by-employments. Historians have stressed the role of the merchant capitalist in soaking up cheap rural labour via the *Verlagsystem*, and implied that artisan structures and the *Kaufsystem* were less progressive or less developed forms of organisation destined to disappear or to be taken over by the putting-out system in the fullness of time. There has been too little recognition of the importance of rural *Kaufsystems*, of their relationship to particular agrarian contexts and of their adaptability (as Thomson suggests in his essay in this volume) to specific market circumstances. The Smithian framework, outlined in Berg's essay in this volume, found in the production and market relations of the independent artisan great and lasting benefits to both economic growth and welfare. The recent neglect of artisan production has been a function of the desire to isolate the progressive forces in socio-economic formations and of an excessive zeal for models of linearity. *Kaufsystems* may well have very important consequences for the dynamics of rural production, as Schremmer has recently suggested. In rural Bavaria and Württemberg smallholders were 'dynamic carriers of the process of ruralisation of handicraft production; but later it was this very group which tended to block modern industrialisation'.[77]

The growing recognition of the importance of institutional and political factors in the early stages of industrialisation has ensured that the work of Kisch has recently been reprinted and re-examined.[78] There are many examples of rural industry developing in areas of Europe dominated by a feudal institutional structure. In Silesia and Bohemia, for example, great feudal landowners set up or encouraged putting-out industries among the serfs and peasants on their estates. As much of this proto-industrial activity catered for markets outside the region, the servile status and low incomes of the local populace did not restrict demand for the textiles and other goods produced. Rigidities could and did, however, occur on the supply side, in the markets for labour and capital.

Kisch has argued that in the case of Silesia and the Rhineland, the reasons for the differential development of industry in adjacent regions of broadly similar topography was a result primarily of the varying strength of feudal institutions. He argued that the contraction and stagnation of the Silesian linen and cotton industries from the late eighteenth century was a result of their development within the constrictions of a feudal structure. This structure was dominated by

---

77   E. Schremmer, 'Proto-industrialisation', p. 123. On urban *Kaufsystems* organised outside the guild see Robert Duplessis and Martha C. Howell, 'Reconsidering the Early Modern Urban Economy', *Past and Present*, 94 (1982).

78   H. Kisch, 'The Crafts and their Role in the Industrial Revolution: The Case of the German Textile Industry', unpublished Ph.D. thesis (University of Washington, 1958); also his articles, 1959, 1981, reprinted in Kriedte, Medick and Schlumbohm, *Industrialization Before Industrialization*.

Junker landlords extracting surpluses through an array of traditional obligations and taxes and dealing with foreign merchants – all of which limited the
growth of an indigenous bourgeoisie. In the mountainous areas weavers had to
pay a fee to carry on their trade, for commutation, for having children, for
marriage, for death, and for the sale of land. In such circumstances one could
hardly except the creation of demographic and market dynamics of the type
theorised by Mendels. By contrast, in the neighbouring Rhineland, where feudal
bonds had been progressively weakened from the fifteenth century, a prosperous
class of tenant farmers had emerged and these became the nuclei of rural industry
and capital accumulation.

In other contexts, as Klima has demonstrated of Bohemia, the development of
rural industry could have a profoundly disintegrating effect on the existing feudal
hierarchy and authority. Competition between manufacturers for labour had
become so intense by the 1770s that it prompted the effective renouncement of
the orders of the feudal system operative until that time. The abolition of serfdom
in the Bohemian lands followed in 1781, and the decree pronounced on the
favourable effects which abolition would have on agriculture and industry.[79]
More often than not, however, it appears that the political and social structure of
feudalism placed fetters on the development of rural industry and the extent to
which the growth of this industry could 'pave the way for industrialisation
proper'. As Schremmer has said concerning East Prussia in the early twentieth
century,

the structure accepted or permitted only those factor flows and factor combinations which
did not endanger the existing structure ... pressures [towards industrialisation] existed ...
but were counterbalanced ... by political forces which had an interest in stabilising the
traditional structure and which became artificially maintained by a steady flow of
monetary subsidies into the regions controlled by the Junkers.[80]

Kisch acknowledged more than twenty years ago that the relationship between
social institutions and the economic process remained an 'empty economic
box'.[81] Despite some recent work, it appears that the contents of that box are still
far too few.

Town and country

The theory of proto-industry discusses the contribution of towns in the pre-
factory period only in terms of their role in serving the rural economy. Towns

---

79 A. Klima, 'The Domestic Industries and the Putting-Out System in the Period of Transition
from Feudalism to Capitalism', *Second International Conference of Economic History*, 1963.
80 Schremmer, 'Proto-industrialisation', p. 133.
81 H. Kisch, 'The Textile Industries in Silesia and the Rhineland: A Comparative Study in
Industrialization', *Journal of Economic History*, 19 (1959), 564.

provided a market, capital, entrepreneurial talents, and a site for the finishing processes, but any independent dynamic which they had is seen as subordinate to the pulse of rural expansion. This is perhaps as misleading as the tendency of earlier industrial historians to concentrate solely on guild production and organisation. It fits with the idea of towns becoming increasingly restrictive, 'feudal' institutions from the fourteenth century, but conflicts with the evidence of the rise of new unincorporated towns, especially in England in the sixteenth and seventeenth centuries.[82] Furthermore, it clashes with the somewhat blurred distinction which one finds in practice between rural and urban manufacture in the pre-factory period.

The town/country dichotomy has also been emphasised by other historians who admit that the protectionism of European towns from the fourteenth century was no more than a phase. These historians see the role of towns changing through a series of cycles dictated by the moving conjuncture of different macro-economic variables. Kellenbenz, for example, has argued that the population rise of the sixteenth century resulted in greater increases in the prices of agricultural than of manufactured goods.[83] This led to a drop in the real incomes of the towns, ultimately resulting in unemployment and migration of craftsmen to the countryside. In the seventeenth century, when population declined or stagnated throughout Europe, low food prices stimulated demand for manufactured goods and induced a shift in favour of rural manufacture.[84]

Macro-economic models of this kind, though making important and interesting connections between rural and urban incomes and demand patterns, fail to enquire into the composition of both. The components and assumptions of these models must be scrutinised at a micro-level if a real understanding of town–country relations is to emerge. One must turn attention to the study of the family economy in both town and country, the structure of mercantile business, and the relationship between urban and rural property, urban and rural wealth.

The rural wage in proto-industrial areas was not, as these models have suggested, based only on the harvest and diminishing returns in agriculture but

---

82 M. Beresford, *New Towns in the Middle Ages* (Cambridge, 1963), Chs. 3 and 7; *Cambridge Economic History of Europe*, Vol. III (1963), Ch. IV; J. Merrington, 'Town and Country in the Transition to Capitalism', in Hilton (ed.), *The Transition from Feudalism to Capitalism*; P. Clark, 'The Early Modern Town in the West: Research since 1945', in P. Clark (ed.), *The Early Modern Town* (London, 1976); P. Clark and P. Slack, *English Towns in Transition 1500–1700* (Oxford, 1976).

83 H. Kellenbenz, 'Rural Industries in the West from the End of the Middle Ages to the 18th Century', in P. Earle (ed.), *Essays in European Economic History 1500–1800* (Oxford, 1974).

84 J. de Vries, *The Economy of Europe in an Age of Crisis* (Cambridge, 1976), p. 85. For an interesting model involving cycles of town–country dynamism, see P. Hohenberg, 'Towards a Model of the European Economic system in Proto-industrial Perspective, 1300–1800', unpublished paper circulated at the Eighth International Economic History Conference, Budapest, 1982.

also on movements in the international markets for manufactured goods. Rural income was not therefore solely, or even usually, dependent on the movement of town–country terms of trade. Changes in the composition of urban production and demand, resulting from higher urban rents in periods of declining returns on the land, considerably affected the terms of trade between agriculture and industry, but it is necessary to ask what those rents were spent on. What was the composition of both urban production and demand patterns?

The consumption of urban property holders and wage earners spawned a whole range of urban employments, yet we know little of the structure and dynamic of these urban trades. Did they merely exist, or did they, like proto-industry, create a dynamic which tended either in the direction of factory production and mechanisation or towards industrial backwardness? These trades were the major suppliers of the basic necessities of life: processed food, drink, transport and shelter as well as luxury production using high-cost materials and sophisticated techniques. Their total size in terms of capital and employment must have been massive. How did their growth adapt to and in turn affect patterns of urban life and culture?

Whilst, thanks largely to the proto-industry literature, we are beginning to understand a great deal about the relationship between rural manufacture and rural social structures, there has been little comparable research into urban social structures and the urban trades. Two of the essays in this volume go some way in addressing this topic. Berg's essay examines Adam Smith's analysis of the town–country relationship and the different types of urban growth in Britain which Smith compared to his model of the town–country dynamic. And Michael Sonenscher begins to ask some important questions concerning the workings of the urban social, economic and 'moral' economy: the relationship of the wage to custom and perquisite, changing attitudes of masters and men, the effects of these and associated values and mentalities on capital accumulation and technical and organisational change.

At a regional level it is necessary to enquire into the effects of great metropolises and provincial towns and cities on rural manufacture. To what extent did urban and rural manufacturing activity compete with each other for capital, labour and markets? Did strong urban growth in a region attract surplus labour from the land and inhibit rural manufacture, or did rural by-employments tie an otherwise insecure agricultural population to the land in such a way that urban growth and the development of centralised manufacture was slowed down?

Historians of proto-industry have not only tended to neglect urban manufacture; they have also created a false dichotomy between town and country manufacture. In practice, especially in England, it is very difficult to place the two in distinctly separate categories. The rapid growth of urban villages, suburbs and unincorporated towns in the eighteenth century was accompanied by the proliferation of low-wage industries in these areas. Parts of the London suburbs were alive with activity in the low-wage unregulated trades,[85] and many of the Black Country towns were specifically associated with the rapid expansion of new manufactures for transatlantic markets.[86] These developments led to the contemporary notion of a division between the honourable and the dishonourable trades, but in no way was this division exclusively connected with a town–country contrast.

Too much of the distinction between town guilds and 'free' rural industries is based upon deductions from corporate regulations rather than upon any examination of the real workings of urban trades, about which only too little is known. The guilds of eighteenth-century England, as of elsewhere, await their historians. Until very much more research has been done, it would be helpful to suspend judgement upon the differences between urban and rural regulation of manufacture and the economic implications of these differences.

The lack of any clear distinction between town guilds and 'free' rural industry was not confined to England. Poni, for example, has noted the existence of underground workshops spinning silk waste in Bologna. The same unregulated practices existed in Nîmes and Avignon.[87] Other historians have pointed out the existence of guild industries in the European countryside, and organisation among rural workers, especially in England, could be very powerful and was by no means uncommon. Perhaps, as Thomson suggests below, rather than posing stark contrasts in the fundamental nature of production, town and country manufactures were to a large extent complementary and interchangeable. Major oscillations in overseas demand may have brought one or other to the forefront at different times depending on their type of organisation and their adaptability to different market conditions.

Custom and culture

Much of the discussion of divisions between town and country manufacture, of the proto-industry literature generally and of traditional economic history comes back time and again to the importance of relative labour costs and associated distinctions between urban and rural forms of labour organisation and resistance, traditions, mentalities and values.

Economic historians turn to such 'social values' when their preferred

---

85   I. Prothero, *Artisans and Politics in Early Nineteenth Century London* (Folkestone, Kent, 1979);
     R. Samuel, 'The Workshop of the World', *History Workshop Journal*, 3 (1977), 6–72.
86   Rowlands, *Masters and Men*.
87   C. Poni, 'Measure for Measure: Entrepreneurs and Silkspinners in Northern Italy', unpublished
     paper, 1980; M. Sonenscher, 'Royalists and Patriots', unpublished Ph.D. thesis (University of
     Warwick, 1978).

explanations in terms of differential productivities and comparative advantage run out. As Mathias has put it, the old world survived into the new by way of the 'non-economic determinants of cohesion'.[88] But these historians have in general been very unwilling to explore in greater depth just what these values were.

'Pre-industrial' social values and practices seem everywhere to have profoundly affected the emergence and extent of factory manufacture and the displacement of rural domestic production. The transition to the factory was not just an economic question concerning the relative merits or efficiency of one form of organisation and technology over another, but a social and political issue.

An appeal to such 'pre-industrial' values and motivations, in other words to non-market behaviour, at the level of the peasant household has been made in recent literature to explain both the early success and dynamism of proto-industry, and its subsequent limitations and failures:

The family functioned as an internal engine of growth in the process of proto-industrial expansion because subjectively it remained tied to the norms and rules of the traditional familial subsistence economy... In an advanced state of proto-industrial production this structural foundation became one of the negatively determining causes of the transition to industrial capitalism or led proto-industry into its cul-de-sac, i.e. into de-industrialisation or 'repastoralisation'.[89]

One of the major pillars of the proto-industry research on peasant household behaviour has been Chayanov's analysis.[90] For Chayanov the object of productive labour of the peasant household economy was to bring into equilibrium the labour consumer balance. If the returns of the family economy fell, it increased its expenditure of work even beyond the amount customary in an economic system dependent on capitalist wage labour. If, on the other hand, the returns of the family economy rose – perhaps because of rising prices of their farm or manufactured products – the household had no need to increase its expenditure of work, opting in preference for leisure, and a backward-sloping supply curve for labour ensued. Thus labour was often withdrawn at a time of maximum potential profit for the capitalist. This mechanism of both self-exploitation and leisure preference may, of course, have been very different in the case of *Kaufsystems* or kulak producers, but variations between motivations and behaviour and the organisational structures from which they derived have not yet been explored.

It is perhaps surprising that the recent proto-industry debate has not

---

88 P. Mathias, comment in conference discussion, SSRC Conference on Manufacture in Town and Country. See also the kind of explanation put forward by Duncan Bythell, *The Handloom Weavers* (Cambridge, 1969).
89 Medick, 'The Proto-industrial Family Economy', pp. 300–1.
90 Chayanov, *The Theory of the Peasant Economy*.

attempted to go beyond the Chayanov thesis, despite the fact that this work, evolved in connection with purely agrarian behaviour, has met criticism even in that context, and must need considerable refinement if and when applied to the rich diversity of proto-industrial forms. Generalisations concerning the backward-sloping supply curve for labour, for example, presuppose a narrow range of consumer choice and hence desires, and a high leisure preference which would depend on the socio-cultural environment as well as on the opportunity cost. Writers have pointed out that women took on a stronger position in the household during the proto-industrial period and that the younger generations were freed from those patriarchal controls so dominant in a purely peasant agricultural environment.[91] If the position of women and children within the power structure of the household was changing, this would surely imply changing consumption patterns and horizons and a lack of cohesion in decision making within the family. Even without these socio-cultural developments associated with proto-industry, the general applicability of the Chayanov model to all or even most of the very different types of household involved in rural manufacture must remain very dubious.

The whole debate concerning pre-factory manufacture, its structure and its 'dynamic', comes back time and again to 'non-economic' variables and, in particular, to custom and culture embodied in minds and in institutions. They can only begin to be understood by an historical approach freed from pre-occupation with the course and cause of human 'progress' or 'retrogression'. Since the 1920s anthropologists from Malinowski to Sahlins have been debating the validity of applying economic analysis and economic categories to the working of primitive societies.[92] Even the presence of a 'market society' with a negligible subsistence sector does not ensure the applicability of market analysis. Nor does it imply the decline of reciprocal and 'gift' relationships framed and conditioned outside of the market and the market mentality.

It is these areas of custom and culture which must be described and analysed before we become immersed in and blinkered by supply and demand analysis, indifference and utility curves and comparative advantage models in our quest to understand the meaning of manufacture before the factory.

THE PAST AND THE PRESENT

Although the proto-industry literature has provided valuable stimuli to research on a broad front, the most misleading and dangerous aspect of its essentially

91   Medick, 'The Proto-industrial Family Economy', pp. 312–14; R. Braun, 'The Impact of Cottage Industry on an Agricultural Population', in D. S. Landes (ed.), *The Rise of Capitalism* (Cambridge, 1966).

92   B. Malinowski, *Argonauts of the Western Pacific* (London, 1922); M. D. Sahlins, *Stone Age Economics* (London, 1974). See also P. Clastres, 'Les Marxistes et leur anthropologie'. *Libre*, 3 (1978), 135–50.

linear perspective is the current attempt to link the theory with contemporary development issues.

The proto-industry model as applied to Europe between the seventeenth and nineteenth centuries will possibly always be 'valid' within the range of assumptions and variables which it addresses. Regional 'testing' of the hypothesis will inevitably reveal complex realities in which it will be impossible to isolate the agency of particular variables to prove or disprove their mechanism in any particular circumstance or set of circumstances. The certainty of particular relationships and reactions is thus insufficient to begin to apply elements of the model in a prescriptive way to Third World industrialisation.

It is certainly the case that interesting and informative parallels can be drawn between Europe in the pre-factory period and Asia, Latin America or Africa at a later date. Providing that the very different circumstances of the world economy and of power structures within it are recognised for different time periods and that the complication of induced rather than autonomous transition is noted, such parallels may be very illuminating. It appears that there is an obvious proclivity of capital at all periods and stages of development, but particularly in crises such as the seventeenth and the late twentieth centuries, to seek out cheap labour. The marked shift in favour of rural production in seventeenth-century Europe has its parallel in the transfer of many labour-intensive production processes to Second and Third World countries at the present time.[93] The siting of such processes in areas of the world with repressive labour laws, with cheap and submissive female and juvenile labour and with attractive tax concessions, implies a subsidy to industrial profits from the social infrastructure and the social wage.

However, this contemporary parallel highlights the most fundamental problem of conceptualising a progression of phases whereby domestic dispersed production paves the way and is destined to be superseded by the more progressive and efficient factory. The persistence and resurgence of domestic and workshop industry – in the garment trade of New York and in the 'Third Italy' for example[94] – provoke scepticism about viewing changes in the organisation and concentration of industry as the major index of fundamental economic change. Both technological innovation and the market are currently favouring the trend away from centralised labour. Numerically controlled machine tools make flexible production on a small scale entirely viable, and the introduction of video computers and word processors is enabling clerical and executive personnel to work from home away from the social and collective world of labour. Meanwhile

---

93 See Ruth Pearson, 'Reflections on Proto-industrialisation from a Contemporary Perspective', unpublished paper, delivered to SSRC Conference on Manufacture in Town and Country. Also See F. Froebel, J. Heinrichs and O. Kreye, *The New International Division of Labour* (Cambridge, 1980).
94 M. Diaz Perez, 'The Re-emergence of Domestic Industrial Labour in the New York City Garment Industry', research paper presented to Urban Research Seminar, Sociology Dept, Graduate School, New York, 1979.

the lack of developed mass markets in the Third World, and their atrophy in advanced countries is directing production towards the satisfaction of wants which are diverse and customised rather than homogeneous.

The present recession and the strength and alienation of organised labour provide a further stimulus to dispersal of production. For the centralisation of industry also increases the potential power of labour. Encountering this barrier, a part of industry at least may now be seeking renewed development based on the greater mystification and complexity of the capital–labour relationship which dispersal inevitably entails.[95]

Against this current backcloth of world recession with the survival of artisan forms, the increase in small businesses and the resurgence of domestic outwork, particularly in the Third World, the need to comprehend the nature and durability of these structures in an earlier period assumes a new relevance and imperative.

95   P. Hudson, 'Proto-industrialisation: The Case of the West Riding Wool Textile Industry in the 18th and Early 19th Centuries', *History Workshop Journal*, 12 (1981).

2

Political economy and the principles of manufacture 1700–1800

MAXINE BERG

The problem I wish to confront in this essay is the extent to which contemporaries noticed and formulated the economic significance of the spread of manfacturing industry in the period just prior to the Industrial Revolution and the factory system. Historians have recently asserted the existence of a distinctive proto-industrial period, characterised by the proliferation of rural manufacturing by-employments.[1] It therefore seems worthwhile to investigate the terms in which contemporaries themselves understood such development. What principles of manufacturing industry did these writers outline? Did they draw attention to the specifically rural nature of early industry, seeing in domestic industry the matrix of economic development as is now so fashionable and popular among historians and economists alike? What other concepts and principles of manufacture did they offer, and how did these intersect with wider economic and social awareness?

In order to compare contemporary perceptions with the historians' picture I propose to look at the analysis of manufacture in some of the economic writings of the mercantilist era and its aftermath in the later eighteenth century. This essay will focus on a relatively narrow group of writers – those whose works attempted to analyse economic improvement. Furthermore, it confines itself to a specific problem – the association, if any, made by these writers between manufacture and wider economic growth and welfare. The essay will look only at British writers whose description and analysis is related to the British experience of economic change and British institutions. The continental experience, notably that of France, was quite different. When the Industrial Revolution came to France, small-scale artisan production was conceived in a new light. In fact and

---

1 See F. F. Mendels, 'Proto-industrialization: The First Phase of the Industrialization Process', *Journal of Economic History*, 32 (1972); Hans Medick, 'The Proto-industrial Family Economy', *Social History*, 3 (Oct. 1976); E. L. Jones, 'Agricultural Origins of Industry,' *Past and Present*, 40 (1968).

in theory this type of manufacture was not just part of a transition to a British style of industrialisation – it was the 'appropriate technology' for an alternative path of economic development. There, artisan production, combined with slow population growth and gradual urbanisation, allowed for steady increase in per capita output without enclosure and the factory system. In juridical terms too there were major differences. French cities were much more sharply divided from the countryside than was the case in Britain. Guild regulations were not so strictly enforced in Britain, and there were many new unincorporated towns and suburbs where industry could flourish without bureaucratic control. This more flexible institutional structure reinforced continuities rather than contrasts between agriculture and industry, country and town. It is very likely that these differences in economic and social structure between the two nations would be conveyed in the contemporary economics of both. This essay, however, will examine only the British case.

'Manufacture' was a subject of considerable interest and debate in the seventeenth century. It was part of the armoury of arguments over trade restriction and liberalisation. Rural manufacture and houses of industry were the long-paraded pet projects of Poor Law reformers. Concern over the spread of manufacturing and the nature of its social impact lay behind recurring misgivings over migration and population change, luxury and subsistence. With this social and political context in mind, we might ask what contemporary economic writings made of this manufacture. To what extent was the analysis they offered affected by these social and political issues, or how much did it ultimately rest on an economic context of changing wages and prices, tariff barriers and market institutions?

Historians have looked at ideas on pre-industrial manufacture only through the related but quite different subjects of attitudes to labour and unemployment and to foreign trade. The bulk of this debate has, however, centred on the seventeenth century in the work of Coleman, Wilson, Thirsk and Appleby.[2] Most of the eighteenth century has been regarded as a rather murky period, undistinguished before the dazzling light of Adam Smith in its last quarter. Thirsk leaves off her study at the beginning of an era which she alleges misunderstood the intentions and achievements of seventeenth-century writers, and which despised the full employment policies and the rural-artisanal path to economic development which they advocated.[3] Appleby, like Wilson, Viner and McCulloch before her, associates the eighteenth century with stagnation in

---

2 See Charles Wilson, 'The Other Face of Mercantilism,' in D. C. Coleman (ed.), *Revisions in Mercantilism* (London, 1969); Joan Thirsk, *Economic Policy and Projects: The Development of a Consumer Society in Early Modern England* (Oxford, 1978); Joyce Appleby, *Economic Thought and Ideology in Seventeenth Century England* (Princeton, 1978).

3 Thirsk, *Economic Policy*, Ch. 6.

economic theory. It was a dark age between the liberal free trade economics of the seventeenth century and Adam Smith.[4]

If, however, the economic literature of the eighteenth century is examined in terms other than the narrow categories of free trade and protection, the artificial division between the seventeenth and the eighteenth centuries would break down. A study of contemporary reflections on the sources and impact of industrial change, instead of being refracted through particular projects or trade policies, could be related to an overall view of the economy. For ideas on manufacture in the eighteenth century were connected with a whole range of wider economic issues, including the growth of output, the relation of town to country and industry to agriculture, the condition of labour, capital accumulation, and the relation of organisational and technical improvements to social change. In fact the most significant continuity between the centuries is in the discussion of manufacturing progress and economic growth. Appleby's group of free traders paid significant heed to the importance of England's manufacturing industries and to the means of raising their productivity. And when Defoe hailed the period since 1680 as 'a projecting age when men set their heads to designing Engines and Mechanical Motion', these writers took notice and wrote that it was higher consumption and the creation of new demands which provided the greatest incentive to efficiency, industry and invention.[5]

One of these writers whose work and political activity spanned the late seventeenth and eighteenth centuries calls into question the meaningfulness of creating a sharp distinction between the two periods. Henry Martyn, claimed by Appleby for a free trader of the 1690s, also falls within the framework of those eighteenth-century writers who focussed on division of labour and technical change. His remarkable piece, *Considerations on the East India Trade* (1701), though quarried in passing by Appleby, seems to have received little notice by most historians except for J. R. McCulloch, who described it as the 'ablest and most profound' of his collection, *Early English Tracts on Commerce* (1856). Martyn was the writer who 'has set the powerful influence of the division of labour in a very striking point of view, and has illustrated it with a skill and felicity which even Smith has not surpassed, but by which he most probably profited'.[6]

Martyn's tract was a powerful analysis of the connections between the extension of the market, the division of labour and technical change. He trounced the view that there was some moral or economic advantage to

4 Appleby, *Economic Thought and Ideology*, pp. 251–2.
5 *Ibid.*, pp. 165–7.
6 J. R. McCulloch (ed.), *Early English Tracts on Commerce* (1856) (Cambridge, 1952), pp. xiii, xiv. The tract was not, however, in Adam Smith's library. A biographical and expository sketch of Martyn and his tract can be found in Marcus Arkin, 'A Neglected Forerunner of Adam Smith', *South African Journal of Economics*, 23 (Dec. 1955).

employing labour-intensive trade strategies or technologies: 'If the same work is done by one, which was done before by three; if the other two are forc'd to sit still, the kingdom got nothing before by the labour of the two, and therefore loses nothing by their sitting still.'[7] He compared the effects of the expansion of trade to those of technological innovation and better means of transport and communication, and denounced 'make-work' policies for 'reducing the business of the people by making our manufactures too dear for foreign markets'. The unemployed might be much more profitably used in trades producing other more standardised commodities than those imported from the East Indies. Displaced labour might go to less skilled trades, 'the plainest and easiest', or to the 'single parts of other manufactures of most variety because the plainest work is soonest learned'. This specialisation between trades and division of labour within trades would soon reduce costs and thus prices in home manufactures. The East India trade would reduce the price of some commodities to the English consumer, and new techniques such as framework knitting would reduce the price and increase the number of stockings sold in this home trade.[8] The East India trade would not only thereby provide cheaper consumer goods; it would also provide the incentives for higher productivity at home, by leading to 'the invention of Arts, Mills and Engines to save the labour of hands in other manufactures' so that 'other things may be done with less and cheaper labour and therefore may abate the price of manufactures, tho' the wages of men should not be abated'.[9]

Martyn then went on to develop an extremely interesting analysis of the relationship between international trade and technical change. More trade, he argued, would help to rationalise the amount of skill assigned to each industrial process. The East India trade would introduce 'more Artists, more order and regularity' in English manufactures, would rid trades of superfluous skill and bring about division of labour in manufacture. In Martyn's words it 'would be the cause of applying proper parts of works of great variety to single and proper artists, of not leaving too much to be performed by the skill of single persons – this is what is meant by introducing greater order and regularity into our English manufactures'.[10] He illustrates this principle with detailed descriptions of the division of labour in textiles, watch making and shipbuilding, pointing out that the maker of any individual part 'must needs be more skilful and expenditious at his proper business, which shall be his whole and constant employment, than any man can be at the same work whose skill shall be pusled and confounded with variety of other business'.[11] Such 'order and regularity'

---

7 Henry Martyn, 'Considerations on the East India Trade' (1701), in McCulloch (ed.), *Early English Tracts*, p. 569.
8 *Ibid.*, pp. 586, 590.
9 *Ibid.*, p. 589.
10 *Ibid.*, pp. 590–1.
11 *Ibid.*, p. 591.

would have the effect of reducing labour costs, though not necessarily wages, and ultimately the prices of British manufactured goods.

A comparison of the Dutch and English herring fisheries gave him a good example of the close connections between the extension of the market, the division of labour and low competitive prices. In Holland he saw a large and stable demand for herring, which generated a large labour force in the trade, and a highly efficient boatbuilding industry. It was not only one which displayed a high degree of division of labour, but also one which seems to have discovered the potential of interchangeable parts:

Busses and other things, are works of great variety: to make them, there is as great variety of Artists; no one is charg'd with so much work, as to abate his Skill or Expedition. The model of their Busses is seldom chang'd, so that the Parts of one would serve as well for every Buss; as soon as any such thing can be bespoke in Holland, presently all the parts are laid together, the Buss is raised with mighty expedition.[12]

The foreign trade which would provide an incentive for the introduction of labour-saving machinery should be encouraged, as should the machinery itself, and Martyn found justification for his views in the number of mills and engines in Holland: 'But has more than only one sawmill been seen in England?... by a wonderful policy the people here must not be deprived of their labour; rather every work must be done by more hands than are necessary'.[13]

Martyn's emphasis on markets, division of labour and technical change was to be a recurrent theme throughout the eighteenth century. John Cary, the Bristol sugar merchant who wrote in the 1690s, was still read widely enough in the eighteenth century for new editions of his works to appear in 1719 and 1745.[14] Usually associated with workhouse schemes and the promotion of state intervention to distinguish between trades useful to the public and those yielding only private advantage, Cary's very detailed work on wages and productivity, new manufactures and technical change, has been ignored by his historians.[15] He argued that there was really no need to reduce British wages, for the same effect might be achieved through technical change, as a whole series of industries, including sugar refining, distilling, tobacco manufacture, woodworking and lead smelting, had recently demonstrated:

There is a cunning crept into the trades – the clockmaker hath improved his art to such a degree that labour and materials are the least part the buyer pays for. The variety of our

12 *Ibid.*, p. 613.
13 *Ibid.*, p. 615.
14 John Cary, *An Essay on the State of England* (Bristol, 1695, new editions 1719 and 1745); and *An Essay Towards Regulating the Trade and Employing the Poor of this Kingdom*, 2nd edn (London, 1719). Joyce Appleby lumps Cary with the group of free traders, even though his arguments favoured protection for home industries and he condemns the East India trade.
15 See Wilson, 'The Other Face of Mercantilism'.

woollen manufacture is so pretty, that fashion makes a thing worth twice the price it is sold for after ... artificers, by tools and laves fitted for different purposes, make such things as would puzzle a stander by to set a price on, according to the worth of men's labour ... new projections are every day set on foot to render the making of our woollen manufactures easy, which should be rendered cheaper by the contrivance of manufacturers not by the falling price of labour; cheapness creates expense, and expense gives fresh employments, whereby the poor will be still kept at work.[16]

Cary's views were confirmed by Joshua Gee, who in 1729 outlined a whole series of new industries which had appeared in England since the war with the French. He was particularly impressed by the advances in the copper and brass industries, and by the emergence of the new hardware, steel and toy trades. Recognising an increase in foreign competition in the woollen industry, he thought that other manufactures would have to supply its place in providing employment for the poor. For this task he was particularly keen on promoting the English manufacture and use of pig and bar iron from the colonies.[17] But an interest in employment did not preclude Gee from praising labour-saving technical change, in particular the Italian silk throwing machine 'which with a few hands to attend it will do more work than an hundred persons can do at throwing by our method'.[18]

Daniel Defoe's *Tour* of 1724–6 provided another variation on Martyn's theme of division of labour and technical change. Observation and detailed journalistic description, not economic analysis, led Defoe to highlight a very different aspect of the new industries and new techniques others had praised. His *Tour* contained a remarkably detailed description of the highly sophisticated domestic system of the West Riding of Yorkshire. Here was a countryside which seemed 'one continuous village'. To every considerable house was attached a 'manufactory or workhouse'; each had its own stream of running water and easy access to coal fuel; and each kept a horse or two and a cow or two with enough land to feed them. Amongst the manufacturers' houses were 'scattered an infinite number of cottages or small dwellings, in which dwell the workmen which are employed, the women and children of whom are always busy carding and spinning'. The workmen were all employed in the clothiers' manufactories, 'a houseful of lusty fellows, some at the dye-fat, some dressing the cloths, some at the loom, some one thing, some another, all hard at work and full employed upon the manufacture, and all seeming to have sufficient business'.[19] Yet this detailed description of a phenomenon which historians have told us was much more widespread, and

16 Cary, *An Essay Towards Regulating the Trade*, p. 99.
17 Joshua Gee, *The Trade and Navigation of Great Britain Considered* (London, 1729), pp. 5, 69.
18 *Ibid.*, p. 10.
19 Daniel Defoe, *A Tour Through the Whole Island of Great Britain* (1724–6), ed. Pat Rogers (Harmondsworth, 1971), pp. 493–4.

indeed the most significant development of the pre-industrial economy, did not stimulate an economic analysis. Why was this? Was it, as Defoe claimed, because earlier writers 'had not properly explored the countryside'? He himself had found it necessary 'to dwell in it and go across the country backwards and forwards'.[20] Or was it because this very sophisticated form of industrial organisation displayed a principle of far greater interest to economic writers than the mere fact that this was rural not urban industry? For what Defoe described was not a region of peasants practising by-employments, but a workforce dwelling in the countryside. The system therein described depicted a division of labour between agriculture and industry. For Defoe saw few people out of doors in the area and little corn. Their corn came from Lincolnshire, Nottinghamshire, and the East Riding, and the clothiers bought their beef in the market in Halifax. He also described a division of labour within the workshops. This was not family production in peasant households, but the employment of workers in assigned tasks and, as a result, it was a 'populous and wealthy region'.[21]

The overall picture presented by Defoe was not one of the predominance and progress of particularly rural industries, but one of industrial regions in Lancashire, Yorkshire and the Midlands where town and country formed a continuity. Such regions became known for the manufacturing industries in which they specialised. It was not the fact that this was rural industry that impressed even Defoe, but that it was specialised manufacture. And what impressed writers on political economy in the mid eighteenth century was that this specialised manufacture was subject to all the gains in productivity to be had through the division of labour and technical change.

Defoe's picture of industrial organisation in the mid-eighteenth-century West Riding of Yorkshire was echoed at the end of the eighteenth century in Sir Frederick Eden's survey of the poor, but with rather less optimistic overtones. It was still the case that manufacturers occupied small farms chiefly laid to pasture and that they kept a cow or two for the use of their families. But with the reduction of wages caused by the war with France there was also in evidence a large group of poor women, who had before earned a bare subsistence by spinning, but 'were now in a very wretched condition'.[22] In fact, many of the industries cited in the economic commentaries of the early and mid eighteenth century had already made the transition from rural by-employment to specialised town or country industry. Joan Thirsk notes that the seventeenth-century connection between dairy farming and stocking knitting was broken by the eighteenth century. Knitters now lived increasingly in towns with little part-time interest in farming. There were many who 'never tasted the independence of the hand

---

20 *Ibid.*, p. 485.
21 *Ibid.*, p. 496.
22 Sir Frederick Eden, *The State of the Poor*, 3 vols. (London, 1797), III, 821.

knitters. From the outset they were enslaved, like the spinners and weavers of cloth working for a clothier for small wages, so that they lived very poorly.'[23] In the seventeenth-century west of England clothing industry, weavers had lost their connection with the land. Most owned no more than a garden; some owned houses in the towns, and were rent payers and the tenants of the clothiers. Their earnings depended not on the supplementary produce of a farm, but on the price of provisions and the industrial employment opportunities for all members of the family.[24] Even the linen industry, which had a long history of small-scale production for domestic use and localised markets, was changing by the early eighteenth century. Where formerly nearly one-third of the labouring population was supposed to have been involved in the linen industry as a by-employment, it was now evident that home and localised production and consumption was being replaced through commercial channels. Linen became instead a staple industry in particular regions of Yorkshire and Co. Durham, Northumberland, Lancashire, Somerset, Dorset, Devon and Wiltshire,[25] as well of course as Scotland and Ireland.

Specialised manufacture, be it in town or country, was evidently what met the eye and caught the imagination of the 'economist' in the early years of the eighteenth century. When we turn to the middle of the century it was this theme and not rural industry which continued to fascinate writers. But by the middle of the century the analysis of manufacture also included an awareness of some of industry's social implications. New industries, technical change and division of labour were carefully weighed against some social considerations in the writings of Josiah Tucker, Malachy Postlethwayt, and the author of *Reflections on Arts, Commerce, and Foreign Artists*. Postlethwayt broadened the ever-recurring enquiry into the costs of labour to a consideration of other ways of reducing costs of production, and of ways of creating new markets. He argued that 'the general perfection of the manufactures of a state consists in obtaining the preference of every class of consumers': this was to be achieved by the maximum variety of output and by the cheapness of commodities. 'The choice of various kinds of goods multiplies the desires of other nations.'[26]

An abundance of cheap British manufactures might be achieved despite high labour costs if there was some prospect of labour-saving technical change. The

---

23 Joan Thirsk, 'The Fantastical Folly of Fashion: The English Stocking Knitting Industry, 1500–1700', N. B. Harte and K. G. Ponting, *Textile History and Economic History: Essays in Honour of Miss Julia de Lacy Mann* (Manchester, 1973), p. 71.

24 J. de L. Mann, *The Cloth Industry in the West of England from 1640 to 1880* (Oxford, 1971), pp. 102, 104.

25 N. B. Harte, 'The Rise of Protection and the English Linen Trade, 1690–1790', in Harte and Ponting, *Textile History and Economic History*, p. 96.

26 Malachy Postlethwayt, *Britain's Commercial Interest Explained and Improved*, 2 vols. (London, 1757), II, 400.

possibilities seen in this by Henry Martyn in 1701 had by the mid eighteenth century become a subject of some debate, and the pros and cons of labour-saving inventions were carefully considered. This discussion of some of the social aspects of technical change was made, however, against a background of concern over employment and home markets. Thus, while there was certainly an awareness among these mid-eighteenth-century writers of the geographical dispersion of industry, there was no conclusive analysis of the role of rural industry in terms other than the long-standing problem of setting the poor to work. The author of *Reflections on Arts and Commerce* argued that the machines 'did the work truer and better than the hand', and that the labour saved by them was so great 'that they who use the machine must undersell the others in a vast disproportion'.[27] Still, he did not consider it easy to determine the pace at which technical change ought to be allowed to proceed. He finally decided that 'engines' might be introduced with no problem, in the first case where they did jobs that could not be done at all by hand, as with pumps, fire engines, looms, wine and oil presses, and secondly where the commodities concerned could not be produced at all except by machine, as in paper-making and iron-processing machinery, and fulling mills. Another consideration was the type of economy – was this a country with a large sector of foreign trade, or a fairly isolated community? Commercial states that had to produce cheaply to gain foreign markets had no option but to use labour-saving techniques. But those with little trade, where the technological unemployment created might adversely affect home markets, did have some justification for holding back or preventing the use of machinery.[28]

Postlethwayt rejected such arguments, limiting his reservations to the use of machinery in agriculture. He thought that the skill of workmen would lead naturally to invention, invention which would not, contrary to popular opinion, reduce employment. It would lead, instead, to more employment 'by multiplying works and increasing the produce of the balance, which never ceases to increase home consumption':

We do not see any objection that can be made to the economising of time, or facilitating the work of manufactures which may not be equally well made to all inventions of new fashions, or of new stuffs, by which the old are forgot ... I believe no man will say it is the interest of a nation to prohibit new manufactures, in order to favour the workmen employed in the old.[29]

27 *Reflections on Various Subjects Relating to Arts and Commerce Particularly the Consequences of Admitting Foreign Artists on Easier Terms* (London, 1752), p. 24. This is ascribed in the Kress Catalogue to Richard Parrott, and by T. S. Ashton in his *An Economic History of England: The 18th Century* (London, 1961) to Dean Tucker. The arguments in this pamphlet, however, contradict those in Tucker's *A Brief Essay on France and Britain with Regard to Trade* (1749).
28 *Reflections on Arts and Commerce*, p. 24.
29 Postlethwayt, *Britain's Commercial Interest*, II, 416, 420.

But still, Postlethwayt believed with the author of *Reflections on Arts and Commerce* that home markets had to be maintained in order to prevent any English industry being undermined by foreign imports. The best security for this market was in the 'cultivators of the soil', and 'every machine tending to diminish their employment would really be destructive of the strength of society, of the mass of men, and of home consumption'.[30]

Industrial location seemed to matter only to those who noticed differences between the incorporated and unincorporated town, between large and small towns, and between the metropolis and the provinces. Tucker condemned the French 'matrises' as a 'cloy upon trade', and commended Birmingham, Manchester, Leeds and four-fifths of London because they had no companies.[31] And Postlethwayt praised the Dutch who refused to allow limitations on the number of workmen in a trade and on the quantity of work produced.[32] The author of *Reflections on Arts and Commerce* disagreed with Postlethwayt on the place of large cities and the metropolis in the industrial hierarchy. The anonymous author argued that though the lower branches of manufacture were by far the most important for numbers employed, the more refined branches succeeded best in large and rich towns. They not only held out the prospect of a greater market, but also held more attractions 'for curious workmen than common food'. But many industries seemed to have a tendency to move northwards, 'from the dearer to the cheaper place'. Even the Spitalfields silk trade might soon be carried on in the north. This movement away from the metropolis, 'the general market and magazine for the world', might be a dangerous development in the long term, for 'small towns find their conveniences near them and produce scarce any effect further than about thirty miles round, whereas London puts the whole nation in motion'.[33] Postlethwayt defended the claims of the country. Provisions were too expensive and the city and workmen would fall prey to 'superfluous wants', 'dissipation', and 'neglect of work'. The higher wages offered in the city would 'tempt workmen from other places and industry would be absorbed by a few towns'. The country was also the best place for the early introduction of improvements: 'it is indifferent to the State whether a manufactory be in one town or fifty miles off in a village, which will become a town in its turn. Experiments are there made quietly by a small number of chosen workmen and their example by degrees invites others thither'.[34] And Tucker threw his weight behind the iron manufacturers dispersed throughout the

30   *Ibid.*, p. 420.
31   Josiah Tucker, *A Brief Essay on the Advantages and Disadvantages which Respectively Attend France and Great Britain with Regard to Trade* (London, 1749), p. 5.
32   Postlethwayt, *Britain's Commercial Interest*, II, 414.
33   *Reflections on Arts, Commerce and Foreign Artists*, pp. 10, 21, 42.
34   Postlethewayt, *Britain's Commercial Interest*, II, 416, 420.

countryside and villages of the Midlands. These were 'men of middling fortune', and the 'nailers amongst them were ranked among the lowest class of life'. But the 'whole of their fortunes together' and the immense yearly value of their labour led him to reckon their trades the 'second manufacture of the kingdom'.[35]

Economic commentators of the early and mid eighteenth century, then, were not very interested in pursuing an analysis of the location of industry as the special feature of its progress. It was the potential markets, the skill, ingenuity and suitable price of labour, and the possibilities of labour-saving technical change which attracted much more attention as the means of encouraging the creation of new industries in Britain and allowing her to dominate world markets in old and new trades.

By the 1760s and 1770s, A. Anderson's *Historical Deduction of the Origins of Commerce* was organised around cataloguing new manufacturing industries and describing the new machinery daily being introduced into particular trades. William Kenrick, another commentator, unreservedly assumed that any well-governed nation would expedite the introduction of labour-saving machinery as the best means of gaining foreign markets. By this time too, writers on political economy were concerned with problems of labour discipline and looked for alternatives to the present system, alternatives not yet perceived in machine technology, but certainly seen in some form of factory organisation.[36] Where Postlethwayt had claimed that the poor were industrious and deserved good wages, J. Cunningham in 1770 objected that the so-called industry of the poor was only predicated on a series of Elizabethan statutes to enforce labour and regulate its price. But this had clearly proved insufficient, for

the lower sort of people in England from a romantic notion of liberty, generally reject and oppose everything that is forced upon them; and though, from a fear of punishment, you may oblige persons to labour certain hours for certain wages, you cannot oblige them to do their work properly. If they work against their wills, they may slight their work, and our foreign trade may be hurt.[37]

The answer to the problem might be found in the type of factory discovered by him at Abbeville. Six hundred workers came to work and left it at the beat of a drum, and 'each branch had a distinct foreman who disciplined the workmen so as to make them excel in every branch of the whole'.[38]

The stage was thus set by the later eighteenth century for Adam Smith's analysis of the significant connections between the expansion of markets, the

35   Josiah Tucker, *The Case of the Importation of Bar Iron from our Own Colonies of North America* (London, 1756), p. 5.
36   A. Anderson, *Historical and Chronological Deduction of the Origins of Commerce from the Earliest Accounts to the Present Time*, 2 vols. (London, 1764); W. Kenrick, *An Address to the Artists and Manufacturers of Great Britain* (London, 1774).
37   J. Cunningham. *An Essay on Trade and Commerce* (London, 1770), p. 92.   38 *Ibid.*, p. 130.

division of labour, and technical change, acting in concert to turn the engine of economic progress. The eighteenth century was not marked by a gap between the insights of the seventeenth-century mercantilists and the advances of Adam Smith, but by continuous analysis from the later seventeenth century onward of the connections between markets, technical change and industrial expansion.

It was on this edifice built up through the eighteenth century that Adam Smith developed the division of labour into a principle underlying the whole mechanism of the economic and political institutions he was analysing in *The Wealth of Nations*. But his analysis was also one which has seemed to some historians to denounce the whole proto-industrial structure, yielding what Joan Thirsk calls a 'simplified, partial and occasionally harsh view of the domestic system', and a 'grotesque caricature of the weaver-farmer'.[39] But, as I will now argue, this is a partial and simplified view of Adam Smith.

Smith's comments on domestic industry cannot be fully understood outside the framework of his model of economic growth and development. The basic elements of this model – the division of labour, the expansion of markets and the accumulation of capital – were specified in Books I and II, and the dynamic of the model outlined in the important but often neglected Book III, 'Of the Different Progress of Opulence in Different Nations'. Smith argues that the division of labour or the specialisation of economic activities, the original source of improvement, generates gains in productivity because of greater dexterity, time saving, and new inventions. But right from the outset he specifies that this hinges on the development of the market and upon capital accumulation. Specialisation took place accordingly in different areas in response to the size and condition of the market:

It is found that society must be pretty far advanced before the different trades can all find subsistence.[40]

The labourer who had to take on multiple employments because the market was not large enough to sustain any single occupation could not increase his dexterity, save his time, or apply himself to technical improvements. There were, therefore, strict limitations to his potential productivity. The labourer's own subsistence from these multiple occupations would be affected not just by his low productivity, but by his own position in the labour market:

Where a person derives his subsistence from one employment, which does not occupy the greater part of his time; in the intervals of his leisure he is often willing to work at another for less wages than would otherwise suit the nature of the employment.

39   Thirsk, *Economic Policy and Projects*, pp. 150–1.
40   Adam Smith, *Lectures on Justice*, cited in *An Inquiry into the Nature and Causes of the Wealth of Nations* (1776), 2 vols. (Oxford, 1976), Vol. I, Book I, Chap. ii, pp. 31ff. All subsequent references are from Vol. I.

The Scottish cotters were a prime example of this:

The produce of such labour comes frequently cheaper to market than would otherwise be suitable to its nature. Stockings in many parts of Scotland are knit much cheaper than they can anywhere be wrought upon the loom. They are the work of servants and labourers, who derive the principal part of their subsistence from some other employment...

The spinning of linen yarn is carried on in Scotland nearly in the same way as the knitting of stockings, by servants who are chiefly hired for other purposes.[41]

The extent of specialisation was also determined, as Smith continued, by the size and rate of increase of the capital stock. An employer's capital had to be sufficient to employ a particular labourer at any single occupation. Any increase in a capital stock would also tend to raise wages, which in turn created incentives for a division of labour and higher productivity:

The owner of the stock which employs a great number of labourers, necessarily endeavours, for his own advantage, to make such a proper division and distribution of employment, that they may be enabled to produce the greatest quantity of work possible.[42]

In Book III Smith demonstrated how this framework – division of labour, market and capital – came together in a dynamic model of the development of agriculture and industry, town and country. The model and the historical economics of Book III form the reference point for views of manufacture expressed by Smith elsewhere in *The Wealth of Nations*. Here Smith argued that there was a natural progression of economic development. The natural (which was not necessarily the actual) course of development was a model of economic growth based in the first instance upon agriculture. 'Manufactures for distant sale' might 'grow up of their own accord, by the gradual refinement of those household and coarser manufactures which must at all times be carried on in even the poorest and rudest countries'. Based on domestic raw materials, they generally sprang up in an inland country which produced an agricultural surplus, which it in turn found it difficult to trade, due to high transport costs. The surplus, however, made basic needs very inexpensive, encouraging the immigration of a larger labour force. These workmen

work up the materials of manufacture which the land produces ... they give a new value to the surplus part of raw produce ... and they furnish the cultivators with something in exchange for it that is either useful or agreeable to them ... They are thus both encouraged and enabled to increase this surplus produce by a further improvement and better cultivation of the land; and as the fertility of the land had given birth to the manufacture, so the progress of the manufacture reacts upon the land and increases still further its fertility.[43]

41　*Ibid.*, I, x., p. 134.
42　*Ibid.*, I, xiii, p. 104.
43　*Ibid.*, III, iii, p. 409.

This was the natural progress from agriculture to manufacture and thence to foreign commerce, praised by Smith for leading both to the most rapid rates of growth and to a balanced economy. Such natural progress, Smith conceded, had actually taken place in certain parts of England, where some cities had arisen on the basis of rural industries which complemented regional agricultural surpluses:

In this manner have grown up naturally, and as it were of their own accord, the manufactures of Leeds, Halifax, Sheffield, Birmingham and Wolverhampton. Such manufactures are the offspring of agriculture.[44]

Smith was also struck elsewhere by the rate of technical progress in the industries of some of these towns. He remarked on the great reductions in prices in recent years in those manufactures using the coarser metals, in the watch making, cutlery, locksmith and toy trades, 'and in all those goods which are commonly known by the name of Birmingham and Sheffield ware'.

There are perhaps no manufactures in which the division of labour can be carried further, or in which the machinery employed admits of a greater variety of improvement than those of which the materials are the coarser metals.[45]

Smith was intrigued by the comparison between these coarse metal industries and the coarse cloth manufacture. Referring to the woollen and worsted industries, he pointed out that prices had not fallen so much, and where they had, this was not a result of technical progress. The coarse manufacture was carried out in 'ancient times in England' in the 'same manner as it always has been in countries where the arts and manufactures are in their infancy'. It was probably a household manufacture, in which 'every different part of the work was occasionally performed by all the different members of almost any private family'. But the prices in this manufacture were already relatively low, indeed much lower than in the fine cloth manufacture. These price differences were not, he thought, due to differences in the quality of the raw material, or to technical progress. Rather the coarse cloth manufacture was a by-employment, and the work which is performed in this manner, 'it has already been observed, comes always much cheaper to market than that which is the principal or sole fund of the workman's subsistence'. The fine cloth manufacture was sold at higher prices because it was manufactured in the 'rich and commercial country of Flanders, and it was probably conducted then, in the same manner as now, by people who derived the whole, or the principal part of their subsistence from it'.

Many industries might exist alongside agriculture, then, but they were not the natural offspring of agriculture unless based on agricultural surpluses. The produce of such industries could indeed be brought to market very cheaply, but

44   *Ibid.*
45   *Ibid.*, I, xi, p. 260.

this was not generally a result of their higher productivity. Their cheapness was due to their labour force which undersold itself doing that kind of work 'only when they had nothing else to do, and not to be the principal business from which any of them derived the greater part of their subsistence'.[46] This practice might yield lower-cost commodities, but it did not necessarily yield the best economic conditions for working men and women, in the way that the natural progress of opulence did. For Smith had also argued in Book I that it was agricultural surpluses and the cheap provisions these entailed which provided the ideal opportunities for the poor. These conditions, he had suggested, allowed men and women to leave their employers and to work much harder, for a larger return, as independent labourers and artisans.

That Smith should have entertained the prospect of growing numbers of independent, artisan labourers is, perhaps, surprising. Concluding the last chapter of Book I, he affirmed that 'the three great, original and constituent orders of every civilized society, from whose revenue that of every other order is ultimately derived' were those of landowners, labourers and employers of stock, or capitalists. This was so because the returns to the landowner, the labourer and the capitalist – rent, wages, and profits – were the three components of the price of commodities.[47] The labouring order, by definition, was dependent on the wage for its subsistence: unlike those who lived in less developed and less differentiated societies, the modern labourer did not receive the whole produce of his labour. Smith was insistent that the modern labourer was thereby neither poor nor unfree. Where the static technologies of underdeveloped economies had provided little more than an equality of poverty, the division of labour in advanced commercial societies assured the labourer not only regular subsistence, but also, through growing surpluses, higher real wages.[48] Where, too, the poor had hitherto been dependent, to the point of servitude, on their lords and masters, the labourer in commercial society was 'really free in our present sense of the word freedom'.[49] The owner at least of his own labour, he enjoyed liberty of person and property under the law. Nevertheless, Smith clearly did not suppose this 'freedom' of the modern wage labourer to extend to complete 'independence': in so far as the labourer's wage, along with his tools and raw materials, were an 'advance' from his master, he must be considered as dependent upon the owner of capital.[50] The labourer's dependence, moreover, must have been enhanced to the extent that the extension of the division of labour presupposed the accumulation and proper employment of capital.[51]

46 *Ibid.*, I, xi, p. 263.
47 *Ibid.*, I, xi, p. 265.
48 *Ibid.*, I, viii, pp. 85–6.
49 *Ibid.*, III, iii, p. 400.
50 *Ibid.*, I, viii, pp. 82–3.
51 *Ibid.*, II, introduction, p. 277.

On this analysis, there would seem to be little room for the fully independent, artisan labourer who sold his own produce. Yet Smith did acknowledge his existence, early in the chapter on wages:

It sometimes happens, indeed, that a single independent workman has stock sufficient both to purchase the materials of his work, and to maintain himself till it be compleated. He is both master and workman, and enjoys the whole produce of his own labour, or the whole value which it adds to the materials upon which it is bestowed. It includes what are usually two distinct revenues, belonging to two distinct persons, the profits of stock, and the wages of labour.[52]

It is true that Smith immediately qualified this acknowledgement, remarking that 'such cases, however, are not very frequent, and in every part of Europe, twenty workmen serve under a master for one that is independent'.[53] Nevertheless, as if tacitly recognising the actual indeterminacy of 'wage labour' in the eighteenth-century European economy, he returned more than once later in the chapter to the significance of the independent artisan. He noted how the produce of such independent labour was frequently ignored by the government and by political arithmeticians: it often consisted of goods which were consumed at home by the family or by neighbours and were never retailed through the market.[54] He observed too how agricultural surpluses and plentiful provisions enabled labourers to 'trust their subsistence to what they can make by their own industry'. He went on:

Nothing can be more absurd... than to imagine that men in general should work less when they work for themselves, than when they work for other people. A poor independent workman will generally be more industrious than even a journeyman who works by the piece. The one enjoys the whole produce of his industry; the other shares it with his master... The superiority of the independent workman over those servants who are hired by the month or by the year, and whose wages and maintenance are the same, whether they do much or do little, is likely to be still greater.[55]

The implications of these observations were particularly far-reaching. In the first place, Smith appears to have been suggesting that as a result of growing agricultural surpluses and higher real wages, there was actually a tendency for increasing numbers of labourers to become fully independent. In the progress of commercial society, wage labour was far from being universalised: to an increasing extent the independent artisan also enjoyed his place. Moreover, secondly, Smith's observation of the greater intensity of the labour of the independent workman strongly suggested that such a workman could make his own contribution to increasing productivity. This contribution would, it should

52 *Ibid.*, I, viii, p. 83.
53 *Ibid.*, I, viii, p. 83.
54 *Ibid.*, I, viii, p. 103.
55 *Ibid.*, I, viii, p. 101.

be noted, be quite consistent with the technical division of labour discussed in the opening chapter of *The Wealth of Nations* and exemplified in the coarse metal trades. The workman who produced but one type of file or but one part of a watch or lock could well be an independent tradesman or artisan. Indeed, such an independent tradesman was for Smith the archetypal workman-inventor who developed and perfected the tools, machines and skills of the trade. As the progress of opulence engendered the artisan, so in turn the artisan contributed to the division of labour on which that progress ultimately depended.

Smith's 'natural progression' which increasingly created these conditions of independence and opportunity for the artisan was not, however, an historical model of *European* economic development. With regret, Smith traced how European policies and follies had generally resulted in an opposite course of development – not from agriculture to industry and commerce, but from foreign commerce and industry to agriculture. The unnatural course of European economic development had been based on policies which favoured the development of luxury manufactures using foreign raw materials, manufactures introduced to substitute for former imports. Such industries had usually been the 'scheme and project of a few individuals' and were established in maritime towns or inland cities 'according to their interest, judgement or caprice'.[56] Of those manufactures which Smith praised as the offspring of agriculture, he said:

In the modern history of Europe, their extension and improvement have generally been posterior to those which were the offspring of foreign commerce.[57]

After a detailed history of the decline of feudalism in Western Europe, as a history of feudal vanities and mercantile cunning, he pointed out with no little distaste the results. The great proprietors, 'to gratify their childish vanity', had sold their land and relinquished their feudal privileges. The merchants and artificers, 'in pursuit of their own pedlar principle of turning a penny wherever a penny was to be got', exploited the countryside and turned the terms of trade in favour of the town.[58]

The advantages of the town even extended to labour. For corporate regulations ensured higher wages in urban than in rural occupations. These higher wages resulted not from the nature of the work but from the exclusive practices of urban labour:

The inhabitants of the country, dispersed in distant places, cannot easily combine together. They have not only never been incorporated, but the corporation spirit never has prevailed among them. No apprenticeship has ever been thought necessary to qualify for husbandry, the great trade of the country.[59]

56 *Ibid.*, III, iii, p. 408.
57 *Ibid.*, III, iii, p. 410.
58 *Ibid.*, III, iv, p. 422.
59 *Ibid.*, I, x, p. 143.

It was these regulations which drove up the wages and profits of the town above those of the country. The main offender was the Statute of Apprentices, which notably did not cover country villages or trades not already established before the Elizabethan statute was first enacted. Most of the trades of Manchester, Birmingham and Wolverhampton were 'not within the statute; not having been exercised in England before the 5th of Elizabeth', and were therefore exempt from Smith's criticism.[60] This is not to say that wage differences between trades and between town and country would not occur in these new towns. For it was also certainly the case that where all other circumstances were equal wages would be higher in new than in older trades. A projector establishing a new manufacture had to entice workmen from other trades:

Manufactures for which the demand arises altogether from fashion and fancy, are continually changing, and seldom last long enough to be considered as old established manufactures ... Birmingham deals chiefly in manufacture of the former kind; Sheffield in those of the latter; the wages of labour in those two different places, are said to be suitable to this difference in the nature of their manufactures.[61]

It was the policies of labourers and merchants alike which had given the town a false advantage over the country. These had broken down 'that natural equality which would otherwise take place in the commerce which is carried on between them. The whole annual produce of the labour of the society is annually divided between those two different sets of people.' By means of those regulations a greater share of it was given to the 'inhabitants of the town than would otherwise fall to them; and a less to those of the country'.[62] The towns might, in the end, become the cause of the improvement of the country, as urban surpluses spilled over into investment in land, but even where this had taken place development had been slow and uncertain:

Compare the slow progress of those European countries of which the wealth depends very much upon their commerce and manufacture, with the rapid advances of our North American colonies, of which the wealth is founded altogether in agriculture.[63]

Smith's aversion to merchants and the industries they fostered for international luxury markets conveys the impression that his concept of the market was one based on the neighbourhood. Local industries that grew up to supply local needs formed the preferable basis for industrial development. This idea of the industrial market, however, contrasts sharply with his idea of the agricultural market. Where corn was the commodity under discussion, the merchant, in this case the corn middleman, fulfilled an important economic function in evening

60 *Ibid.*, I, x, p. 137.
61 *Ibid.*, I, x, p. 131.
62 *Ibid.*, I, x, p. 142.
63 *Ibid.*, III, iv, p. 422.

out the seasonable availability of bread and in easing the regional disparities between surpluses and scarcities. E. P. Thompson argues that the national market economy perspective of the corn middleman clashed with the regional subsistence and moral economy mentality of the poor.[64] But the division was not so clear-cut. As Smith recognised, the livelihood of the poor in a now transitional economy was not dependent only on local agricultural surpluses or scarcities. Many of them were now at least partially wage dependent. Many involved in industrial employment faced capital and labour markets beyond the locality – national or even international markets. Manufacture destined for international trade, in particular, was dependent on conditions outside the region, 'on circumstances affecting demand in the countries where they are consumed; upon peace or war, upon the prosperity or declension of other rival manufactures, and upon the good or bad humour of their principal customers'.[65] Local customary markets now intersected with national and international markets. The domestic economy of artisan and rural producers was becoming a microcosm of macro-economic variables. Smith argued that whatever the corn middleman's motives, his interests coincided with those of the wider population:

it is the interest of the people that their daily, weekly, and monthly consumption, should be proportioned as exactly as possible to the supply of the season. The interest of the inland corn dealer is the same.[66]

In order to maximise his profit, the middleman brought to bear a knowledge of the state of the crops and a judgement on markets which should have effectively adjusted seasonal supplies of corn at the least cost. In addition, the corn market was not, in Smith's view, easy to monopolise. He thought it of all commodities 'the least liable to be engrossed or monopolised by the force of a few large capitals'. The capital required to do so would be enormous, and production was too dispersed to control in this manner:

it is necessarily divided among a greater number of owners than any other commodity; and these owners can never be collected into one place like a number of independent manufacturers, but are necessarily scattered through all the different corners of the country, and their dispersed situation renders it altogether impossible for them to enter into any general combination.[67]

The actions of the corn middlemen, then, ought to increase competition and widen local markets. But it was also true that because they made their profits in years of scarcity of this basic subsistence commodity, they were the victims of 'public odium'. People of 'character and fortune' therefore avoided the trade,

64 E. P. Thompson, 'The Moral Economy of the Crowd', *Past and Present*, 50 (1972).
65 Smith, *The Wealth of Nations*, I, viii, p. 103.
66 *Ibid.*, IV, v, p. 525.
67 *Ibid.*, IV, v, p. 526.

abandoning it to 'an inferior set of dealers; and millers, bakers, mealmen, and meal factors, together with a number of wretched hucksters'.[68] Such characters were not presumably the men of knowledge and judgement best suited to direct this trade, yet, in spite of themselves, they too generally assisted the operation of the market.

If this was the case with corn merchants, why was Smith so pessimistic about the effect on the local economy of the actions of merchants in industrial commodities? These merchants, it seems, did not act to widen local markets, but rather to append local labour and capital to the whims and dictates of international markets. They moved in with patents and regulations, and could establish monopolies where the corn merchants could not. They fostered a breach between the wealth and specialisation of the towns and the poverty and subsistence economy of the country. International markets, therefore, coexisted with local subsistence economies – they did not, as they ought to, grow out of the commercialisation of a region. These international markets did eventually enter the countryside, but only after it had been reduced to a disadvantage beside the town. The market then created in the countryside was distorted. The labour employed was not wage labour: it was the labour of by-employments, easily and cheaply bought, and easily cast off. The capital invested was accumulated but not built, for it shifted at least as quickly as the trade cycle. The existence of an international division of labour manifest in a local community was not therefore evidence of regional growth and welfare.

It is from within the framework of Smith's model of economic growth, based on specialisation, markets and capital, whose dynamic entailed the emergence of industry out of agricultural origins, that we can understand his favour for the corn middleman and his criticisms of rural by-employments run by merchants. It was because of the gains of specialisation and the demands of markets that 'in every improved society the farmer is generally nothing but a farmer, the manufacturer nothing but a manufacturer'. It was because there was inadequate capital to provide full-time occupations that the underemployed country weaver 'sauntered a little in turning his hand from one employment to another'. And it was because of inadequate capital invested in the land, combined with the exploitation of the country by the towns, that rural workers were paid lower wages for their by-employments than rates of wages paid for full-time employment would have warranted. These workers, underemployed in agriculture, would work in their free time for less than customary wages or prices in another trade. The existence of these by-employments, seen by Smith at their worst in the Highlands of Scotland, was a sign of the poverty and exploitation of rural society. The merchants and the towns, of course, benefited, and the

68   *Ibid.*, IV, v, p. 528.

domestic system was from their standpoint a success. It gave merchants access to an easily exploitable rural labour force which created a lucrative source of differential profit. The domestic industries and by-employments criticised by Smith had been created out of rural poverty, not out of agricultural wealth. They were not manufactures which had grown up naturally out of agriculture (as in Leeds, Halifax, Birmingham and Wolverhampton), but unnatural extensions of commerce, monopolistic restriction and mercantile greed from the towns into the country. The countryside and its workforce had been put at a disadvantage by a long history of economic policies designed to promote the interests of urban incorporated industries at the expense of agriculture and other rural enterprises. And urban artisans had falsely credited themselves with superior skills, established and buttressed by resort to monopolies and corporate restrictions. Smith was indeed critical of these developments, but in his model of the natural progress of opulence what better, sustained analysis and prescription for the agricultural origins of industry? What greater praise for the significance of basic domestic commodities catering to a home market, and for the importance of the rural industries which gave rise to the fastest growing urban areas of the period? Smith was a theorist whose economic analysis was a social and moral tribute to the growth of agriculture and the development of the country region, with its own integrated towns, as opposed to the wealthy mercantile city. And he was a theorist who found in tenant farmers, country labourers and independent artisans a class whose individual interests and attributes were pre-eminently conducive to the growth of the wealth of the nation.

Smith's asides on the poverty of those domestic industries practised as by-employments did not constitute an analysis of that industrial organisation in itself. Smith and his eighteenth-century predecessors avoided a direct discussion of the merits and demerits of rural industry because they were more interested in the fundamental principles of improvement in rural *and* urban industry and in agriculture. Some of Smith's contemporaries and followers did, however, confront the issue head-on. The result was a substantial debate between James Anderson, Arthur Young and Dugald Stewart. This foreshadowed the much more extensive debate on the social benefits of rural industry as against machinery that was to take place at the end of the eighteenth century and in the early years of the nineteenth century. We will now turn to these debates, which form both a contrast to and a culmination of the analysis of manufacture to be found in the work of earlier eighteenth-century commentators and of Smith himself.

Anderson chose the problems of Scottish economic development to frame his denunciation of the domestic system:

if manufacture be of such a nature as to admit of being carried on in separate detached houses in the country, and may be practiced by any single person independent of others, it must invariably happen, that the whole of the money that is paid for the working up of these foreign materials flows directly into the hands of the lower ranks of people, often into those of young women and children; who becoming giddy and vain, usually lay out the greatest part of the money thus gained, in buying fine clothes, and other gaudy gewgaws that catch their idle fancies.[69]

He complained that rural industries would lure labour away from agriculture and encourage landlords to break up their tenancies into small plots to rent to cottagers instead of to tenant farmers. This would lead to a very unstable social order and totally undermine the order of rich substantial tenants, resulting ultimately in lower agricultural productivity. Anderson preferred industries that needed 'to be carried on by people in concert' who would all 'work in one place'. Kept some distance from farming areas, and protected by apprenticeship barriers, such industries would provide markets for agriculture without interfering with it or seducing away farm labour.[70]

Anderson's worries over the effects of domestic industry on agriculture also loomed large in Arthur Young's work. In his controversy with Mirabeau between 1788 and 1792, in the *Travels in France* and the *Tour of Ireland*, he pursued the issue entirely with regard to the productivity of labour in agriculture. He found those provinces known for their manufacturing – Normandy, Brittany, Picardy and the Lyonnais – to be 'among the worst cultivated in France'. 'The immense *fabrics* of Abbeville and Amiens have not caused the enclosure of a single field.' 'The agriculture of Champagne is miserable, even to a proverb: I saw there great and flourishing manufactures, and cultivation in ruins around them.' Examples drawn from Britain and Ireland confirmed him in his view that poor cultivation was to be attributed entirely to 'manufacture spreading into the country, instead of being confined to the towns'.[71]

Young's vituperative denunciation of domestic industry induced Dugald Stewart to raise a spirited defence against both Young and Anderson. Young's bias in favour of manufacturing towns went too far, Stewart claimed, for he never enquired into the type of manufacture, in particular whether it was for luxury or common commodities. The manufacture of common commodities was a much safer development, for luxury commodities were more subject to market fluctuations:

The manufacturers of Norwich who deal in fine crepes and other delicate stuffs are laid idle three times for every once that the Yorkshire manufacturer who deals in low priced serviceable cloths experiences a similar misfortune.[72]

69 James Anderson, *Observations on the Means of Exciting a Spirit of National Industry, Chiefly Intended to Promote the Agriculture, Commerce, Manufactures and Fisheries of Scotland*, 2 vols. (Dublin, 1779), I, 39.
70 *Ibid.*, p. 53.
71 Cited in Dugald Stewart, *Lectures on Political Economy*, Vol. I, in *Collected Works*, ed. Sir W. Hamilton (Edinburgh, 1855), Vol. VIII, pp. 164, 165.
72 *Ibid.*, p. 177.

And in defence of Smith's 'sauntering weaver' he argued:

(Though it follows that a domestic manufacture must always be a most unprofitable employment for an individual who depends chiefly for his subsistence on the produce of a farm, the converse of the proposition requires some limitations.) A man who exercises a trade which occupies him from day to day must of necessity be disqualified for the management of such agricultural concerns as require a constant and undivided attention... but it does not appear equally evident how the improvement of the country should be injured by his possessing a few acres as an employment for his hours of recreation.

'Occasional labour in the fields' was better than 'those habits of intemperate dissipation in which all workmen who have no variety of pursuit are prone to indulge'.[73] But with this, Stewart had actually changed the terms of the debate. It is notable that he was not discussing a farmer-weaver, but a worker in a rural area who kept his own garden.

Stewart's views on some of the advantages of rural by-employments were similar to some of Sir Frederic Eden's observations on the work and living conditions of the poor. Eden found widespread evidence of such by-employments at the end of the eighteenth century. Woollen and worsted spinning by women provided a small supplement to family incomes in Oxfordshire, Leicestershire, Norfolk, Yorkshire and many other counties. He found Scotland to be the epitome of the rural by-employment. There labourers produced nearly all their own consumption goods, for 'every man there is Jack of all trades'.[74]

Discussion of the advantages and problems of rural as opposed to urban industry became inevitably linked to a growing concern over the issue of hand techniques versus machinery. By the end of the eighteenth century the debates on rural industry and on machinery had virtually merged. This was already evident in the work of Lauderdale and, in particular, of Dugald Stewart. I will now conclude this essay with a discussion of how the debate on the principles of manufacture earlier in the eighteenth century was becoming a debate on machinery by its end.

The eighteenth-century discussion of the connections between manufacturing progress and economic growth and welfare became in the work of Stewart and Lauderdale a direct debate on the social consequences of the division of labour and technical change. The social advantages Stewart attached to the continued existence of rural industry were justified by his scepticism over the division of labour. He believed Smith had placed far too much weight on the relation between division of labour and increases in productivity. It was unlikely that the

---

73 *Ibid.*, pp. 175–6.
74 Eden, *State of the Poor*, I, 558–9.

dexterity of the workman who acquired other abilities would be impaired. And he was certainly not impressed with Smith's example of pin making. He knew of few manufactures 'where great manual dexterity is less required than in that of pin making', and Lauderdale was right to argue that 'even in pin making without the use of machinery to supersede the work of the hand, no great progress could have been made in the rapidity with which pins are formed'. He conceded that it was true that one of the advantages of the division of labour was to increase the rapidity of manual work, but he had much lower expectations than Smith of the significance of this for productivity gains.[75]

Both Stewart and Lauderdale were perhaps most critical of the connection Smith drew between the division of labour and the invention of machinery, for they thought that these operated on different principles. Lauderdale argued that the principle behind the invention of machinery was to combine and embrace within one machine the execution of the greatest possible variety of operations in the formation of a commodity. But the division of labour was destructive of the chain of reasoning necessary to the perfection of machinery. Smith had, of course, admitted this in Book V of *The Wealth of Nations*, but the point was driven home by Stewart, who argued that:

among the many complicated machines which the manufacturers of this country exhibit, while many of them may be traced to men who never entered the workshop, but in order to gratify a mechanical curiosity, hardly one can be mentioned which derives its origin from the living automatons who are employed in the detail of the work.[76]

Where the division of labour had any effect, it operated on the inventive powers not of the workman, but of his employer. What motive, in addition, would the workman have to invent machines which would only throw himself and his companions out of work? The effect of the division of labour was much more fundamentally to analyse an operation into its various separate steps. Such an analysis would discover that some of these steps could only be performed by the human hand while others admitted of the substitution of machines. It was the invention of machines which was really important, for this enabled one man to perform the labour of many, and it produced an economy of time by separating the work into its different branches, all of which could be carried into execution at the same moment. But equally the 'general experience of the utility of machines has led ingenious men to push, in some cases, the division of labour to a far greater length than was useful'. Stewart drew on Ferguson's *Essay on the History of Civil Society* to back up his apprehensions. 'Manufactures accordingly prosper most where the mind is least consulted, and where the workshop may,

75 See James Maitland, Lord Lauderdale, *An Inquiry into the Nature and Origin of Public Wealth* (Edinburgh, 1804), pp. 167, 294–5; Stewart, *Lectures on Political Economy*, I, 314.
76 Stewart, *Lectures on Political Economy*, I, 318.

without any great effort of imagination, be considered as an engine, the parts of which are man.'[77]

Stewart and Lauderdale also addressed themselves to the issue of machinery and employment. Lauderdale argued that whatever the longer-term considerations might be, the real reason for introducing machinery was to save labour. The new machine looms in stocking knitting proved his point that 'the profit of stock employed in machinery is paid out of a fund that would otherwise be destined to pay the wages of the labour it supplants'.[78] And the effect of this was demonstrated in the social conflict of his own time:

It derives ample testimony of its truth from the conduct of the unlettered manufacturers themselves, as is sufficiently evinced by the riots that have taken place on the introduction of various pieces of machinery, and particularly at the time when the ingenious machines for carding and spinning were first set agoing.[79]

While Stewart recognised the problem, he dismissed the 'slovenly reasoning' of some of his British predecessors. He argued that workmen displaced by machinery would soon be able to find jobs in other branches of industry. But machinery would anyway open new home and foreign markets, increase a country's capital, and therefore eventually increase employment. Machinery, furthermore, provided the only means by which some nations might compete in international markets: 'It is only by such contrivances, combined with that division of labour which is intimately connected with them, that nations among whom the wages of labour are comparatively high, can maintain that competition in foreign markets.'[80] Stewart's careful assessment of the economic and social benefits and problems of the division of labour and machinery finally came out in favour of the pursuit of both. The argument which clinched the matter for him was this: 'The competition among commercial nations at present was not merely a competition of *industry*, but of ingenuity and skills and it is likely to become so in a greater and greater degree as the progress of Science and of Art advances.'[81] Both machinery and the division of labour, instead of displacing the importance of skill, would make it all the more important. Mechanical contrivances would ultimately be substituted for much manufacturing work, but this would 'open a field for human genius in the nobler departments of industry and talent.'[82]

77 *Ibid.*, p. 325.
78 Lord Lauderdale, *An Inquiry*, p. 167.
79 *Ibid.*, pp. 294–5.
80 Stewart, *Lectures on Political Economy*, I, 195.
81 *Ibid.*, p. 195.
82 *Ibid.*, p. 331. See M. Berg, *The Machinery Question and the Making of Political Economy 1815–1848* (Cambridge, 1980), Chapter 1, for a discussion of the emergence of the machinery question.

The analysis of manufacture in eighteenth-century Britain had, then, come full circle. Britain's advantage at the end of the century, as at the beginning, was recognised to be the 'wonderful skill and ingenuity of her artisans'. It was not the existence of rural by-employments, nor even of machinery *per se*, that was recognised to be the source of Britain's path to economic improvement, but her skilled artisans, who worked in concert with advanced technology and new industries.

PART I

The structure of manufacture

3

Variations in industrial structure in pre-industrial Languedoc*

J. K. J. THOMSON

INTRODUCTION

The province of Languedoc contained the largest concentration of textile production of any area of France during the pre-industrial period.[1] As one French historian has written, the cloth industry occupied a similar place in the region's traditional economy to that occupied by the vine today,[2] and, as anyone who has travelled across the Lower Languedocian plain will be aware, this 'place' occupied by the vine today is overwhelming – the area has been described, without exaggeration, as a 'wine factory'.[3] Indeed, it is possible, in view of the fact that the province was the largest textile centre in what was probably Europe's greatest industrial producer in the pre-industrial era,[4] that it is accurate

---

*   The author gratefully acknowledges valuable advice received from the editors concerning various drafts of this essay and help received from Mrs Margaret Thomson in translating French historians cited.

1   'We consider Languedoc to be the most important region of the French woollen industry at the beginning of the 18th century, more significant than Normandy... more significant than Champagne or Picardy...': T. J. Markovitch, 'L'Industrie Lainière à la fin du règne de Louis XIV et sous la Régence', *Cahiers de l'Institut de Science Economique Appliquée*, 2 (1968), 1629–30. See also his *Histoire des industries françaises*, I, *Les Industries lainières de Colbert à la Révolution* (Geneva, 1976), pp. 205–310; L. Fontvieille, 'Les Premières Enquêtes industrielles de la France : 1692 et 1703', *Cahiers de l'Institut de Science Economique Appliquée*, 3 (1969), 1109–34, 1270–3 and S. Chassagne, 'L'Industrie lainière en France à l'époque révolutionnaire et impériale (1790–1800)', in *Colloque Albert Mathiez–Georges Lefebvre : voies nouvelles pour l'histoire de la révolution française* (Paris, 1978), pp. 153–5. Chassagne shows Languedoc's superiority to have increased considerably during the eighteenth century.

2   C. Fohlen, 'En Languedoc vigne contre draperie', *Annales, Economies, Sociétés, Civilisations*, 4 (1949), 290.

3   The phrase is that of R. Dugrand, *Villes et campagnes en Bas-Languedoc : le réseau urbain du Bas-Languedoc méditerranéen* (Paris, 1963), p. 402. His, too, is the best description of the pastoralisation of the province; see especially pp. 243–427.

4   Thus France's gross, but not per capita, industrial production was greater than England's. F. Crouzet, 'England and France in the Eighteenth Century', in R.M. Hartwell (ed.), *Causes of the Industrial Revolution* (London, 1967), pp. 151–2.

to describe Languedoc as Europe's most important proto-industrial centre. Yet this region has received little attention from historians in recent years, and only passing mention from participants in the discussions about proto-industrialisation.[5] So large a historiographical gap would, in itself, justify the devotion of space to the consideration of the province's industrial development, and there would seem to be all the more advantages obtainable from doing so in that the province's industry was of a type, and its experiences of a nature, that have not, as yet, received much attention from participants in the proto-industrialisation debate. Thus the most important sectors of the industry consisted in high-quality, expensive, woollen broadcloth (whereas the major preoccupation in the debate has been with cheap, low-quality goods, and largely linens); in addition, the major centres for the trade were urban (whereas analysis has to date largely been focussed upon rural production), and Languedoc's extensive proto-industrial development, despite apparent, impressive industrial growth during the eighteenth century, was a preliminary not for industrialisation but for a near-total de-industrialisation.[6] And although Mendels and others have

5   This gap has been bridged in part, it is to be hoped, by my book *Clermont-de-Lodève, 1633–1789: Fluctuations in the Prosperity of a Languedocian Cloth-Making Town* (Cambridge, 1982). Other recent publications include the following: F. Jaupart, 'L'Industrie drapière et le commerce des draps dans le diocèse de Carcassonne au XVIIIe siècle', *Bulletin de la Société d'Etudes Scientifiques de l'Aude*, 61 (1960), 185–218; C. Carrière and M. Morineau, 'Draps du Languedoc et commerce du Levant au XVIIIe siècle', *Revue d'Histoire Economique et Sociale*, 56 (1968), 108–21; C. Carrière, 'La Draperie Languedocienne dans la Seconde Moitié du XVIIe siècle: contribution à l'étude de la conjoncture levantine', in *Conjoncture économique, structures sociales: hommage à Ernest Labrousse* (Paris, 1974), pp. 157–72; P. Wolff, 'Esquisse d'une histoire de la draperie en Languedoc du XIIe au début du XVIIIe siècle', in *Produzione, commercio e consumo dei panni di lana. Atti della seconda settimana di studio (10–16 April 1970)* (Florence, 1976), pp. 435–62; R. Descimon, 'Structures d'un marché de draperie dans le Languedoc au milieu du XVIe siècle', *Annales, Economies, Sociétés, Civilisations*, 30 (1975), 1414–46; L. Teisseyre, 'L'Industrie lainière à Nîmes au XVIIe siècle: crise conjoncturelle ou structurelle?', *Annales du Midi*, 88 (1976), 383–400; G. Bernet, 'Jean Giscard, marchand-drapier toulousain sous Louis XIV', *Annales du Midi*, 91 (1979), 53–70. In addition L. Dermigny's chapter 'De la Révocation à la Révolution', in P. Wolff (ed.), *Histoire du Languedoc* (Toulouse, 1967) and Markovitch, *Les Industries lainières*, pp. 216–307, contain information and some older studies remain extremely useful, particularly L. Dutil, *L'Etat économique du Languedoc à la fin de l'Ancien Régime* (Paris, 1911), especially pp. 277–527; E. Appolis, *Un Pays languedocien au milieu du dix-huitième siècle: le diocèse civil de Lodève* (Albi, 1951), pp. 455–561, and three articles by P. Boissonnade – 'Colbert, son système et les entreprises industrielles d'Etat en Languedoc: 1661–1683', 'La Restauration et le développement de l'industrie en Languedoc au temps de Colbert' and 'L'Etat, L'organisation et la crise de l'industrie languedocienne pendant les soixante premières années du XVIIe siècle', *Annales du Midi*, 14, 18, 21 (1902, 1906, 1909), 5–49, 441–72, 169–97.

6   In addition to Fohlen and Dugrand (see notes 2 and 3 above), G. Cholvy refers to this unsolved problem in his article 'Histoires contemporaines en pays d'Oc', *Annales, Economies, Sociétés, Civilisations*, 30 (1975), 864, 869–70. The timing of the turning-point in Languedoc's industrial destiny has been identified by Chassagne, 'L'Industrie lainière', p. 163: his analysis of the imperial industrial survey of 1810 shows Languedoc by then to have 'entré pour toujours dans une décadence'. See also C.H. Johnson, 'Proto-industrialisation and De-industrialisation in Languedoc: Lodève and its Region, 1700–1870', unpublished paper given at the preparatory

raised the question of de-industrialisation, they have not attempted to explain it systematically, and their main interest in proto-industrialisation is, it is clear, occasioned by their belief that it did, generally, represent a preparatory stage in the industrialisation process.[7] In addition, Languedoc's was an old industry: the province's industrial and commercial tradition was long, and thus there exists the possibility of examining its proto-industrial development over the long term and of compensating for two other imbalances which, Pierre Jeannin has noted, have revealed themselves in the recent proto-industrialisation literature. These are the relative neglect of early periods of economic development in favour of that immediately preceding industrialisation and the lack of consideration given to the influence of conjunctural tendencies on proto-industrialisation.[8]

The ideal would be to survey the province's industrial development, with the issues raised by the proto-industrial debate in mind, from the Middle Ages until the nineteenth century, for that approximate half millennium during which an almost unchanging 'economic system' functioned in Europe.[9] This, unfortunately, it is not possible to do, as my own researches have been confined to the seventeenth and eighteenth centuries and what published work exists for the prior and succeeding periods is not sufficiently detailed to permit well-founded generalisation. So this essay will be confined, largely, to the period from 1600 to 1800. What I shall demonstrate is that leading centres of the province's cloth industry experienced two major cycles during these years, which followed approximately the general, conjunctural movement of the French economy, and that these cycles took the form of fluctuations in the organisation of production – movements between *Kaufsystems* (a production system characterised by small-scale, artisanal, familial production units which were subjected, generally, to the dominance of merchant capital) and *Verlagsystems* (large-scale production units, with significant division of labour, dominated by the *marchand-fabricant* or 'gentleman clothier' and known as putting-out systems in

---

conference for the 8th International Conference of Economic History, held at Bad Hamburg, Germany, 11–14 May 1981. Johnson argues that the significance attributed by some historians to the collapse of the Levant trade has been too great and that Lodève, and Bédarieux, took over the leadership of the provincial industry which remained competitive and advanced until the 1870s.

7 This is shown purely by the title of F.F. Mendels's seminal article on the subject – 'Proto-industrialization: The First Phase of the Industrialization Process' (*Journal of Economic History*, 32 [1972], 241–61). Mendels mentions, however, the question of de-industrialisation (p. 246) and the complications involved in analysing older industrial regions which 'experienced not one, but several broad changes in their spatial organization since the Middle Ages' (p. 248).

8 P. Jeannin emphasises the omissions in a review of P. Kriedte, H. Medick and J. Schlumbohm, *Industrialisierung vor der Industrialisierung* (Göttingen, 1977), now translated as *Industrialization before Industrialization* (Cambridge, 1981): 'La Proto-industrialisation: développement ou impasse?' *Annales, Economies, Sociétés, Civilisations*, 35 (1980), 52–65.

9 'Histoire et sciences sociales: la longue durée', in his *Ecrits sur l'histoire* (Paris, 1977), pp. 53–4.

England).[10] Having documented these fluctuations I shall then hazard some speculations about their significance for the understanding of proto-industrial development.

I

In view of the lack of information about Languedoc's commercial and industrial past, it is necessary first to describe briefly the basic characteristics of the regional economy. The province was from many points of view a privileged region within *ancien-régime* France. It was privileged legally and institutionally, firstly in that it was a *pays d'état*, with a relatively effective provincial assembly, and thus was protected from the worst excesses of fiscalism, and secondly in that its seigneurial system was mild and unrestrictive.[11] But, more important in view of the theme of this book, the province was privileged economically and socially in that, in addition to that exceptional proto-industrial development just mentioned, it enjoyed many other elements of 'modernity'. This was especially true of Lower Languedoc, which despite a relative poverty in natural resources was the more prosperous half of the province. Intendant Basville at the end of the seventeenth century attributed this prosperity to the skills and energy of the area's inhabitants, whom he contrasted with the 'habitants ... grossiers, peu laborieux, peu industrieux' of the agriculturally richer upper province. He drew the moral that 'la nature vouloit compenser par les talents dont elle leur est libérale, la perte qu'ils souffrent de l'infertilité de la terre'.[12] But if the area's soil was poor, other elements in its geographical and climatic environment were less disadvantageous. The closeness of its mountain regions to the sea, as in so many Mediterranean areas, meant that the lower province contained within it the most varied of climatic and natural conditions, which permitted an exceptional degree of agricultural specialisation. All areas during the *ancien régime* devoted considerable proportions of their land surfaces to grain production, and Lower Languedoc was no exception to this rule, but the extent to which its agricultural production was commercialised was exceptional: the olive oil, wine, almonds and wheat of the plain and foothills of the Massif Central were exchanged with

10 For definitions of these and other production forms see F. Braudel, *Civilisation matérielle, économie et capitalisme, XVe – XVIIIe siècle* (Paris, 1979), II, 259–61. For fuller definitions of the *Kauf-* and *Verlagsystems* see J. Schlumbohm, 'Relations of production – productive forces – crises in proto-industrialization', in Kriedte, Medick and Schlumbohm, *Industrialization Before Industrialization*, pp. 98–107.

11 Information on the institutional history of the province can be found in R. Mousnier, *Les Institutions de la France sous la monarchie absolue, 1598–1789* (Paris, 1974), pp. 474–86. On the weakness of the seigneurial system see P. Goubert, *L'Ancien Régime*, vol. I, *La Société* (Paris, 1969), p. 83.

12 In H. de Boulainvilliers, *Etat de la France* (London, 1727), II, 511–12.

the timber, chestnuts, livestock, industrial raw materials and milk products of the mountains, while surplus grain was drawn from the great wheat-growing plains of Upper Languedoc.[13] A sign of the extent of agricultural commercialisation is provided by price patterns. Languedoc's wheat, for example, as in other Mediterranean zones, sold at international prices, defined by Jean Meuvret as 'relatively high price levels and moderate fluctuations', proof that the province was spared the disasters of either abundance or scarcity which caused the sharper price fluctuations elsewhere.[14] A crucial contributory element permitting this capitalisation on the comparative advantage of mountain and plain, and allowing this synchronisation of prices, was the quality of Languedoc's communications. To add to the advantages of its roads, invariably admired by travellers,[15] were two major navigable rivers, the Rhône and the Garonne, from the 1660s a superb canal, 'du Midi' or 'des deux mers', connecting these two, and the sea – the Languedocian coastline was dotted with small ports (though no major ports: to its eventual, crucial disadvantage) which facilitated intra- and inter-provincial as well as international trade.[16] And, of course, and this it is important to emphasise, international trade was largely Mediterranean-based until the mid seventeenth century, and far from Atlantic-dominated until the late eighteenth century – the Mediterranean remained, as recent research has shown, Europe's most important export market until the mid eighteenth century.[17] And Languedoc was crucially and advantageously placed to profit from this trade. It provided not only an important overland route between Spain and Italy in a period in which sea transport was far from possessing overwhelming predominance as a means of communications,[18] but also major trade routes for those north–south exchanges which characterised a European economy

13 On Languedoc's varied agriculture see E. Le Roy Ladurie, *Les Paysans de Languedoc* (Paris, 1966), I, 53–76. On local trading in agricultural commodities see P. Boissonnade, 'La Production et le commerce des céréales, des vins et des eaux-de-vie en Languedoc dans la seconde moitié du XVIIᵉ siècle', *Annales du Midi*, 14 (1905), 240–2.
14 'Les Prix des céréales dans la France mediterranéenne au XVIIᵉ siècle', in his *Etudes d'Histoire Economique* (Paris, 1971), p. 104.
15 For instance A. Young, *Travels in France and Italy* (London, 1976), p. 42: 'I know nothing more striking to a traveller than the roads of Languedoc', and Marquise de la Tour du Pin, *Journal d'une femme de cinquante ans, 1778–1815* (Paris, 1913), I, 53: 'on entrait, une fois le Rhône franchi, sur une route aussi belle que celle du jardin le mieux entretenu'.
16 On the Canal du Midi, M. Maistre, *Le Canal des Deux Mers* (Toulouse, 1968), and on Languedocian ports and coastal navigation, L. Dermigny, 'Une Concurrence au port franc de Marseille: armement languedocien et trafic de Levant et de Barbarie', *Provence Historique*, 5–6 (1955–6), 248–62, 53–81.
17 R.T. Rapp, 'The Unmaking of the Mediterranean Trade Hegemony: International Trade Rivalry and the Commercial Revolution', *Journal of Economic History*, 35 (1975), 502–5. See also G.D. Ramsay, *English Overseas Trade During the Centuries of Emergence* (London, 1957), p. 60.
18 See F. Braudel, *The Mediterranean and the Mediterranean World in the Age of Philip II*, 2 vols. (London, 1972), I, 284–93.

dominated by the Mediterranean,[19] the principal ones being provided by the Rhône and Garonne valleys and subsidiary ones by the valleys of the Cévennes, the southern promontory of the Massif Central. Symbolising the openness, internationalism and prosperity of the Languedocian economy was the fair of Beaucaire, held in late July each year, and described by Ernest Labrousse as the 'great commercial event of the Midi, and even of Europe'.[20]

The social structure and the personality of the inhabitants of the region were in harmony with this strong material infrastructure which had been consolidated by the many centuries during which the province had played a central role in Europe's major commercial circuits. Social mobility was, to all appearances, considerable in comparison with more isolated regions of France,[21] and the region's inhabitants were independent, undeferential, ambitious and highly commercialised, whether they were involved in industry or in agriculture. Basville, intendant at the end of the seventeenth century, an outsider who had previously worked in the more commercially inert province of Poitou, was struck by these characteristics:

de tous les pays du monde où l'auteur croit que l'intérêt met les peuples en action il prétend qu'aucune ne produit des hommes si vifs sur cet article que celui ci, qu'il est ordinaire d'y manquer à des devoirs essentiels pour le moindre profit, et que cette avidité les éloigne des sciences et des lettres en les leur faisant envisager comme un métier stérile qui ne produit qu'une réputation infructueuse... d'ailleurs ils sont sobres et ménagers, ne donnant jamais dans aucune dépense superflüe; ils sont aussi polis, flateurs et prévenans envers les étrangers, le tout par rapport à leur profit.[22]

So, to conclude on Languedoc's general characteristics, the province was, by the standards of the pre-industrial era, prosperous and highly commercialised. It was an area which attracted migrants from poorer regions and whose population was highly mobile. 'Here is a France which is on the move, migrant', writes Le Roy Ladurie of the region, in sharp contrast to the north-west, 'quieter, more

19 Though from the mid seventeenth century, as Braudel emphasises, latitudinal, west to east, commercial movements began to predominate. See F. Braudel, P. Jeannin, J. Meuvret and R. Romano, 'Le Déclin de Venise au XVIIᵉ siècle', in *Civiltà Veneziana*, 9 (1963), 30–1, 35, 62–3.

20 *La Crise de l'économie française à la fin de l'ancien régime et au début de la révolution* (Paris, 1944), I, lll. On Beaucaire see P. Léon, 'La Foire de Beaucaire', *Revue de Géographie de Lyon* (1953), 311–27.

21 Thus E. Appolis's studies on the Lodévois showed most noble families to have been linked in some way with cloth production and trading and that, in some cases, the roles of noble and *négociant* were combined: 'Les Seigneurs du diocèse de Lodève', in *Cahiers d'Histoire et d'Archéologie* (Nîmes, 1947), pp. 226–7. Likewise E. Roschach writes in the *Histoire du Languedoc* of the cloth industry and cloth trade of the province as 'The national industry par excellence' and adds that 'Almost all the wealth of the country derives from it, and the nobility as well... the majority of the feudal families having disappeared': Dom C. De Vic and Dom Vaissète, *Histoire générale du Languedoc* (Toulouse, 1872–92), XIII, 166.

22 Boulainvilliers, *Etat de la France*, II, 512.

stay-at-home',[23] and for the inhabitants of the improverished Gévaudan, Lower Languedoc was regarded as 'le bon Pais'.[24] These qualities Languedoc shared with other areas bordering the Mediterranean. As Jean Meuvret writes, 'bourgeois or peasant, those near the sea have always worked to sell. Here an "exchange" mentality is long standing.'[25] It seems doubtful, and this is an issue to which we shall return, that proto-industrial development in the period leading up to the Industrial Revolution was necessary to act as a modernising agent – and this seems to be the role attributed to it in some areas of Europe – in a region which was already so commercially aroused.

II

Languedoc's large textile industry was far from uniform. The major distinction was between the industries of Upper and Lower Languedoc. That of the upper province was confined almost entirely, and well into the eighteenth century, to low-quality production, and the universal production form was the *Kaufsystem*: small-scale, artisanal producers, from both rural and urban areas, sold their low-quality products, generally in an unfinished state, to merchant-buyers, especially from the towns of Albi, Lavaur and Toulouse, who supervised the finishing processes, marketed the final product and absorbed – they were few and concentrated and the cloth sellers were many and widely spread – the majority of the profit. Lacking was the *marchand-fabricant*. Lacking, too, was the possibility of an accumulation of industrial capital. And the industry was immobile. A recent study has shown that the same production centres were producing the same types of cloth for the same markets in the sixteenth as in the fourteenth century, and this situation, with minor exceptions, persisted into the eighteenth century. The industry of the upper province would thus not qualify for consideration by students of proto-industrialisation whose definitions require industrial production for non-local markets and whose interests are not in continuity but in social, economic and structural change.[26] By contrast, such students would be interested by the industries of the lower province. There were major differences – and differences, it should be noted, which became more marked during the early modern period. An important sector of Lower Languedoc's industries, in addition to supplying local markets, was involved in those wider national, and international, commercial circuits for the profiting

23 *Paysans*, p. 93.
24 Archives Départementales de l'Hérault (henceforward referred to as ADH) C2554, Petition of *journaliers, artisans et laboureurs* of Mende to Saint-Priest, 1781.
25 'Prix des céréales', p. 100.
26 See P. Deyon and F. Mendels, 'Programme de la section A2 du Huitième Congrès International d'Histoire Economique: la proto-industrialisation: théorie et réalité (Budapest, 1982)', *Revue du Nord*, 63 (1981), 11–20.

from which the province was so well placed geographically. The port of Marseilles, local ports, and the international fairs of the littoral – above all those of Beaucaire, Pézenas and Montagnac[27] – linked the cloth-making centres of Lower Languedoc to the world economy[28] and thus subjected them to those sorts of experiences, denied to the artisanal industries of the upper province, which interest students of proto-industrialisation. The conditioning factor in the demand for cloth came from outside the province; the province's industry was subjected to those not easily explained, but nevertheless most definitely established, conjunctural fluctuations which occurred in the prosperity of the international economy; and industrial accumulation of capital and merchant investment in industrial production occurred. This industrial investment had the consequence that improvements in the production process occurred: improvement in organisation (division of labour, through the development of *Verlag*-, or putting-out systems); investment in equipment (and particularly in that necessary for fulling, dyeing and finishing cloth); investment in the labour force (skilled workers from other textile areas were employed to instruct native workers in specialised cloth-making skills); investment in marketing (and in particular in the copying or devising of new cloth styles).[29]

The geographical division between the textile industries of the two halves of the province became, if anything, more pronounced between the fourteenth and seventeenth centuries, though in the eighteenth century some elements of the upper province's industry were drawn into the orbit of that of the lower province. As R. Descimon writes, 'Lower Languedoc, maritime and "international", whose nerve centre in the sixteenth century is Marseilles rather than Montpellier, contrasts with Upper Languedoc, centred on Toulouse, which is more continental and French.'[30] This increasing geographical division from the upper province's industry was not the only change experienced. Within Lower Languedoc there were, it would seem, significant shifts in the distribution of industry. Until the fourteenth century, the industry was dominated by the great trading cities of the Languedocian plain – Narbonne (the capital of the industry in the fourteenth century), Béziers, Montpellier and Nîmes. But between the fourteenth and

27 On Pézenas and Montagnac see L. Dermigny, 'Les Foires de Pézenas et de Montagnac au XVIIIe siécle', *Congrès Régional de la Fédération Historique du Languedoc*, 26 (1957), 97–116.
28 On this contrast between the industries of the two halves of the province see Descimon, 'Structures d'un marché', pp. 1414–46
29 The concentration of technical progress on the finishing processes, and the importance of variations in cloth styles, are emphasised by D.C. Coleman, 'Textile Growth', in N.B. Harte and K.G. Ponting (eds.), *Textile History and Economic History: Essays in Honour of Miss Julia de Lacy Mann* (Manchester, 1973), pp. 2–14, and M. Aymard, 'Production, commerce et consommation des draps de laine du XIIe au XVIIe siècle', *Revue Historique*, 499 (1971), 9. On the general consequences, and implications, of investment in industrial production in the pre-industrial period see J. Schlumbohm, 'Relations of production – productive forces', pp. 101–17.
30 'Structures d'un marché', p. 1415.

seventeenth centuries there was a shift in the centre of gravity of the industry to a range of hill-towns situated at the base of the Pyrenees and the Massif Central – Limoux, Carcassonne, Castres, Saint-Pons, Saint-Chinian, Clermont-de-Lodève, Sommières, to name the principal ones. The rise to predominance of these towns (they had produced cloth before but there had been a dependence on the cities of the plain) would seem to have a dual explanation: it was the cities which were most exposed to, and damaged by, the repeated civil and religious disturbances which affected the province between the fourteenth and sixteenth centuries, whereas these (generally fortified) hill-towns not only escaped the worst of these disruptions but also possessed those sorts of advantages which have frequently been shown as important for the attraction of proto-industry – abundant labour supplies, relatively weak guild systems, water facilities (for driving fulling mills as well as for washing wools and cloth) and easy access to raw materials.[31] Textile production was not totally abandoned by the cities of the plain – Montpellier continued, for instance, to produce higher-quality velvets and blankets, and Nîmes retained a large interest in cloth production until the seventeenth century and then switched to silk[32] – but the principal activities of these towns became, certainly, commercial ones to add to traditional (and in fact growing) administrative roles.[33] Languedoc's hill-towns thus emerged during these centuries to exercise a dominance over the provincial industry which was to endure until its disappearance, and Carcassonne developed into the provincial cloth-making capital and, indeed, was regarded by some, and well-informed, observers as the most important cloth-making centre in France. Louis Cauvière for example, newly appointed inspector at Marseilles, described the town in 1694 as 'la fabrique du Royaume la plus Considérable par le grand nombre de draps qu'il s'y fait, et par la quantité de marchands qui font ce commerce'.[34]

It was only a part of Lower Languedoc's industry which escaped from localism to develop more sophisticated production methods and organisational forms. The production of the more remote areas of the Cévennes was confined to lower qualities, and the industry took there the form of *Kaufsystem* and was dominated by urban merchants. This primitive, traditional industry was larger than the more advanced industry which we have just described but, like the industry of Upper Languedoc, it was technologically and organisationally static.[35] These

---

31 On the industry of Lower Languedoc, and the geographical shifts in this industry, see Thomson, *Clermont-de-Lodève*, pp. 32–9.
32 Teisseyre, 'L'Industrie lainière à Nîmes', pp. 383–400.
33 On the change of Montpellier from commercial to administrative centre see A. Germain, *Histoire du commerce de Montpellier antérieurement à l'ouverture du port de Cette* (Montpellier, 1861), II, 65.
34 ADH C2200, Memoire of Cauvière, inspector at Marseilles, 1694.
35 Markovitch, 'L'Industrie lainière', pp. 1622–30 and *Les Industries lainières*, pp. 216–19.

are our grounds for ignoring it and concentrating our attentions on the fortunes of two of the principal towns of the more advanced industry, Carcassonne and Clermont-de-Lodève, over the approximate two centuries about which we are informed.

III

The cloth industries of these two towns shared in that general conjunctural movement which characterised the French economy as a whole between the sixteenth century and the French Revolution. Thus there are a few signs of prosperity in the mid sixteenth century, evidence of a disruption at the end of the sixteenth century and beginning of the seventeenth, fuller documentation for a considerable industrial recovery until the mid seventeenth century, as the province's industry shared in that last burst of Mediterranean prosperity documented by Braudel, and then widespread evidence for a sharp, complete and prolonged industrial decline until the end of the 1680s.[36] As elsewhere, the prosperous 'eighteenth century' had its beginnings in these two towns in the late seventeenth century, in the 1690s. These were shaky beginnings, but important and definite ones. They were followed by steadier expansion until the mid 1750s. The industries of both towns were unprecedentedly prosperous during these years. The 1750s saw a turning-point, however, not so much in the quantity of cloth produced but in profitability, and from these years until the Revolution the industries of both towns were in severe difficulties. Neither town after 1800 was ever again to be very prominent in the provincial (let alone national) industry; neither was to play a leading role in industrialisation.[37]

Not only did the level of prosperity in the two towns fluctuate during these two hundred years. There were variations, too, in the nature of industrial organisation, in the quality of cloth produced and in the balance between urban and rural production. These variations I shall now, briefly, describe.

The first detailed information about Clermont's industry is from the 1630s. The town's industry was large – no less than fifty *marchands-drapiers* attended a meeting of its cloth-making *confrérie* in 1633 (and others failed to attend, it was noted) – and, interestingly, distinctly larger than the industry of its cloth-making neighbour, and rival, Lodève. The state of prosperity of these town's industries was generally opposed between the seventeenth and nineteenth centuries for

36 Clermont's production in the mid sixteenth century was being sold directly to Greek merchants at the fair of Beaucaire: F. Teisserenc, *L'Industrie lainière dans l'Hérault* (Montpellier, 1908), p. 46. On the fortunes of the provincial industry between 1570 and 1680 see Thomson, *Clermont-de-Lodève*, pp. 89–103. On the last upsurge in the Mediterranean economy in the seventeenth century see Braudel, Jeannin *et al.*, 'Déclin de Venise', p. 33.
37 On the fortunes of these two industries between 1680 and 1800 see Thomson, *Clermont-de-Lodève, passim*, and works of Carrière and Dutil cited in note 5.

reasons to which we shall return.[38] Division of labour was extensive, and the crucial finishing processes were carried out by specialised skilled workers in the town. Thus shearers and cloth dressers were included among the members of the clothiers' *confrérie*, and in the 1650s there is evidence for the presence in the town of two non-Languedocian dyers, one from Tulle, near Limoges, the other from Orange, in Provence, as well as a specialised shear grinder. The industry produced a wide range of cloths, of uniform sizes and qualities (and thus, evidently, for market consumption). This is revealed by a cloth regulation recorded by the clothiers' *confrérie* in the 1650s. Seven cloths are listed, ranging in quality from 'draps fins façon dollande', with 3200 threads to the warp, and 'draps raffins vingthuitains', with 2800 warp threads, to 'vingtains, façon de Seau' and 'douzains' with a mere 1200 warp threads. The existence of Dutch-style cloth and 'vingtains, façon de Seau' amongst the repertoire of the town's clothiers illustrate that the industry was technologically advanced. The complex Dutch-style cloth-making methods had only recently been introduced into France and 'draps façon de Seau' had just been developed near Rouen in Normandy.[39] That the bulk of the town's production was destined for distant sale is suggested by the year-round presence in the town in the 1640s of cloth commissioners from Lyons, Nice and Genoa to buy cloth. Divisions, both social and economic, and apparently of quite recent creation, existed between clothiers and weavers. The latter in 1633 had recently been excluded from the 'merchant' *confrérie*, which had previously grouped together all participants in the production process, and had thus been obliged to form their own organisation. There was evidence, too, of disputes between the two groups over payment for cloth production. A type of *Verlagsystem* thus clearly existed, and there are signs, too, of rural workers operating to the orders of Clermont's clothiers.

I have less information on Carcassonne's industry during these years. Some of its dominant characteristics, however, are revealed by a surviving register for a *subvention* (or tax) raised on cloth made in the town for the period October 1642 to March 1643. As at Clermont, a wide range of uniform cloth types was produced, some of the highest quality ('suprafins façon dollande', 'suprafins de Sagobie large', 'raffins larges', 'draps larges façon d'Espagne' etc.) and some, by their names, revealing contact with, and imitation of, other cloth-making centres – thus, in addition to 'draps de Seau', 'draps de Berry' or 'draps façon de Berry' were being produced. The total production of the town was large – if the five months recorded are representative, some 10 000 pieces of cloth per annum.

38 E. Martin, *Cartulaire de la ville de Lodève* (Montpellier, 1900), p. 335: recorded is the fact that there were only 34 *marchands-drapiers* in Lodève's industry at this date. Cited by Johnson, 'Proto-industrialisation', p. 11.

39 On Dutch-style cloth-making techniques see J. de L. Mann, *The Cloth Industry in the West of England from 1640 to 1880* (Oxford, 1971), pp. xiv–xvii, 9–13.

No less than 152 individuals, of a variety of different statuses and resources, were responsible for this production, but the majority of the cloth was made by a relatively restricted number of clothiers. Two partners, Maffre and Castel, for example, produced during these five months 275 pieces or approximately one-twelfth of the total output of the town. At Carcassonne, and the same was true at Clermont too, there was considerable investment in industrial production by men of merchant and bourgeois status. (Or, as may have been the case, there were clothiers of bourgeois status, or who combined cloth making with trading and thus described themselves as merchants.) The principal markets produced for would seem to have been Spain and the Levant. It was the latter trade, Basville wrote later in the century (when a considerable commercial decline had occurred), which was 'autrefois le grand commerce de la ville de Carcassonne'.[40] And, finally, at Carcassonne as at Clermont, there was considerable division of labour within the cloth industry, which was organised on a putting-out basis, with the major participants in the production process – *pareurs*, *drapiers*, *cardeurs* and *tisserands* – organised in different *confréries*.[41]

This industrial prosperity observable in Languedoc, like that in other French industrial centres, did not endure.[42] The exact timing of the turning-point in the industry's fortunes is difficult to establish. Identification of the causes of the decline is, similarly, problematic. Already in the 1640s difficulties were being experienced. These were reported on by the Estates of Languedoc, who blamed the crisis on the 'infidelité' of the province's dyers. By the 1650s severe depression had set in. Leading members of Clermont's industry were deserting industrial activity, and the clothiers' *confrérie* registered new regulations in an attempt to reverse the general decline in cloth qualities which was occurring – a decline which, it was believed, was the cause, rather than the consequence, of mis-sale. Basville accounted for the crisis in terms of Dutch and English competition. Clearly this was a contributory factor, and it was in the seventeenth century that the Dutch and English trades achieved their maximal prosperity, having ousted Venetian and French producers from Levantine markets.[43] Extremely damaging to the economy of the province, too, were the wars with Spain, for these not only obstructed imports of Spanish wools, which were essential for the production of

---

40 Boulainvilliers, *Etat de la France*, II, 561.
41 For all these, and more, details on Languedoc's cloth industry during these years see Thomson, *Clermont-de-Lodève*, pp. 100–3
42 P. Deyon, 'La Production manufacturière en France au XVIIᵉ siècle et ses problèmes', *Le XVIIᵉ Siècle*, 70–1 (1966), 54, 58, and *idem*, 'Variations de la production textile aux XVIᵉ et XVIIᵉ siècles', *Annales, Economies, Sociétés, Civilisations*, 18 (1963), 951–2.
43 See D. Sella, 'The Rise and Fall of the Venetian Woollen Industry', in B. Pullan (ed.), *Crisis and Change in the Venetian Economy* (London, 1968), p. 120; R. Davis, 'England and the Mediterranean, 1570–1670', in F.J. Fisher (ed.), *Essays in the Economic and Social History of Tudor and Stuart England* (Cambridge, 1961), p. 123; Rapp, 'The Unmaking', pp. 499–525.

higher-quality broadcloth, but also hampered trade with what was the province's most important market for textile exports. But possibly the more profound explanations for the crisis were internal ones. Overvaluation of the *livre*, civil strife, demographic crisis and a collapse in agricultural prices and incomes contributed to depressing the domestic economy and hence the internal demand for cloth and also the demand for return products from foreign markets;[44] and the Levant, as several studies have shown, was one trade whose prosperity was determined by the demand in exporting countries for return cargoes.[45]

More than the cause it is the consequences of the depression which are of central interest to us. Declining foreign and domestic demand for Languedoc's cloth led not only to a quantitative decline in the industry but also to structural and qualitative changes. Thus at both Clermont and Carcassonne the ability to make the highest-quality cloth was lost – Dutch-style production skills disappeared completely. And not only did the number of clothiers decline: the nature of the profession was changed too. The extent of division of labour decreased. The gap between clothier and salaried worker was narrowed. Specialised, skilled workers in the crucial finishing processes no longer found adequate employment for their services and declined in number, some leaving for Lyons, a solitary oasis of prosperity in late-seventeenth-century France,[46] others changing profession.

The fixed capital investment in the industry was minimised, and those clothiers who remained in it rather than directing the labour of others increasingly carried out the majority of the production processes themselves. The extension of their role is revealed by an apprenticeship contract recorded in the 1680s. Instruction to the would-be clothier was promised in the 'métier de facturier ... consistant à carder embourrer excardasser emprimer et les teintures ordinaires': apart from spinning and weaving, virtually the whole cloth-making process is included in the list. That a similar contraction, and transformation, of the clothier's role occurred at Carcassonne is revealed by retrospective statements made by the local sub-delegate in the eighteenth century. Referring to this period he wrote that 'les fabriquands de ce temps là ne faisoient qu'un commerce borné; ils possédoient touttes les qualités des maîtres des differends arts et ne croyoient pas dérogés d'être continuellement autour de leurs ouvriers': they were 'eux mêmes tisserands cardeurs pareurs'. Centralist founders of royal manufactures in the province during these years found that there was a lack of both local entrepreneurial talent and skilled labour for specialised processes of textile production. This lack, indeed, was the main reason for the foundation of such concerns.

44 On the timing, and cause, of the crisis see Thomson, *Clermont-de-Lodève*, pp. 100–3.
45 E.g. R. Davis, *Aleppo and Devonshire Square* (London, 1967), pp. 24–9.
46 J. Meuvret, 'Circulation monétaire et utilisation économique de la monnaie dans la France du XVIe siécle', *Etudes d'Histoire Moderne et Contemporaine*, 1 (1947), 24–6.

Finally, there was a change in the nature of the relationship between urban and rural producers. If for the first half of the century there are signs that rural producers were working to the orders of urban clothiers within ordered putting-out systems, during the depression rural producers freed themselves from their urban employers to produce independently: the clothiers of Clermont and Lodève complained about this development and in particular about the activities of rustic cloth makers in the neighbouring villages of Ceilhes and Cornus, 'où il se fait une grande quantité de ... méchans draps'. The return to *Kaufsystem* was not total, but a considerable shrinkage in the *Verlagsystem* had occurred.

Early industrial surveys, carried out in the 1690s, reveal that although some recovery was already taking place in Carcassonne's industry, boosting the number of looms to the clothier, Clermont's eighteen clothiers only shared twenty-nine looms between them.[47] And although some of the cloth produced by these clothiers was being finished and dyed on the spot, some was also being sold in the white to local and Lyonnais merchants for finishing and dyeing elsewhere. And such an arrangement was universal for those rustic clothiers whose activities have just been described. The survey of *arts et métiers* carried out in 1692 reveals that their small-scale productions (between four and fifteen pieces of cloth a year) were entirely destined for sale in the white to merchants who either attended the local fairs or bought the cloth on the spot in the villages.[48] It was not the case, of course, that either Clermont's or Carcassonne's experiences were in any way unusual. Such a shrinking in size, and changing in form, of the basic industrial production unit was universal in times of depression in pre-industrial production zones. It occurred at Amiens, too, where Pierre Deyon has noted a return to 'a more fragmented organisation of production in the trade, return to the family enterprise', as well as a shift in the centre of gravity of production from urban to rural areas.[49] And that it was representative of other industrial zones in France is suggested by Meuvret's categorisation of seventeenth-century French industrial producers as 'casual workers' for whom industrial earnings 'merely provided a means of making up their incomes'.[50]

---

47 Fontvieille, 'Les Premières Enquêtes'. One entrepreneur was also utilising 12 looms. I have not included him in my calculation as his case was a special one, connected with state intervention. See Thomson, *Clermont-de-Lodève*, pp. 105–16.

48 On the effects of the depression on Clermont's and Carcassonne's industrial structures see Thomson, *Clermont-de-Lodève*, pp. 103–16.

49 On the frequency of such shifts between urban and rural production see Aymard, 'Production, commerce et consommation'. pp. 6–7 and Braudel, *Civilisation matérielle*, II, 270–1: 'The industrial revival of the town partly took place in the 16th century, when the countryside took its revenge in the 17th century, only to start losing ground again in the 18th century.' On Amiens, see P. Deyon, *Etude sur la société urbaine au XVIIᵉ siècle: Amiens, capitale provinciale* (Paris, 1967), and on a French 'realisation' see Deyon, 'Variations de la production textile', p. 952: 'The great depression in the 17th century transferred part of the weaving of *sayetterie* [type of worsted] to the countryside.'

50 Circulation monétaire', p. 19

It was on the basis of production for the Levant that an industrial recovery began in the 1690s. The growth was vigorous, but subject to sharp reversals on account of the disruptions of warfare and agrarian and demographic crises. This, indeed, was without doubt the major originality of the period and what caused it to be so testing a one for the new commercial and industrial dynasties which were arising from the debris of France's seventeenth-century economy. As Pierre Deyon writes, 'Everything happens, in this second part of the reign of Louis XIV, as though a contradiction had arisen between the new technical and commercial possibilities of a section of our manufacturing industry, and the obstacles to this activity resulting from the frailty of the Kingdom's agricultural economy and its megalomanic foreign policy'.[51]

Again it is not the causes of the recovery which interest us so much as its consequences for industrial organisation, the role of the clothier, the quality of production, and the relationship between rural and urban production. By the 1720s a new industry had developed which was in sharp contrast to that of the seventeenth century which has just been described. Fully fledged *Verlagsystems* had re-emerged. Clermont's clothiers, for example, controlled an average of eleven to twelve looms each, which would have meant that they employed labour forces of around three hundred.[52] The total labour force of the town was estimated at 5649 by an inspector of manufactures in 1732,[53] and a survey carried out in 1754 showed that the inhabitants of no less than fifty-six villages and towns in six dioceses were weaving, spinning or carding for these urban clothiers. The fixed capital investment in the industry had been much enlarged and, bar a few shearing and finishing shops, was entirely owned by the clothiers, the richest of whom had built impressive 'maisons de fabrique' (their expression) to house their offices, store-rooms and the crucial finishing processes. Carcassonne's industry had developed in a similar manner. Its clothiers employed workers in no less than eighty-one different villages in 1754,[54] and the sub-delegate described eloquently the change which had taken place in the nature of their roles since the seventeenth century: 'Il en est bien autrement aujourdhuy, les fabriquands sont des gens comerçans ils font leurs affaires dans leur bureau et peu vont chez leurs ouvriers, ce sont des commis ou des facteurs quon y envoye.' This superior organisation of production, in both towns, was mainly devoted to high-quality cloth production. The Dutch-style cloth-making techniques had been relearnt and five different cloths, with between 2400 and 3600 threads *to* the warp, were being

51 'Variations de la production textile', p. 954. See also his *Amiens*, pp. 171–2 and Thomson, *Clermont-de-Lodève*, pp. 230–3.
52 Archives Nationales (henceforth AN), F12 1380, Production for *département* of Montpellier, 2nd semester 1724.
53 ADH C5595.
54 ADH C2090.

produced.[55] Finally, independent rural producers had, once again, been absorbed within these vast new putting-out industries. This is revealed by the 1754 survey just referred to, and as early as 1727 it was reported that independent artisanal production within the diocese of Lodève had been abandoned – 'les ouvriers qui sont dans le voisinage de Clermont et de Lodève ne s'occupent plus…à la fabrique des cadis', the inspector noted.[56] The countryside was producing to the orders of the towns and this, as well as the extraordinary extent of movement and activity to which the new industry had given rise (one is reminded of George Wansey's description of a boom in the West Country trade in the 1760s: 'we have this year had a very great trade, which has thrown the country into a strange hurry, even into a kind of madness…'),[57] is well illustrated by a description made by an inspector at Carcassonne in 1731:

On ne fait autre chose dans la même ville et dans touttes les paroisses du diocèse que de donner les façons nécessaires aux draps, ce qui occuppe même le peuple dans quatre ou cinq diocèzes voisins et par là à proprement parler Carcassonne nest dans un sens qu'une manufacture de draps remplie de cardeurs tisserands fileuses et tondeurs de draps, toutte la campagne fourmille et des fabriquands et des ouvriers.[58]

The surveys carried out on the province's labour force in the 1750s in fact caught the industry at its height. A crisis began during the Seven Years War from which there was never to be complete recovery. The decisiveness of the turning-point is now fully established: 'a serious and prolonged slump begins in Languedoc's cloth industry,' Carrière and Morineau write.[59] Both Carcassonne and Clermont were to continue to produce cloth, in large quantities in some years, but their industries were never again to attain the prosperity which they had enjoyed in the first halves of the seventeenth and eighteenth centuries, and they lost permanently that definite leadership which they had enjoyed within the provincial industry until this time. Again it is not the causes of the crisis which so much concern us (although we shall return to them, for in this case it is a permanent, not purely a temporary, margination and depression which is the object of our attention), but the effects of the crisis on the structure of the industry. There was a return to some of the characteristics which the industry had shown in the seventeenth century. In this case our information is largely confined

---

55 Thus included in the regulation for Languedoc's Levant industry for 1708 were the following cloth types: 'mahous', 'mahous seconds', 'londrins premiers', 'londrins seconds', 'londres larges' and 'londres ordinaires', with 3600, 3000, 3200, 2600, 2400, and 2000 threads to the warp respectively. The bulk of the province's production, though, was to consist in 'londrins seconds'.

56 AN, F12 74, folio 314, *Procès-verbaux*, Bureau de Commerce, 24 April 1727.

57 Letter of 15 July 1760, in J. de L. Mann (ed.), *Documents Illustrating the Wiltshire Textile Trades in the Eighteenth Century* (Devizes, 1964), pp. 40–1.

58 ADH C4677, Report of sub-delegate, de Murat, 1731. On the growth of Languedoc's industry during these years see Thomson, *Clermont-de-Lodève*, Chapters 8–9.

59 'Draps de Languedoc', p. 121.

to Clermont, where the crisis was more severe than Carcassonne. Quality of production declined; richer clothiers moved out of the trade; clothmaking became a less regular activity; some cost-cutting was achieved by a reduction of dependence on the industry – for example, both clothiers and clothworkers buttressed industrial incomes with agricultural earnings – and by clothiers participating more extensively in the physical sides of the production process. Furthermore, fixed capital investment in the industry was sharply decreased, looms being sold to weavers and costly *maisons de fabrique* abandoned; again the social and economic gap between employer and employed was decreased. So there was a regression towards, though not a complete return to, the *Kaufsystem*. The extent of the regression was not as great as in the seventeenth century, and the crisis in the province was not so general, as it affected above all those industries which had prospered in the first half of the century,[60] other industrial centres, and particularly Castres, Mazamet, Bédarieux, Riols, Chalabre and Lodève, progressing fairly vigorously.[61]

IV

So the survey of Clermont's and Carcassonne's industrial experiences in the seventeenth and eighteenth centuries has revealed two repetitive cycles of development, cycles during which all aspects of the production processes were changed. What specific issues arise from the survey? Firstly, it is apparent that the types of development which historians of proto-industrialisation regard as important precursors of the Industrial Revolution had, to all appearances (and Languedoc's, of course, is far from the only proto-industrial region which reveals this),[62] been anticipated in previous centuries and, in addition, operated in a cyclical, rather than a linear, fashion. In other words they could represent, and apparently did represent in the case of Languedoc's industry, a stage in a parabolic curve of industrial expansion and decline. Secondly, it is apparent that

---

60 On the crisis, and structural regression, see Thomson, *Clermont-de-Lodève*, pp. 374–7 and 431–9.
61 On these towns see Thomson, *Clermont-de-Lodève*, pp. 385, 426, 433, 449; Wolff (ed.), *Histoire du Languedoc*, p. 406; Baron Trouvé, *Description générale et statistique du département de l'Aude* (Paris, 1818), pp. 608–12; E. Baux, 'Les Draperies audoises sous le Premier Empire', *Revue d'Histoire Economique et Sociale*, 38 (1960), 418–32; H. Creuzé de Lesser, *Statistique du département de l'Hérault* (Montpellier, 1824), pp. 472–3, 541–70; see also Johnson, 'Proto-industrialisation', pp. 2–9.
62 The industries of Amiens, Hondschoote and England's West Country provide three examples of pre-eighteenth-century developments of *Verlagsystems*. See Deyon, *Amiens*, pp. 200–28; E. Coornaert, *Un Centre industriel d'autrefois: la draperie sayetterie d'Hondschoote, XIVe–XVIIe siècles* (Paris 1941), pp. 288–9, 304, and E.A.L. Moir, 'Gentlemen Clothiers: A Study of the Organization of the Gloucestershire Cloth Industry, 1730–1815', in H.P.R. Finberg (ed.), *Gloucestershire Studies* (Leicester, 1957), pp. 226–39. Also Braudel, *Civilisation matérielle*, II, 276–7, provides details on a variety of early *Verlagsystems* from the thirteenth century.

the nature of the production unit in Languedoc's industry was influenced by market conditions. In periods in which there was a regular demand for high- and medium-quality cloth the urban producer dominated with a more capital-intensive production unit, and in periods of less regular demand, for lower-quality cloth, the market was shared between impoverished, 'artisanal', urban clothiers and rustic producers. Thirdly, it is apparent that, although the economic development of textile centres was 'parabolic', different towns' development cycles were not necessarily synchronised – some centres might be in upward phases of their cycles when others were on the way down. The variance of Lodève's cloth-making fortunes with those of Clermont in the seventeenth century we have already mentioned, and during the second half of the eighteenth century the lack of synchronisation was yet more marked.

These three issues – the cyclical development patterns observable in some of Languedoc's industrial centres during these years, the variations in industrial structure consequent upon changing market conditions, and the lack of synchronisation observable in different towns' development patterns – are clearly of more than local interest. The rest of this essay will be devoted to discussing them and to commenting on three other aspects of Languedoc's experience which are of relevance to the proto-industrialisation debate – the questions of de-industrialisation, of the relevance of high-quality proto-industrial development for later industrialisation and of the utility of proto-industrialisation models devised largely on the basis of observing proto-industrialisation growth in originally static areas of the European economy to commercially advanced regions such as Languedoc.

Cyclical development patterns

The cyclical nature of the fortunes of different textile centres, the 'frailty of wool towns', 'the succession of rapid growths followed by violent crises or long declines', have frequently been commented on by economic historians.[63] A number of factors are probably involved. A first point is the following: as has often been emphasised, production for different markets could be highly specialised. This was particularly true for more distant markets. Competition was greater for such markets, and thus a steady upward pressure was applied to cloth qualities and, as in modern industries subject to such competitive pressures, greater and greater product variation occurred. Success in such markets depended on developing a cloth which would sell well and then ensuring, by

---

63   Such cyclical patterns in industrial destinies are discussed most suggestively, but rather inconclusively, by Braudel, *Civilisation matérielle*, II, 302–5. The quotations are from Aymard, 'Production, commerce et consommation', p. 8.

regulations enforced by guilds or by the state at the point of export, that the quality and style of this cloth should be maintained. Regulations, as Aymard writes, fulfilled the function of the exact milling of a machine in a modern industrial economy.[64] But the process which consolidated a success in a market could also, the argument goes, give rise to inflexibility, which prevented adaptation to a change in consumer tastes or to a competing product from another industrial centre. More was involved than a matter of attitudes – cloth workers became accustomed to working in a certain way, with certain materials, and to retrain them to produce different cloths could be a costly and risky business.[65] It is also the case that changing market conditions could shift the comparative advantage for industrial production from one centre to another. Possibly, for example, in the seventeenth century the depression favoured areas capable of producing cheaper, harder-wearing cloths, as against those (which had flourished in the previous period) equipped to produce high-quality, expensively finished and dyed products. This might, for example, explain the greater success of Lodève in the second half of the seventeenth century – this town, in contrast to Clermont, was particularly well provided with the water power necessary for the more heavily fulled, coarser broadcloths which sold well in the second half of the seventeenth century.[66] Similar arguments have been used to explain the success of England's *New Draperies* during these years.[67]

Factors of this sort would certainly be of some relevance in explaining the cyclical variations in the prosperity of Carcassonne's and Clermont's industries during these years. Problems of inflexibility, a difficulty in adapting, are apparent. However, a close observation of the development of these industries leads me to believe that, in addition to these geographical and technological factors which might have caused difficulty in adapting to changing market conditions, elements intrinsic to the very growth processes of 'pre-industrial', industrial centres affected their competitiveness. Aspects of this growth process I shall now describe with this question of competitiveness in mind.

64 'Production, commerce et consommation', p. 6, and see also D.R. Ringrose, 'Comments on Papers by Reed, de Vries and Bean', *Journal of Economic History*, 31 (1973), 226, for an explanation of the need for regulations.

65 Such inflexibility in Venice's industry is noted by Rapp, 'The Unmaking', pp. 515–19; Sella, 'The Rise and Fall', pp. 122, 124, and C. Cipolla, 'The Economic Decline of Italy', in Pullan, *Crisis and Change*, pp. 135–8.

66 Lodève possessed the best water-power facilities in the province. In the mid eighteenth century there were forty-seven fulling mills in operation. A visitor to the town in 1674 commended the 'très bons draps' being produced there, and in 1694 an inspector reported that Clermont's industry had declined because 'les ouvriers de Lodève qui font le même travail y réussissent beaucoup mieux': Bibliothèque Municipale de Toulouse, MS 603, folio 360, and ADH C2200, Report of Cauvière, 1694.

67 D.C. Coleman points out that it could have been either supply factors (cheaper methods of production) or demand ones (increased incomes bringing more buyers into the market) which accounted for the success of these cloths: 'An Innovation and its Diffusion: The New Draperies', *Economic History Review*, 21 (1968), 423–4.

All *Verlagsystems* began as *Kaufsystems*. This seems certain. Invariably there were artisanal beginnings to large-scale putting-out systems.[68] Now it would seem likely, and evidence from Languedoc supports this, that such industries enjoyed special advantages during the early stages of their growth. (They would suffer some disadvantages, too, and notably from capital shortage, but this I would argue would not be likely to be so serious a handicap as it would be in a modern industrial economy, in view of the limited extent of fixed capital investment and the fairly ready availability of credit for circulating capital in the pre-industrial economy.) The entrepreneurs in such 'young' industries, who, at least on the basis of Languedoc's example, were largely of artisanal origin, and, in line with H. Pirenne's surmises,[69] generally unlinked to the previous, dominating commercial elite, were distinguished in two principal ways. They tended, firstly, to be particularly ambitious, as changing market conditions provided them with previously unhoped-for possibilities of industrial expansion, and hence of profit and social mobility, and, secondly, to be particularly hard-working, coming as they did from artisanal sectors of the economy, and thus having no inhibitions about involving themselves in all aspects of cloth making – manual, managerial and commercial. They were fully committed to, indeed obsessed by, their crafts, and their participation in manual work, together with shared social origins, encouraged sympathetic relationships with their labour forces.[70] The nature of these labour forces, too, held certain advantages for the clothier in the early stages of industrial expansion. The sudden growth of production could, of course, only be met by the migration of labour from rural areas or from other textile centres, or by the employment, often, initially at least, on a part-time basis, of rural or urban workers previously involved in other activities. This new labour force, while it might be lacking in skills, had advantages of other kinds. Migrants were generally young, male, and without dependents, and the advantages of having such employees were similar to those obtained from employing immigrant labour in the twentieth century: whereas the salary of a national worker must include some elements for the support and

---

68 A point emphasised by Coleman : 'such peasant textiles were not in the same class as the products of *la grande industrie*. But it was from such peasant by-employments... that there were fashioned... the rural industries, organized on a putting-out basis and which came to serve wider markets. Consequently, the technical processes, methods, and designs of such peasant manufactures *before* they were so organized constituted a reservoir of potential innovations' ('New Draperies', p. 421). I would also emphasise (see below, pp. 81–3) other types of inheritance.

69 'The Stages in the Social History of Capitalism', *American Historical Review*, 19 (1914), 494: 'I believe that, for each period into which our economic history may be divided, there is a distinct and separate class of capitalists. In other words, the group of capitalists of a given epoch does not spring from the capitalist group of the preceding epoch.'

70 On the influence of such factors on Languedoc's industrial progress in the first half of the eighteenth century see Thomson, *Clermont-de-Lodève*, pp. 287–90.

education of children, and for the care of the aged, these costs in the case of an immigrant are borne by the community of departure. In addition, such migrant workers often possessed some financial reserves, for their new employment provided them with the opportunity of liquidating their assets, including their inheritance rights, in their communities of origin. Finally, in a young and expanding industry, the scope for social mobility was likely to be high. This would have given an incentive to the labour force generally lacking in old, established and stable industries.

Having listed some of the advantages enjoyed by a young industry, the nature of some of the disadvantages from which old industries were likely to suffer can already be construed. The very success which the first generation of clothiers achieved made it less likely that their sons or grandsons would be as dynamic as they. Industrial decline was frequently attributed by contemporaries to entrepreneurial decay, and there seems no reason to doubt these verdicts. For a variety of reasons the quality of entrepreneurship was even more crucial in the pre-industrial period than it is in the industrial one – the fact that production units were not centralised complicated managerial problems; demand for industrial products was generally exceptionally unsteady; managers could rarely be relied upon; and the fact that economic outlets were so limited in the pre-industrial world had the consequence that those few opportunities which did exist were fought over particularly harshly – the unobservant clothier would be cheated at every stage of the production process.[71]

A decline in the quality of the labour force, likewise, was an aspect of industrial decline much emphasised by contemporaries, and again, it would seem, with justification. Possibilities of social mobility became fewer as the scale of industrial concerns grew, and the consequence of this tended to be a growing lack of interest shown by cloth workers in their employment. The types of society in which extensive putting-out systems were likely to develop were those in which the majority of the population would have enjoyed a certain degree of economic independence. It was the fact, or the prospect, of this enjoyment of independence, and hopes for social mobility through the purchase of land or the building up of stock, which were the major contributors to the maintenance of social harmony.[72] There were as yet no alternative rewards, such as those provided by a growing availability of consumer goods, which would have served to reconcile a wage earner to his lot. Possibilities of social mobility existed in a growing

71 For such views held by contemporaries in France see *ibid.*, pp. 360–2.
72 David Levine makes a similar point when explaining why the existence of wage labour did not have demographic consequences in the Middle Ages. The 'social solidarity of the peasant community' prevented this, he argues, and emphasises that within such a society 'social maturity' was 'equated ... with economic independence' and labourers were 'regarded ... as unfree'. [*Family Formation in an Age of Capitalism* New York, 1977], p. 148. I would argue that such values continued to be influential up to, and beyond, industrialisation.

industry, and this would have contributed to cloth workers' involvement in, and enthusiasm for, their tasks, but such possibilities became more and more scarce in established industries. The result of this was an alienation and estrangement which was all the more notable in so far as the general condition in the pre-industrial economy was the possession of at least a degree of independence. Contemporaries, in plenty, remarked upon the phenomenon which, it must be emphasised, was not a universal feature of pre-industrial labour but purely one of pre-industrial labour in situations (usually at fairly advanced stages of commercial and industrial development) *in which the possibilities of social mobility and career advancement had been cut off.* Thus Josiah Tucker believed that the chief reason for the growing advance of Yorkshire's cloth industry over that of the West Country lay in the better conditons provided for its labour force. In the case of West Country cloth workers, he wrote, 'The motives of industry, Frugality and Sobriety are all subverted by this one consideration, *viz.* That they shall always be chained to the same Oar, and never be but Journeymen. Therefore their only Happiness is to get Drunk, and to make Life pass away with as little Thought as possible.'[73] David Hume was sensitive to the same phenomenon. The reputation for debauchery and irresponsibility which cloth workers in putting-out industries possessed was a sign of their alienation, he realised – 'an attempt to compensate through pleasure for want of liveliness resulting from a thwarting of the design of interesting action'.[74] Discontent and disillusion were all the more likely in view of the fact that employment was often irregular and wages increasingly inadequate – cloth workers would by now have dependents, both young and old. Disillusioned, impoverished workers meant badly made cloth, embezzled raw materials and growing indebtedness.

All pre-industrial activity was extremely labour-intensive, and there could have been no more significant element sapping an industry's strength than this gradual impoverishment and disillusionment of its labour force. The much-discussed conversion of English political economists to a high wage policy in the mid eighteenth century may have been partly caused by an awareness of growing prospects for technological change and an increasing appreciation of the role of domestic demand in boosting industrial progress, but it must, too, have been contributed to by an awareness of the tragic social and damaging economic consequences of the low wage policies which had been adopted to boost output

---

73 *Instructions for Travellers* (London, 1757), pp. 24–5. Many historians have described labour problems in putting-out industries and the term 'backward-sloping supply curve for labour' has been coined for the strong leisure preference shown by individuals denied possibilities of social mobility. See, for example, J. de L. Mann, *Cloth Industry in the West*, pp. 105–16; Moir, 'Gentlemen Clothiers', pp. 247–58 and, especially, A.W. Coats, 'Changing Attitudes to Labour in the Mid Eighteenth Century', *Economic History Review*, 11 (1958), 39–43.

74 These are Hume's views as interpreted by E. Rotwein in his introduction to D. Hume, *Writings on Economics* (London, 1955), pp. 17–18. Cited by Coats, 'Changing Attitudes', p. 40.

(necessity was proving the only efficient stimulus) in areas of putting-out industry.[75] As we have noted, an 'asset' of a young industry was the vigour, enthusiasm and financial resources of its labour force. The wealth of weavers at early stages of putting-out industries' development has frequently been commented on. But the gradual inpoverishment and proletarianisation of cloth workers in putting-out industries has also been frequently emphasised. Effectively what occurred was a process of human-asset-stripping which ultimately damaged the industry itself in many ways, the most fundamental being the destruction of workers' motivation (speed and quality of production were determined by this, still, and not yet by the rate at which machines turned).[76]

Variations in industrial structure

Our second point, that of variations in type and geographical distribution of production units in different periods depending upon the demand situation being stronger for high-quality or lower-quality cloth, is, I think, simpler to explain. Different types of production system suited different types of cloth. Thus the production of high- or middling-quality cloth could only be carried out successfully if it was undertaken on some scale: specialised workers were required for certain processes, and their wages could only be paid if a large output was achieved; uniformity of cloth sizes, qualities, dyes, etc. could, likewise, only be achieved if production was carefully regulated and carried out in some volume; the right raw materials at the right prices could only be obtained if buying was done in bulk; and, finally, in a European economy which was becoming more and more competitive, the entrepreneur, who co-ordinated all aspects of the production process, from the buying to the packing and presentation of the final article, was becoming more and more essential if success in international markets was to be achieved. The importance of growing international competition to industrial progress in the period preceding the Industrial Revolution certainly requires emphasis, and the fact that industrial progress was attainable only by investment in the production process by *marchands-fabricants* is stressed by Deyon: 'The only progress that we have been able to confirm occurred where the actual cloth-makers had some monetary reserves'. In another context he notes that the merchants, in contrast, had an

---

75 Coats, 'Changing Attitudes', pp. 46–51.
76 Vincent de Gournay, visiting Languedoc's industry in the 1750s, commented on the decline in resources of weavers at Carcassonne: some had had possessions up to a value of 4000 *livres*, had owned land and eaten meat regularly, but extreme poverty had become universal (ADH C5552, Memoir of 1753, and Thomson, *Clermont-de-Lodève*, p. 365). The decline in West Country weavers' resources is noted by J. de L. Mann, *Cloth Industry in the West*, p. 105: weaving had originally been a high-status profession, the Tudor Statute of Artificiers restricting the right of apprenticeships into the trade to sons of parents with land worth at least £3 a year.

interest in leaving unchanged 'production conditons which would guarantee their economic domination'.[77] So, in other words, production of cloth for specialised markets was subject to considerable economies of scale, and in addition international competition was making more and more necessary a dynamic control of the entire production process. In such circumstances the small-scale producer, be he rural or urban, could not compete. However, in the production of lower-quality cloth, for more scattered domestic markets, the richer clothier possessed few, if any, advantages. The premium for standardisation in the production of such cloth was not so high. The skills involved were less complex, and processes such as dyeing and pressing, which in the case of high-quality cloth needed to be carried out by specialised, skilled workers, could be carried out by the clothier himself. Above all, the artisan, and even more so the rustic producer, could cut costs both by increasing his own and his family's labour input into cloth production and by subsidising his production by obtaining income from other generally agricultural, sources. Evidently the large-scale producer, given both his status and volume of affairs, was quite incapable of contributing significantly to the labour input of his cloth production. He was obliged to continue to employ labour and, of necessity, to pay for it at above subsistence level. He was also, clearly, far more vulnerable than the small-scale producer to any interruption in demand and, further, he lost those economies of scale which he had enjoyed in the production of high- or medium-quality cloth of uniform sizes.[78]

The lack of synchronisation in development patterns of different towns

In commenting on our first point, we have argued that the competitiveness of industries could vary, depending on their 'age' and on the point reached in their development cycles. This argument, in itself, would partly account for the varying performances of different Languedocian industrial centres in the second half of the eighteenth century, and it is indeed the case that those cloth-making

---

77 *Amiens*, p. 197, and 'Le Mouvement de la production textile à Amiens au XVIIe siècle', *Revue du Nord*, 44 (1962), 209.

78 The pre-industrial, as well as the industrial, economy was characterised by 'dualism'. The contrast in the manner of functioning of market and subsistence rural concerns has frequently been emphasised. See, for example, J. de Vries, *The Economy of Europe in an Age of Crisis, 1600–1750* (Cambridge, 1976), pp. 73–5, and Le Roy Ladurie (*Paysans*, pp. 165–74), who emphasises the more favourable performance of smaller, peasant properties during periods of labour shortage. Similar points are made by Levine, *Family Formation*, p. 14 ('For the full time proletarianized rural industrialist such competition [from areas in which rural and industrial work was combined] was unfair because while he needed to derive *all* his income from his wages, the cottager needed only to gain his margin of subsistence'.). See also Thomson, *Clermont-de-Lodève*, pp. 119–21 for an attempt to compare the functioning of large, market-oriented and small, family textile production units.

centres which fared well had young industries, with industrial structures in the process of developing from *Kaufsystem* to *Verlagsystem*. What concerns us at this point in our argument, though, are the reasons for the lack of synchronisation in the development cycles of the province's industries when uniformity might have been expected in view of the supposed universal dominance of the agrarian situation on textile production.[79]

The lack of synchronisation is far greater for the eighteenth than for the seventeenth century, it would seem, but even in the seventeenth century the case of Lodève (to the limited extent that we are informed about it) suggests the possibility of there having been exceptions to the general industrial decline. And inconsistent industrial performances in pre-industrial periods have been noted in the case of other industrial economies, and particularly the Italian. A first possible explanation, and it is one which has been put forward by other historians, is that demand shifts, by changing the extent of comparative advantage of different industrial centres, might occasion depression in one industry whilst stimulating another. Such a shift in demand towards lower-quality, harder-wearing, depression cloth might have favoured Lodève's cloth industry. But, as has been noted, the production of such types of cloth was generally most economically carried out within the small-scale production unit, and it is indeed the case that Lodève's organisation of production was 'artisanal' until well into the eighteenth century. Effectively, then, the contrasting fortunes of Lodève and Clermont in the seventeenth century simply illustrate that variation between *Verlagsystem* and *Kaufsystem*, depending on market circumstances, described in the previous section. In the eighteenth century, on the other hand, there were varied industrial responses to what were, on the whole, favourable market situations throughout. Thus in the first half of the century the *Verlagsystems* of Carcassonne, Clermont and Saint-Chinian (which shared in the growth pattern described) were isolated phenomena within the province, Bédarieux's, Lodève's and Mazamet's industries, for example, remaining frozen at the *Kaufsystem* stage, whereas in the second half of the century the reverse was the case.

There would seem to be two principal factors responsible for this increased variety. First, the extent of intervention in industrial life had been greatly increased in the eighteenth century in France, and this had inevitably resulted in some areas of the economy being favoured at the expense of others, and in some towns being allowed an exceptional share of markets, while others were completely excluded from the right to produce. This had contributed to a greater

---

79 That a close, and inverse, relationship continued in most areas to exist between total industrial production and grain prices is shown by C. E. Labrousse, *Esquisse du mouvement des prix et des revenus en France au XVIIIe siècle* (Parix, 1933), II, 316–20, 546–50.

variety of industrial experience than would normally have been the case, and by the mid eighteenth century, when many restrictive policies were reversed, there existed some towns like Clermont at a ripe stage of their development cycles, and others, like Castres, Mazamet and Bédarieux (and it was not without significance that these were all Protestant towns) which had been deliberately excluded from production for certain markets, and which had thus retained industrial structures characterised by the artisanal production unit.[80] The second factor contributing to a greater diversity of experience is more closely linked to the Industrial Revolution: changes were occurring which affected both supply and demand conditions. Thus new products, and notably cotton cloth, were being developed, and the rise of the Atlantic trades, in which continental economies as well as Britain participated, had led to a widening of industrial markets and for the first time to a growth in the overseas demand for lower-quality textiles and metal goods, which could be produced efficiently by the smaller-scale production unit, be it artisanal or rustic. It was on the production of coarser-quality cloths, not for Mediterranean but for Atlantic markets, that the initial industrial expansion of Mazamet and Castres was based.[81]

This widening and diversifying of the market situation thus increased the possibility of varying economic performance in the second half of the eighteenth century. In particular there was a sharp reversal in the circumstances of the non-participants and participants in the expansion of the first half of the century. Towns excluded from the early growth found after the mid-century change in industrial policy that they were doubly favoured. Firstly, their *Kaufsystem* organisation of production enabled them to profit from growing Atlantic demand for lower-quality, hard-wearing cloth. Secondly, should they want to produce for more traditional markets like the Levant (and it was on production for this market that Bédarieux's early expansion was based), they could do so by employing ex-members of Carcassonne's or Clermont's labour force, and could do so advantageously as their industries, so long checked by administrative intervention, would be enjoying the advantages which accrued to all industrial centres moving from *Kaufsystem* to *Verlagsystem*. In sharp contrast, the industries of the traditional producers for the Levant would have been doubly penalised. Firstly, they were ill equipped for profiting from the rising demand in the New World for lower-quality goods, for the cost reasons discussed above and

80 For information on the effects of state intervention on French industry see P. Clément, *Histoire de la vie et de l'administration de Colbert* (Paris, 1846); P. Boissonnade, *Colbert et le triomphe de l'étatisme* (Paris, 1932); A. des Cilleuls, *Histoire et régime de la grande industrie en France aux XVIIᵉ et XVIIIᵉ siècles*, 2nd edn (New York, 1970); E. Levasseur, *Histoire des classes ouvrières et de l'industrie en France avant 1789*, 2 vols. (Paris, 1901), and also Thomson, *Clermont-de-Lodève*, Chs. 1, 6, 9, 10, 11 and 12.
81 On this see L. Dermigny, 'Les Foires de Pézenas', pp. 102–3, 113–14. By 1773 Mazamet was exporting 10 000 pieces of cloth a year to Canada.

because of the inflexibility to which all pre-industrial centres, and heavily regulated centres in particular, were prone. Secondly, they were unable to compete very effectively with fresh producers in the supplying of traditional markets with high-quality broadcloths because of the advanced stages of their development cycles.

So, once again, the competitive advantages of industries in the process of moving from *Kaufsystem* to *Verlagsystem* asserted themselves. It should be noted, though, that the possibility of such supplanting of old industrial centres by new was not to last for long. The mechanisation of spinning and other production processes gradually eroded those cost advantages which the family economy had previously enjoyed over the large concern. The nature of industrial development was thereby totally changed, and above all its cyclical characteristics were moderated. Mechanisation and the enclosure of production not only provided economies of scale in the production of lower-quality goods, but also furnished the decadent entrepreneur of the *Verlagsystem* with a partial solution to his declining powers: by enclosing his labour force, and mechanising, his entrepreneurial tasks were greatly eased. In addition, as the entry cost to industrial activity was increased by these new types of capital investment, he was likely to find himself more protected than previously from the competition of dynamic entrepreneurs rising from the labour force.

De-industrialisation

What we would like to establish in connection with the issue of de-industrialisation is the following: are the criteria which governed industrial success in the pre-industrial period of relevance in explaining the varied success of proto-industrial towns in adapting to industrialisation proper? A priori there seem to be no reasons why these criteria should not be of relevance. Continuity and improvisation have been two characteristics frequently attributed to early industrialisation – continuity with respect to entrepreneurial tasks, capital requirements, ways of managing the labour force, etc.[82] – and it has been argued that the same sorts of qualities determined economic success as in the pre-industrial period.

The validity of these a priori reasonings is substantiated by the characteristics of those Languedocian industrial centres which successfully adapted to the challenges of the nineteenth century. It was, indeed, those industrial centres which were emerging, or had recently emerged, from the *Kaufsystem* to the *Verlagsystem* which were most successful during industrialisation – these were the circumstances of Bédarieux, Mazamet, Castres, Chalabre, Riols and Lodève.

82 See, for example, S. Pollard, *The Genesis of Modern Management* (Penguin edn, 1968), p. 301.

And the examples of Carcassonne and Clermont serve not only to illustrate the difficulties experienced by old putting-out industries in adapting to the new industrial era: they illustrate, too, the even lesser likelihood of continuity when extensive state intervention with industry had occurred. The diseconomies and inflexibilities inherent in pre-industrial development cycles were exacerbated by guild systems, inspectors and government regulations. Areas subject to such intervention rarely distinguished themselves during industrialisation. Thus Jürgen Kocka emphasises the lack of continuity in Germany and points to the contrast between the entrepreneurial qualities apparent in those areas which had experienced industrial and commercial development spontaneously, under the discipline of the market, and those which existed in areas subjected to intervention. Entrepreneurs in the latter areas, Kocka writes:

side-stepped problems of large-scale management which were . . . appearing for the first time, and which were to become typical of the later factory system too . . . adopted known technical advances, but seldom . . . initiated them themselves . . . absent is not concern for profits, market-orientation, or an aptitude for political dealings, but abilities and motivations for rational, systematic, steady entrepreneurship and for innovatory control over the technological processes.[83]

The Languedocian textile centres which best succeeded in adapting to industrialisation were those which had not been corrupted by too much contact with the state and which were progressing, or had recently progressed, from *Kaufsystem* to *Verlagsystem*. In other words, the same sort of criteria applied as those which we have argued caused industrial performance to vary in the pre-industrial period.

A further qualifying note with respect to Languedoc's de-industrialisation needs to be added. It should be emphasised that the section of Languedoc's industry which entered the nineteenth century in a reasonably healthy state was far outweighed by that which entered it in a state of decline. As Chassagne has shown, Languedoc's situation of primacy in France's textile industry had been lost decisively by the turn of the century, and by 1810 'Languedoc and, more generally, the Midi... have begun a permanent decline.'[84] The most fundamental causes for this were probably beyond the control of provincial industrialists. The province which had been near the centre of a Mediterranean-dominated economy was on the periphery of an Atlantic-based one, and it was its agricultural role (as Dugrand emphasised) which was encouraged by French industrialisation. This 'demotion' is well illustrated by the fate of the fair of Beaucaire, which declined from international to local market centre between

83 'Entrepreneurs and Managers in German Industrialization', in P. Mathias and M. M. Postan (eds.), *Cambridge Economic History of Europe*, Vol. VII, Part I (1978), p. 507.
84 'L'Industrie lainière', p. 163.

1789 and 1815 and lost all importance with the railway age.[85] What we have shown, therefore, is not why the province did or did not de-industrialise but why, within what was undoubtedly a generally deteriorating environment for the province's industry, different industrial centres showed varying capacities to adapt. In the longer term there were barely any survivors. As Chassagne writes, in Mazamet 'one finds... the only southern example of successful transition from proto-industrialisation to mechanized industry', and it could be argued that Mazamet's success came not from perseverance with textiles but from the growth of *délainage*.[86] Johnson, likewise, although he attributes great significance to a revival in the province's cloth production largely for military demands in the mid nineteenth century, concedes that little of note survived into the twentieth century.[87]

Significance of high-quality proto-industrial production

It was certainly the case that until the late eighteenth century high-quality production was regarded by contemporaries as the most significant sector determining success in international markets. Proliferation of such production was invariably given pride of place in all mercantilist schemes for industrial development. But it can be argued that the future lay not with luxury production, but with cheaper goods, destined for mass consumption. This type of argument must be one of the premises for the emphasis placed in the proto-industrialisation model on textile production of low quality. This importance of the low quality is, of course, undeniable. We have just observed some of the significant consequences for Languedoc's industry of the growth in concentrated overseas demand for lower-quality goods, and the importance to Britain's early Industrial Revolution of an expansion in the demand for such products, both within and outside Europe, has been much emphasised by historians.[88] Equally stressed, however, in recent years has been the fact that Britain's path was not the only one to industrialisation.[89] In that followed by several continental European countries the production of high-quality luxury goods (in contrast to Britain's case) played an important role. This was particularly true of France, and the concentration there during the industrialisation process on high-quality pro-

85 Léon, 'La Foire de Beaucaire', pp. 325–7.
86 S. Chassagne, 'Industrialisation et désindustrialisation dans les campagnes françaises: quelques reflexions à partir du textile', *Revue du Nord*, 63 (1981), 46–7.
87 'Proto-industrialisation', pp. 2–5, 8–9, 22–38.
88 D. E. C. Eversley, 'The Home Market and Economic Growth in England, 1750–1780', in E. L. Jones and G. E. Mingay (eds.), *Land, Labour and Population in the Industrial Revolution* (London, 1967), pp. 206–59, and R. Davis, *The Industrial Revolution and British Overseas Trade* (Leicester, 1979), pp. 14–15.
89 See, for example, P. O'Brien and C. Keyder, *Economic Growth in Britain and France 1780–1914: Two Paths to the Twentieth Century* (London, 1978), p. 18, and A. S. Milward and S. B. Saul, *The Economic Development of Continental Europe, 1780–1870* (London, 1973), pp. 25–40.

duction, once regarded as virtually reprehensible, and as a possible sign of conservative entrepreneurship, is now seen, and surely quite rightly, as an intelligent response to the internal and European demand situation and as a fruitful capitalisation on two comparative advantages which French entrepreneurs gained from the qualities of their labour force – its cheapness (*vis-à-vis* England) and its skills (*vis-à-vis* continental competitors).[90] But in view of this interpretation credit must be given, and importance attached, to the development and proliferation of skills in luxury trades during the pre-industrial period. Significantly, those Languedocian centres whose first expansion in the late eighteenth century was based on exploitation of the developing markets for lower-quality textiles consolidated their successes during the first half of the nineteenth century on the basis of high-quality production.[91]

Relevance of the proto-industrial model to advanced areas such as Languedoc

At the beginning of this essay we questioned the relevance of the proto-industrial model to an area such as Languedoc. We questioned it not so much on account of the province's de-industrialisation, an eventuality catered for, if not adequately accounted for, in the model, but in that it seems unlikely that a model derived from the observation of the catalytic role played by proto-industrial development in largely agrarian, backward areas, could have much relevance to an area such as Languedoc which was already highly commercialised in the Middle Ages. What the model would seem to be providing, we would argue, and providing most effectively, is not a general explanation of how industrialisation was prepared for in the pre-industrial period *throughout* Europe, but one of how it was prepared for in backward, generally interior areas whose first full contact with the market system and commercial opportunity came from involvement in proto-industrial activity.[92] It may be, of course, that this more sudden and unsettling manner of modernising provided a better preparation for, and

90 Thus P. Landes in 'Business and the Businessman', in E. M. Earle (ed.), *Modern France, Problems of the Third and Fourth Republics* (Princeton, 1951), p. 345, is critical of the emphasis on high quality and the leaving of 'coarser types of cloth, which would best lend themselves to efficient and large scale production... to those backward centres in no position to take advantage of these possibilities', but F. Crouzet, M. Lévy-Leboyer and Milward and Saul all commend the intelligent profiting from comparative advantage: 'French Economic Growth in the Nineteenth Century Reconsidered', *History*, 59 (1974), 177; 'Le Processus d'industrialisation: le cas de l'Angleterre et de la France', *Revue Historique*, 496 (1968), 290–1; *Development of Continental Europe*, pp. 319, 324.

91 The introduction of fine cloth production at Mazamet is mentioned by Chassagne, 'Industrialisation et désindustrialisation', p. 46. For Bédarieux's concentration on high-quality production see Wolff (ed.), *Histoire du Languedoc*, p. 406.

92 S. Pollard, likewise, criticises the failure of the proto-industrial model to 'distinguish between different social settings': *Peaceful Conquest: The Industrialization of Europe 1760–1970* (Oxford, 1981), p. 76.

contribution to, the rupture of industrialisation than the more balanced and gradual type of advance that was experienced in areas like Languedoc. Certainly Languedoc, and the south of France generally, showed a difficulty in adjusting to industrialisation which was much commented on and which it would be sweeping to attribute entirely to the geographical shift just referred to. A contributory element in this difficulty could also be the fact that the many centuries during which the province had played so central a role in the pre-industrial economy had led to its inhabitants possessing rigid attitudes to commercial and industrial activity which, though they corresponded to the circumstances of the pre-industrial economy, were less well suited to success in an industrial one.[93]

93 A contemporary who believed that the south's failure to adapt well to industrialisation was attributable to such factors was Stendhal, who wrote that 'Le midi de la France est dans le cas de l'Espagne et de l'Italie. Son *brio* naturel, sa vivacité, l'empêchent de s'angliser comme le nord de la France'; cited by F. Crouzet, 'Les Origines du sous-développement économique du Sud-Ouest', *Annales du Midi*, 71 (1959), 78. For some speculations on the influence of these sorts of inheritances from the pre-industrial period see Thomson, *Clermont-de-Lodève*, pp. 40–5. The idea that success in one economic epoch might disqualify you from achieving in the next is, of course, not a new one. See, for example, Pollard, *Peaceful Conquest*, p. 49 and J. de Vries on Holland: 'the Dutch Republic stands as an example of an economy whose intense specialization in one direction effectively closed the door to the kinds of social structure and economic policies required for industrial growth. Not every growth path led to the Industrial Revolution' (*The Economy of Europe*, p. 252).

4

Seasonal fluctuations and social division of labour: rural linen production in the Osnabrück and Bielefeld regions and the urban woollen industry in the Niederlausitz (*c.* 1770–*c.* 1850)*

JÜRGEN SCHLUMBOHM

Seasonal fluctuations have been assumed to be one of the main characteristics of pre-industrial production processes. The rhythms of climate and the seasons regulated the economic cycle of societies dominated by agriculture. Natural rhythms rather than time discipline determined the flow of work. And the chronic imbalance of labour supply between the peak and slack times of the year are said to have limited production possibilities. Modern industry has been associated with regularity, continuity and, ultimately, the elimination of fluctuation in output caused by man or nature. A recent version of this characteristic division between traditional and modern societies has been set out by Franklin Mendels: 'We can thus consider primitive agriculture and the assembly line as the end points of a linear evolution marked by a progressively increasing continuity and intensity of work over the centuries, an approach that makes it easier to place "proto-industrialisation" in its proper perspective.'[1]

This essay demonstrates the extent to which this dichotomy and the notion of linear evolution are far too simple. Different regions manifested different production cycles and seasonal fluctuations which do not necessarily accord with what we think about their relative 'progress' or backwardness.

* Revised version of an essay published in *Archiv für Sozialgeschichte*, 19 (1979), 263–98, under the title 'Der saisonale Rythmus der Leinenproduktion im Osnabrücker Lande während des späten 18. und der ersten Hälfte des 19. Jahrhunderts: Erscheinungsbild, Zusammenhänge und interregionaler Vergleich'. Translated by Rachel Norman. I am grateful to the members of the Max-Planck-Institut für Geschichte for their criticisms, especially to Manfred Thaller for his advice and help on questions of EDP. I thank Michael Schwibbe for permission to use the programmes which provided the correlograms. The calculations were carried out at the Gesellschaft für wissenschaftliche Datenverarbeitung mbH, Göttingen.

1 Franklin F. Mendels, 'Seasons and Regions in Agriculture and Industry During the Process of Industrialization', in *Region and Industrialisierung*, ed. Sidney Pollard (Göttingen, 1980), pp. 177–95; the quotation is from p. 180.

Another characteristic separating modern from traditional production processes is supposed to have been the degree of social division of labour. But in the cases studied in this paper we notice that as late as around 1800 a very low degree of social division of labour in a region could be regarded as an economic advantage; and only from the point of view of capitalist industrialisation did it seem self-evident that 'modernisation' meant a growing division of labour.

The purpose of this essay is rather to raise questions than to answer them. It presents some preliminary findings of a long-term research project. The seasonal fluctuations in three German regions are described and the great variety in their extent and character is explained by the social structure of the production processes in the respective regions and industries. Specifically, the social division of labour is looked at on several levels: combination or separation of agriculture and industry, and of the different stages of production within the manufacturing process; and the division of labour by sex and age within the production unit (the farm, the workshop, the household). This description tends to underline the variety of pre-industrial industries. It leads to questions about the relative 'modernity' of different structures and may serve as an introduction to further research into their origin as well as into their impact on the industrialisation or de-industrialisation of the subsequent period.

At the time when the Osnabrück region (which had been a principality of its own before, and was to become part of the kingdom of Hanover in 1815) was part of the French empire, the prefect of the Oberems *département* announced on 4 April 1812 an extensive inquiry into the linen trade. In so doing he referred to the general concern about 'outlets for the linen produced in this region', and, among other things, asked the *maires* of all *communes* to state the quantity and value of the linen produced in their district, not only in the last four half-years but also in the first quarter of 1812.[2] The answers given by the *maires* of the Osnabrück region to this last part of the question, however, were unproductive for the authorities. The number of pieces of linen reported as being ready for sale in the first quarter was very close to zero or zero in practically all areas. 'In the first quarter very little is woven and sold, this only happens in the following quarters'; 'no figures can be given yet for the first quarter, since although the yarn has already been spun, it has not been woven or bleached' – these were some of the responses of the *maires*.[3] In this respect, the purpose of the inquiry, to determine the latest situation in linen production and trade under the continuing

2 *Sammlung der Präfektur-Akten des Oberems-Departements*, vol. 2 (Osnabrück, 1812), No. 68, pp. 141–4. Concerning the administrative history of the time, see Antoinette Joulia, 'Ein französischer Verwaltungsbezirk in Deutschland: das Oberems-Departement (1810–1813)', in *Osnabrücker Mitteilungen* (hereafter referred to as *OsnabMitt*), 80 (1973), 21–102.
3 The *maires* of Bissendorf and Belm in the 'comments' in the respective tables: Staatsarchiv Osnabrück (hereafter referred to as StA OS), Rep. 240, No. 844, fols. 120 r., 241 r.

continental blockade, remained unfulfilled; the trade cycle was hidden behind the seasonal fluctuations.

Thanks to remarkably good sources, it is possible to study the seasonal rhythm of linen production in the Osnabrück region not only at the isolated times of such inquiries, but also in its most important aspects over a continuous period of about eighty-five years. The reason for the good sources for this period is the institution of the *Legge* (staple).[4] In the town of Osnabrück, this office of inspection had its roots in the late Middle Ages. The town *Legge* became effective again in 1770 and the government established several further *Leggen* in the surrounding countryside between 1770 and 1774. These all continued to function far into the second half of the nineteenth century – and in some cases until the beginning of the twentieth – as the authorities responsible for quality control and classification, for measuring the length of the individual pieces and for arranging sale from rural producers to the linen merchants. In spite of various changes in individual cases, in principle it was compulsory until 1869 to take any linen produced for sale to the *Legge*. Of course in spite of this the *Leggen* never completely controlled the linen production of the Osnabrück region. It was never intended that the linen woven for the producer's own consumption should be brought to the *Legge*; and the trip to the *Legge* was not always immediately made compulsory for new sorts of fabric. For some sorts of linen there were by the late eighteenth century individual putters-out who paid the local inhabitants to weave their yarn without then taking the finished product to the staple. Finally, some linen was sold simply by ignoring the *Legge*, either by migrant labourers, or to wandering merchants or merchants in the neighbouring territories. On the other hand, some linen from the nearby Prussian districts or from the Münster region came to the Osnabrück *Leggen*. In spite of these qualifications, it can be assumed that, from the 1770s until the mid nineteenth century at least, the *Leggen* received the greater part of the linen produced in the Osnabrück region by small producers using their own yarn and looms and then selling to a merchant.[5] These pieces of linen which came to the *Leggen* also represent a substantial majority of all the linen produced for sale in the principality of Osnabrück.[6] Therefore, in as far as the *Legge* statistics provide a record of monthly or quarterly quantities, they cover the seasonal fluctuations for most of the linen produced for sale.

4 Hermann Wiemann, 'Die Osnabrücker Stadtlegge', in *OsnabMitt*, 35 (1910), 1–76; Joachim Runge, *Justus Mösers Gewerbetheorie und Gewerbepolitik im Fürstbistum Osnabrück in der zweiten Hälfte des 18. Jahrhunderts*, Schriften zur Wirtschafts- und Sozialgeschichte, vol. 2 (Berlin, 1966), pp. 66ff.; Konrad Machens, 'Der Osnabrücker Leinenhandel', incomplete and unpublished manuscript in the StA OS.

5 Concerning the relations of production in a *Kaufsystem* like this, see Schlumbohm, in Peter Kriedte, Hans Medick and Jürgen Schlumbohm, *Industrialization Before Industrialization: Rural Industry in the Genesis of Capitalism* (Cambridge, 1981), pp. 98ff.

6 Compare the estimation by Friedrich Wilhelm von Reden, *Die Gewerbe des Königreichs Hannover* (Hanover, 1835), col. 155.

Table 1 *Osnabrück Legge 1771–1855: mean number of pieces for individual months*

	Jan.	Feb.	Mar.	April	May	June	July	Aug.	Sept.	Oct.	Nov.	Dec.
1771–1855	30	17	37	183	672	1424	2200	1229	1169	541	378	191
1771–98	40	29	74	416	1252	1495	1872	809	944	592	418	216
1799–1826	24	5	7	65	503	1524	2413	1366	1286	592	414	193
1827–55	26	17	30	72	274	1259	2312	1503	1274	443	303	165

Source: see footnote 7.

On the basis of the *Legge* registers, or of contemporary extracts from them, the number of pieces of linen brought to the Osnabrück town *Legge* can be ascertained month-for-month between 1771 and 1855.[7] In order to get an idea of the average scale of seasonal fluctuations, the mean for the individual months over these 85 years was calculated (see table 1).[8] The enormous imbalance

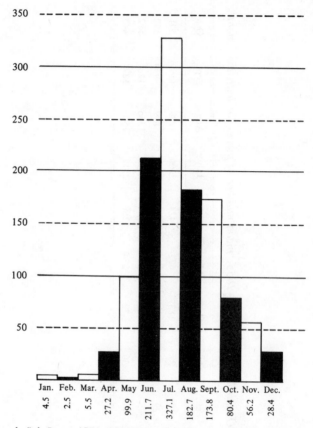

Figure 1 Osnabrück *Legge* 1771–1855: index of the mean number of pieces for individual months (mean annual figure divided by 12 = 100)

7 StA OS, Dep. 3 bV, No. 1041, No. 1059–1110. Before 1810 the business year of the Osnabrück *Legge* ended in the middle of December. The monthly figures and the yearly figures were transferred to the exact calendar months or years before the calculation. In these sources the numbers of pieces of linen are missing for the years 1792 and 1796 and for the months from August to December 1805. These missing values were estimated and added.

8 Because of the relatively approximate nature of the results required, this simple method (see Taro Yamane, *Statistik: ein einführendes Lehrbuch*, Fischer-Taschenbuch, vol. 6308 [Frankfurt-on-Main, 1976], I, 318ff.) appears to be sufficient, and the use of techniques developed for considerably more complicated purposes, in particular for the seasonal adjustment of time series, does not seem to be required.

between the months is immediately striking: in February an average of 17 pieces of linen came to the Osnabrück town *Legge*, but in July the mean was 2200, almost 130 times as many. The results become clearer if the mean number of pieces per month is expressed as a percentage of a fictitious 'normal month' (the mean number of pieces per year divided by 12). The graph of the index shows the relative importance of the individual months (figure 1). Whereas only 1% of the annual yield falls to the first quarter, in April the number of pieces increases and in May it reaches the figure for the fictitious 'normal month'. The four summer months, June to September, bring the peak of linen supply and together provide 75% of the year's total, while July stands out once more with 27%, more than three times the figure for a 'normal month'. Then, from October onwards, the figures fall sharply once more.

In order to see whether this pattern of the relative importance of the various months and the scale of the seasonal fluctuations represents a constant picture over the $8\frac{1}{2}$ decades, or whether there are substantial changes hidden behind the average figures calculated for this long period, the period under study can be divided into three periods of 28 or 29 years respectively (see table 1). The basic result is a clear indication that the extent of seasonal fluctuations rose rather than fell over the whole period. The relative importance of the different months remained basically unchanged. It was overwhelmingly in the summer months that the linen fabric was brought to the staple, and July was always by far the most important month. Within the six summer months, however, there were some shifts: the earlier months (April and May) decreased and the later months (August and September) increased in importance.

Until now the observations have represented the passing of several decades with a static picture of an 'average' year. The auto-correlograms (figures 2.1–2.3) take account of the dynamic character of time series, showing the coefficients of correlation between the original series and the series lagging by 1, 2, 3 ... 49 months.[9] The regular swing between the high positive and the low negative values of r shows the commanding importance of the yearly cycle. After 12, 24, 36, 48 months a high number of pieces follows a high number of pieces, and a low number a low number, with a probability that borders on certainty (the values of r are between $+0.89$ and $+0.95$). In contrast, after 6, 18, 30, 42 months the probability is that a low number follows a high one and a high number a low one. It is worth mentioning that this correlation is clear not only after 12 or 24 months, but also after 36 and 48 months with essentially unchanged intensity, although no attempt has been made to smooth out the effects of longer-term movements (business cycle and trend). These facts indicate that in the short run the seasonal

9   Concerning auto-correlation see Yamane, *Statistik*, II, 806ff. These statistics are used by Reinhard Spree and Michael Tybus, *Wachstumstrends und Konjunkturzyklen in der deutschen Wirtschaft von 1820 bis 1913* (Göttingen, 1978), pp. 142ff.

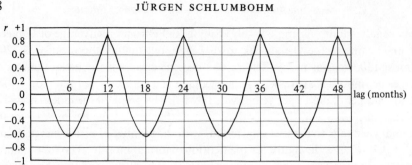

Figure 2.1 Osnabrück *Legge* 1771–98: auto-correlogram of the series 'number of pieces per month'

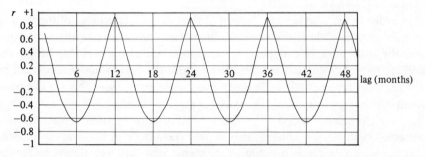

Figure 2.2 Osnabrück *Legge* 1799–1826: auto-correlogram of the series 'number of pieces per month'

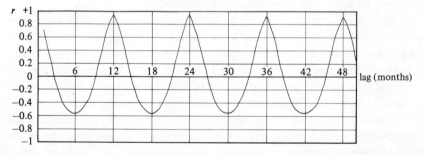

Figure 2.3 Osnabrück *Legge* 1827–55: auto-correlogram of the series 'number of pieces per month'

fluctuations are of more importance than any other influences. As in the case of the scale of the seasonal fluctuations, it can be seen that the regularity of these fluctuations does not alter when the three sectional periods are compared.

For the years 1839 to 1846 not only the number of pieces of linen for the individual months, but also the total length and the total value of all the pieces in

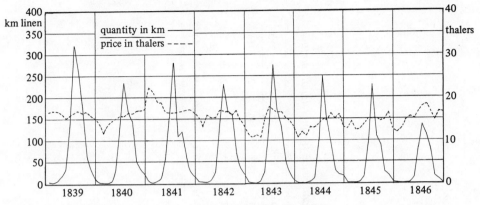

Figure 3 Osnabrück *Legge* 1839–46: quantity of linen (in 1000 metres) and price of linen
(in thalers per 100 metres) – monthly values

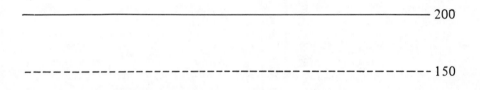

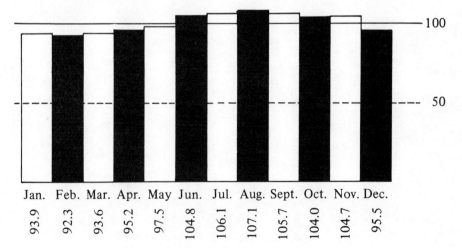

Figure 4 Osnabrück *Legge* 1839–46: index of mean linen prices for individual months
(the mean of the mean monthly prices = 100)

Table 2 Osnabrück Legge 1839–46: mean number of pieces, quantity of linen and price for individual months

	Jan.	Feb.	Mar.	April	May	June	July	Aug.	Sept.	Oct.	Nov.	Dec.
Number of pieces	53	30	36	91	295	1262	2466	1714	1406	546	321	164
Quantity (in 1000 metres)	3.50	2.04	2.39	7.55	28.04	128.60	245.24	157.37	125.92	47.64	26.19	12.35
Price per 100 metres in thalers	14.45	14.20	14.41	14.65	15.00	16.13	16.33	16.48	16.27	16.00	16.12	14.69

Source: see footnote 10.

each month can be discovered from the Osnabrück *Legge* records.[10] On this basis the price in thalers per 100 metres of linen was calculated for each month. Figure 3 shows the curves of the quantity of linen and the linen price. Table 2 contains for the 12 months of the year the mean number of pieces of linen, the mean total length and the mean price, while figure 4 shows the mean monthly prices, translated into the percentage of a 'normal month'.

The figures for these 96 months make it clear that, as far as the short run is concerned, the number of pieces is a good indicator for the quantity of linen brought to the *Legge* ($r = 0.9966$ between the amount of linen in metres and the number of pieces). What is more interesting is the seasonal fluctuation of the linen price. As shown by the monthly price curve (figure 3), there is indeed a seasonal price movement. In general the lowest prices fall in winter and the highest in summer. The price paid by merchants for linen at the Osnabrück *Legge* thus rose and fell rather in the same way as the quantity of linen brought to the *Legge*. However, the seasonal fluctuations in price are not as regular as those in the quantity of linen. While in the quantity series (figure 3) the annual minimum lies in the first three months and the maximum in July every year, in the price series the minima and maxima are far more widely scattered. This is so even if the period from autumn 1840 to autumn 1841 is excluded. (In this year prices moved almost contrary to other years, and it would therefore have to be studied separately.)[11] The minima are in the months January (2), February (2), March, April and May, and the maxima in July (2), August (2), September and November. The scale of the price fluctuation from one minimum to the next maximum is by no means inconsiderable – taking an average of the eight years, the ratio of the minima to the following maxima is 1 : 1.42, which means that within less than 12 months the prices being paid had risen by 42%! If, however, the seasonal fluctuation of the linen prices in these 96 months is summarised as an 'average year' (calculating the mean price for each month over the eight years; see table 2 and figure 4), the scale of the seasonal fluctuations seems clearly smaller – the ratio of the lowest mean monthly price (February) to the highest (August) is 1 : 1.16. The auto-correlogram for the price series (figure 5.1) confirms these results. It is true that there appears to be a small swing between positive and negative correlation coefficients (highest positive values at lags of *c.* 12 or 24 months, lowest negative values at lags of *c.* 6 or 18 months), but the absolute peak of the correlation coefficients is always so small (up to $r = 0.23$), that the knowledge of the linen price for one month does not by any means guarantee the

10   StA OS, Dep. 3 bV, No. 1094–1101.
11   At the same time as the extreme maximum price, in the months from January to April 1841, an extreme minimum in the average length of each piece of linen is noticeable. Compared with the average for the year, in these months the proportion was higher of those sorts of linen which commanded a higher price per ell and whose pieces were shorter than the *Löwend* linen.

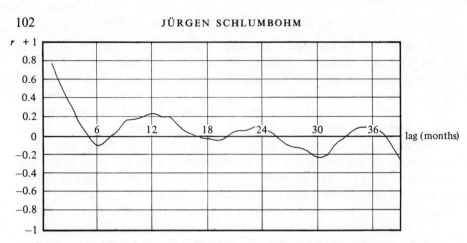

Figure 5.1 Osnabrück *Legge* 1839–46: auto-correlogram of the series 'linen price'

accuracy of a prediction of the price 12 months later. The prices are obviously not primarily determined by a seasonal cycle.

The question of the connection between the seasonal fluctuations of linen prices and quantities can be tackled statistically by calculating the correlation coefficients between the two series. The value of $r = 0.34$ confirms that this connection is positive but not very strong, which means that in the month with high prices more rather than less linen came to the *Legge*. The impression that the seasonal cycles of the price curve and the quantity curve ran synchronously rather than with a time lag can be verified if one series is moved backwards by $1, 2, 3 \ldots$ etc. points in time and then the correlation coefficients between the two series for each of these lags is calculated and presented in a cross-correlogram[12]

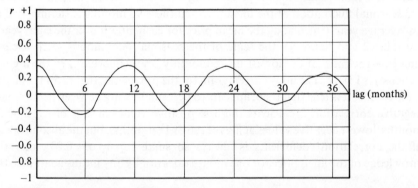
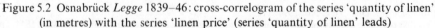

Figure 5.2 Osnabrück *Legge* 1839–46: cross-correlogram of the series 'quantity of linen' (in metres) with the series 'linen price' (series 'quantity of linen' leads)

12 Concerning this method, see Maurice Kendall, *Time-Series*, 2nd edn (New York, 1976), pp. 129ff.

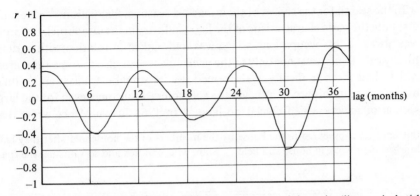

Figure 5.3 Osnabrück *Legge* 1839–46: cross-correlogram of the series 'linen price' with the series 'quantity of linen' (in metres) (series 'linen price' leads)

(figures 5.2 and 5.3). The fact that *r* has the highest positive values when the series are not moved at all (lag = 0) or when lag is *c*. 12 or 24 months, and the lowest negative values with lags of *c*. 6 or 18 months, confirms that in fact the seasonal curves of prices and quantities run alongside rather than opposite each other. A closer observation of the cross-correlograms shows that sometimes the highest and lowest values lie not at the lags 6, 12, 18 and 24, but, when the quantity series leads, at lags 11, 17 and 23, and, when the price series leads, at lags 7, 19 and 25. This could give rise to the interpretation that the price series was leading by a month – that is, that one month after the highest prices were being paid at the *Legge* the greatest quantity of linen was brought, and that one month after especially low prices were being offered very little linen came to the *Legge*. However, the margin between the correlation coefficients at lags 6, 12, 18 and 24 and those of the lags directly next to them is hardly large enough to provide firm support for such an interpretation.

All that this meant for the small linen producers was that they could count on getting generally rather higher prices in the summer months, when year after year they brought most linen to the *Legge*, than in the winter months. But the course of the seasonal price movement was by no means regular enough – as shown in particular by the auto-correlogram for the price series (fig. 5.1) – to allow them to predict the most favourable month on that basis with any certainty.[13]

13 Confirmation for the two main results, which were provided by the additional data about length and value for the period 1839 to 1846, can be obtained from a random sample of the records of the Osnabrück *Legge* for the years 1806–30. If the cases of this sample (whose main purpose was to provide estimates for the average prices and lengths of pieces of linen per year) are grouped together according to the months, and if the mean length and the mean price per 100 metres of all pieces brought to the *Legge* in the same month of the different years is translated into an index (the mean of all pieces being 100), the following results can be shown:

In the search for the causes of these marked seasonal fluctuations,[14] one must first note the basic characteristic of the linen industry in the Osnabrück region. It was always a 'by-occupation', which was undertaken in rotation with agricultural work. In contrast not only to the urban trades but also to some rural areas which had been radically transformed by proto-industrialisation,[15] linen manufacture in this area was never the sole source of income, even for the large section of society which owned no land.[16] In 1768 Justus Möser wrote that

this linen... is prepared in the house by the members of the household after they have finished their work in house and field... Man, wife, children and servants use the spare

	Jan–April	May	June	July	Aug.	Sept.	Oct.	Nov.	Dec.
Length of piece	98.7	108.6	108.0	104.7	98.2	95.7	90.2	90.5	85.4
Price per 100 metres	102.7	102.1	104.1	100.6	99.0	98.1	99.0	98.0	94.8
No. of pieces in sample	14	116	373	779	560	470	217	164	57

These results show that a) in the period 1806–30 the average length of the pieces of linen differs between the various months. Yet these differences are neither so large nor distributed in such a way that it might be necessary to question the usefulness of the monthly number of pieces of linen as an indicator of the linen quantities. b) there are also in this period obvious differences between the mean monthly prices, yet again the scale of these fluctuations is not very large (the ratio of the mean price in December to the mean price in June is 1 : 1.10).

The variations in the mean length of a piece of linen are distributed similarly both in the period 1806–30 and in the later period, as is shown by an index of the mean of the mean length per month for 1839–46 (the mean of the mean length of pieces for all 96 months being 100):

Jan.	Feb.	Mar.	April	May	June	July	Aug.	Sept.	Oct.	Nov.	Dec.
91.0	89.6	84.9	109.7	111.7	116.6	113.0	103.9	101.5	99.7	92.8	86.0

If the mean monthly prices for 1806–30 are compared more closely with those for 1839–46 (see figure 4), in the earlier period the highest prices seem to have been reached earlier in the year: while from 1839–46 the peak in price seems to fall together exactly with the peak in the amount of linen brought to the *Legge*, from 1806–30 the peak in the seasonal price movement lies before the peak in the quantity (compare table 1).

14 In the German version of this essay it is shown on pp. 277–80 that a similar pattern of seasonal fluctuation was in operation in the other *Leggen* of the principality of Osnabrück in the late eighteenth century.

15 See Kriedte, Medick and Schlumbohm, *Industrialization Before Industrialization*, pp. 27, 101, 105.

16 More precise statements are not possible without a detailed investigation of the socio-economic circumstances of those employed in the linen trade. These questions are dealt with in J. Schlumbohm, 'Agrarische Besitzklassen und gewerbliche Produktionsverhältnisse: Grossbauern, Kleinbesitzer und Landlose als Leinenproduzenten im Umland von Osnabrück und Bielefeld während des frühen 19. Jahrhunderts', in *Mentalitäten und Lebensverhältnisse: Festschrift für Rudolf Vierhaus* (Göttingen, 1982), pp. 315–34.

time they have from their other work for spinning. The chair by the spinning-wheel is at the same time a resting-place from other work ... Everybody has his loom in the house ... the time which is spent on it would otherwise have been wasted or put to bad use.[17]

'Men and women return to their spinning from field work, to their weaving from the threshing-floor': this was how Friedrich Wilhelm von Reden, almost 70 years later, described the main feature of this, 'the most important industry of the kingdom of Hanover'.[18] The *Legge* inspector for the district of Osnabrück in 1840 underlined the specific character of the linen industry in his area: 'the production of the same is regarded by our countryman only as secondary work ... and fills up his idle hours as determined by season and weather'.[19]

The seasonal distribution of the maximum and minimum linen sales completely contradicts what we would expect from the usual seasonal distribution of work in agriculture and in the linen trade. Industrial work was done at times when there was little agricultural work: yet in the winter months the inhabitants brought the least linen to the *Legge*, and in the summer months the most. Seasonal fluctuations in the quantity of linen might be the result not of the rotation of the producers from agricultural work to linen production, but of price difference between seasons. For these, as is shown by the evidence from the Osnabrück town *Legge* between 1839 and 1846, ran essentially synchronously with the fluctuation in the quantity of linen coming to the *Legge*. In fact there is evidence that not all linen was brought to the *Legge* as soon as it was woven, but that sometimes people waited until the low prices had given way to higher ones.[20] Only a detailed examination of the social and economic position of the linen producers will be able to show how many of them were in a strong enough economic position to delay the sale of their fabric for some time on a regular basis, and only micro-analysis can determine on what scale the inhabitants really took several pieces to the *Legge* at once when the prices seemed good rather than piece by piece as it was finished. Only if both these assumptions proved to be true for the vast majority of linen producers could the enormous scale of the seasonal

17 Justus Möser, 'Osnabrückische Geschichte: allgemeine Einleitung (1768)', in the same author's *Sämtliche Werke. Historisch-kritische Ausgabe*, vol. 12/1, ed. Paul Göttsching (Oldenburg/Hamburg, 1964), p. 147.
18 von Reden, *Gewerbe des Königreichs Hannover*, col. 141. In the seasonal ordering of the various tasks the sentence quoted is admittedly somewhat misleading, at least in the case of Osnabrück (see below).
19 Report for the year 1839 of 14 January 1840: StA OS, Rep. 335, No. 8018.
20 Runge, *Justus Mösers Gewerbetheorie*, p. 76. The *maire* of Osnabrück *extra muros* to the sub-prefect of the *arrondissement* of Osnabrück in the Oberems-Departement, 2 May 1812 (StA OS, Rep. 240, No. 844, fols. 35–39, esp. fol. 37v): 'For the first quarter of 1812 I am not at all in a position to present an estimate ... not a single piece of *Löwend* linen has yet been finished. The linen which is being brought to the *Legge* is still from last year when the owners did not wish to sell it because of the poor prices.' In this particular instance it can be shown that this was not a case of a mass appearance setting the seasonal cycle, for in 1812 barely 1% of all the year's pieces came in between January and April.

fluctuation in the quantity of linen be explained in this way. There are already other reasons contradicting this explanation which must be mentioned. If 'speculative hoarding' of the linen produced had been the norm for the linen producers, we would expect to find greater flexibility in the exploitation of the year's highest prices, which fell at different months from year to year. By flexibly reacting to every year's individual price curve weavers stood to gain considerably more than by merely exploiting their experience that as a rule prices were better in the summer than in the winter. But if this was too risky for the linen producer, because it was difficult to predict when the highest price would come, and he merely acted on the experience he had gleaned over the years, it makes it difficult to explain why on average between 1806 and 1830 the maximum and minimum quantities of linen clearly came in at least a month after the highest and lowest prices.[21] Even taking these years on average, the country people selling their linen would regularly have missed their target.[22]

To find the basic cause of the seasonal fluctuation in the quantity of linen offered for sale at the *Legge*, we must look to the social structure of the production process. At the time of the statistical survey in the Oberems *département* mentioned above, one of the *maires* of the Osnabrück region tried to discover the specific characteristics of the regional linen trade, whose most important article was *Löwend* linen, a relatively coarse flax or hemp fabric, bleached in the yarn:

The manufacture of *Löwend* linen is quite different from any other industry. This work can in no way be divided into half years and even less into quarters. It starts in the autumn straight after the harvest and finishes at the end of July. In the first months after the harvest the home-grown flax or hemp is steeped, crushed, broken, scutched and brushed.[23] Then the spinning starts: husband, wife, children, servants and maids all spin a certain amount each day. This takes until the middle of the month of April, when the mistress of the house bleaches the spun yarn with the help of some of the servants. If this is finished by the middle of May, then the mistress generally starts weaving while the other members of the household do the necessary work in the fields. The question of how many

21 See above, note 13.
22 Since the seasonal movement of prices at the *Legge* obviously cannot be explained by the simple mechanism of supply (by the linen producers) and demand (from the merchants of the region), but is rather opposed to what we should expect from such a mechanism, nothing definite can be said about the causes of this seasonal fluctuation in price without a thorough investigation both of the relationship between producers and merchants and of the whole inter-regional and international web of trade and traffic connections through which the linen was supplied to the customers, most of whom were overseas. An assessment according to the results of the sample of the Osnabrück *Legge* from 1806 to 1830 shows that the distribution of the different grades of linen over the various months differs, but that this distribution is only partly related to the differences in the mean prices, so that differences in quality can hardly have been the only deciding factor for the differing mean prices of the individual months.
23 A thorough description of the individual stages of production can be found in Eduard Schoneweg, *Das Leinengewerbe der Grafschaft Ravensberg* (Bielefeld, 1923).

workers spin, how many weave and how many bleach does not apply here. The mistress, who is the focal point of the work, spins, weaves and bleaches, each at the correct time, as do the daughter, son, father, servant. There are no particular spinners, weavers or bleachers.[24]

According to contemporary reports, all the various stages of production, from the planting of the flax (or hemp) to the weaving, were generally carried out within one household. To obtain raw materials linen producers needed land of their own *or* had to rent land.[25] It was in this way that the connection between agricultural and industrial work was in fact a basic cause of the seasonal fluctuation in the quantity of linen offered for sale at the *Legge*. As late as 1847 the *Legge* inspector for the district of Osnabrück wrote that

all people living in the countryside, from the largest landowner down to the smallest *Heuermann* try to produce enough [flax] for their own needs themselves... In this province flax and hemp are hardly ever planted in order to sell them. [It has] never become the custom here that the larger landowners should plant more flax than they need themselves and bring it cleaned to market...

With few exceptions, the whole yield of the product [flax and hemp] is worked into yarn... The yarn is exported (but practically only in the district of Grönenberg), used for home consumption, and quite the largest part... turned into *Löwend* linen. [In this] the spinner is quite often also the weaver or lives in the latter's house.[26]

This, incidentally, according to the *Legge* inspector writing the report, was an important reason for the relatively good quality of the yarn spun in the Osnabrück region, since the disadvantages of bad spinning soon became apparent in weaving.[27] 'The same people generally do the spinning, weaving and

---

24 The *maire* of Osnabrück *extra muros* to the sub-prefect of the Osnabrück *arrondissement* in the Oberems-Departement, 2 May 1812: StA OS, Rep. 240, No. 844, fols. 35–9, quotation from fols. 36v–37r. The reason for these comments was particularly that the printed form, which the *maires* were to fill in, had separate columns for the 'number of workers spinning', for those 'weaving' and for those 'bleaching and carrying out other finishing processes', as well as for the 'total number' of workers.
25 Concerning various ways in which those who did not own land took part in flax planting in another part of Lower Saxony, see Walter Achilles, 'Die Bedeutung des Flachsanbaus im südlichen Niedersachsen für Bauern und Angehörige der unterbäuerlichen Schicht im 18. und 19. Jahrhundert', in *Agrarisches Nebengewerbe und Formen der Reagrisierung im Spätmittelalter und 19./20. Jahrhundert: Bericht über die 5. Arbeitstagung der Gesellschaft fur Sozial- und Wirtschaftsgeschichte*, ed. Hermann Kellenbenz, Forschungen zur Sozial- und Wirtschaftsgeschichte, vol. 21 (Stuttgart, 1975), pp. 109–24, esp. 117ff.
26 Report for the year 1846 of 7 January 1847: StA OS, Rep. 335, No. 8018.
27 Report for the year 1838 of 9 January 1839: StA OS, *ibid*. It is indicated for the 1840s that in the production of *Schiertuch*, sailcloth and *greise Leinen* (grey linen) the circumstances differed, in that the households doing the weaving would buy a proportion of their yarn, and for the production of sailcloth even some hemp was imported from abroad; but this quantity of yarn was not of great importance: reports from the *Legge* inspector to the *Landdrostei* Osnabrück for the years 1845, 1846, 1847 (StA OS, *ibid*.)

bleaching as everything happens in rotation', it was said in 1812.[28] The seasonal cycle of these stages of production, including the cultivation and the preparatory treatment of the flax or hemp, was the basic reason for the enormous seasonal fluctuations in the quantity of linen coming to the *Legge*. In the linen industry of this area there was no marked specialisation between households, and indeed even the division of labour according to age and sex within the households was relatively limited: 'This manufacturing of linen is not done in factories by particular people . . . but both sexes, almost every class, young and old take part in it, occupy themselves with it the whole year between their other work . . . produce the raw material themselves . . . process and finish it.'[29] Weaving was, however, usually female work and was, in the Osnabrück region, done either by the mistress of the household or by the maid.[30] Spinning on the other hand occupied 'husband, wife, children and servants' in the 'spare time from their other work', a fact which led Möser to remark: 'Due to folk customs of our region, it is not dishonorable for men to work at the spinning-wheel, although the law-giver is unable to enforce this in other regions.'[31]

Spinning was the stage of production that took by far the most time. Roughly speaking, it probably occupied two-thirds of the total time needed for the production of a piece of linen, while the rest of the time would have been divided almost equally between flax planting and treatment on the one hand, and weaving on the other.[32] The stage of the linen production that took up the most time was therefore done in winter, and it could even be said, that 'in the summer months themselves very little happens [i.e. in the linen production]'.[33] Bearing this in mind, the position of the peak quantity of linen at the *Legge* in the months between June and September no longer seems irreconcilable with the fact emphasised by contemporaries that the linen producers also worked on the land as peasants or *Heuerlinge*, and that they used the times when there was less work in agriculture to produce their linen.

Contemporaries did not regard job specialisation or division of labour as the dominant characteristic of the regional linen trade. Instead, they pointed out that

28 The *maire* of Belm in his comments on table 1 of the survey of 1812: StA OS, Rep. 240, No. 844, fol. 241r.
29 Friedrich Meese, 'Von den westfälischen Löwendlinnen und deren Leggen', in *Beiträge zur Geographie, Geschichte und Staatenkunde*, ed. Johann Ernst Fabri, vol. 1, no. 1 (1794), pp. 120–40, esp. p. 122.
30 Möser, 'Osnabrückische Geschichte', p. 147.
31 *Ibid.*, pp. 147f.; compare von Reden, *Gewerbe des Königreichs Hannover*, cols. 141, 152, 164. For general remarks on the division of labour between the sexes in the period of proto-industrialisation, see Medick, in Kriedte, Medick and Schlumbohm, *Industrialization Before Industrialization*, pp. 61ff.
32 Approximate estimate based on Achilles, 'Bedeutung des Flachsanbaus; pp. 112ff., in conjunction with Friedrich Wilhelm von Reden, *Der Leinwant- und Garnhandel Norddeutschlands* (Hanover, 1838), table belonging to p. 53.
33 The *maire* of Belm, reference as in note 28.

the same workers took part in all the stages of linen production with the changing of the seasons, and also did their share of the work in the fields and with the livestock. This peculiar character, which at the same time was the basic cause of seasonal fluctuations in the *Legge* statistics, had been retained by the linen trade. Its growth, however, which had gone far beyond regional demand, was due to a pronounced inter-regional and even international division of labour so that the Osnabrück linen industry is a clear example of proto-industrialisation. Through trade it was closely bound to the 'world system' of that time, in particular to the asymmetric division of labour in the Atlantic triangle between Europe, Africa and America, not least because the relatively coarse flax or hemp fabric of the Osnabrück region was used in the colonies, to clothe the slaves for example.[34] The assumption made by the French authorities of the Oberems *département*, which informed their statistical survey of 1812, was that only full-time linen weavers produced for sale, while seasonal and part-time weavers only produced for household needs.[35] As demonstrated, this assumption was not true for the Osnabrück region. It was the secondary nature of the Osnabrück linen trade which observers always gave as the most important reason for the goods being relatively cheap and therefore competitive on the international market; this fact was therefore considered as an essential cause of the rise and the continuing importance of this export trade.[36] Of course, the more this regional industry ran into crises and declined in the course of the nineteenth century, the more the

34 Stephanie Reekers, 'Beiträge zur statistischen Darstellung der gewerblichen Wirtschaft Westfalens um 1800: Teil 3', in *Westfälische Forschungen*, 19 (1966), 27–75, esp. 41–8; Edith Schmitz, *Leinengewerbe und Leinenhandel in Nordwestdeutschland (1650–1850)*, Schriften zur Rheinisch-Westfälischen Wirtschaftsgeschichte, Vol. 15 (Cologne, 1967), pp. 85ff.; Hermann Schröter, 'Handel, Gewerbe und Industrie im Landdrosteibezirk Osnabrück 1815–1866', in *OsnabMitt*, 68 (1959), 309–58, esp. 325ff.; von Reden, *Leinwand- und Garnhandel*, pp. 5ff., 18ff. For the fundamentals see Kriedte, in Kriedte, Medick, Schlumbohm, *Industrialization Before Industrialization*, pp. 35ff. It must be taken into consideration that from the 1840s onwards the difficulties which the German linen industry experienced in disposing of its goods in overseas markets increased sharply, so that the industry was forced to try and reorientate itself towards continental and German markets: Horst Blumberg, 'Ein Beitrag zur Geschichte der deutschen Leinenindustrie von 1834 bis 1870', in Hans Mottek *et al., Studien zur Geschichte der industriellen Revolution in Deutschland*, Veröffentlichungen des Instituts fur Wirtschaftsgeschichte an der Hochschule für Ökonomie Berlin-Karlshorst, Vol. 1 (Berlin-GDR, 1960), pp. 65–143, esp. pp. 81ff, 93ff.

35 See the writ of the Prefect of the Oberems-Department referred to in note 2, especially p. 143, and tables 1 and 2 in StA OS, Rep. 240, No. 844. It is worth stressing that in spite of all the problems – caused by such misleading questions – important findings can be obtained from the results of this thorough survey, even beyond those clarifications which have been quoted more than once. See for example the calculation in respect of the 'concentration of weaving looms' (number of weaving looms per 1000 inhabitants): Reekers, 'Beiträge: Teil 3', pp. 42ff.

36 Thus Möser, 'Osnabrückische Geschichte', pp. 147f.; von Reden, *Gewerbe des Königreichs Hannover*, col. 141. Concerning some general preconditions for the validity of this argument, see Schlumbohm, in Kriedte, Medick, Schlumbohm, *Industrialization Before Industrialization*, p. 105 with note 64.

opinions on this method of production changed. In 1845 Wilhelm Roscher wrote of 'the present crisis of production in the Hanoverian linen trade' that 'almost all the faults of our linen trade' could be

expressed in these terms...: on the one hand too little concentration, on the other hand too little division of labour. Industries like this, which work for a market – and a very distant market at that – and yet are only run on a small scale, without any particular connection between the producers, and mostly just as a subsidiary occupation, are becoming increasingly difficult to maintain on the higher levels of the economy.[37]

In the age of industrial capitalism, faced with competition from the partially

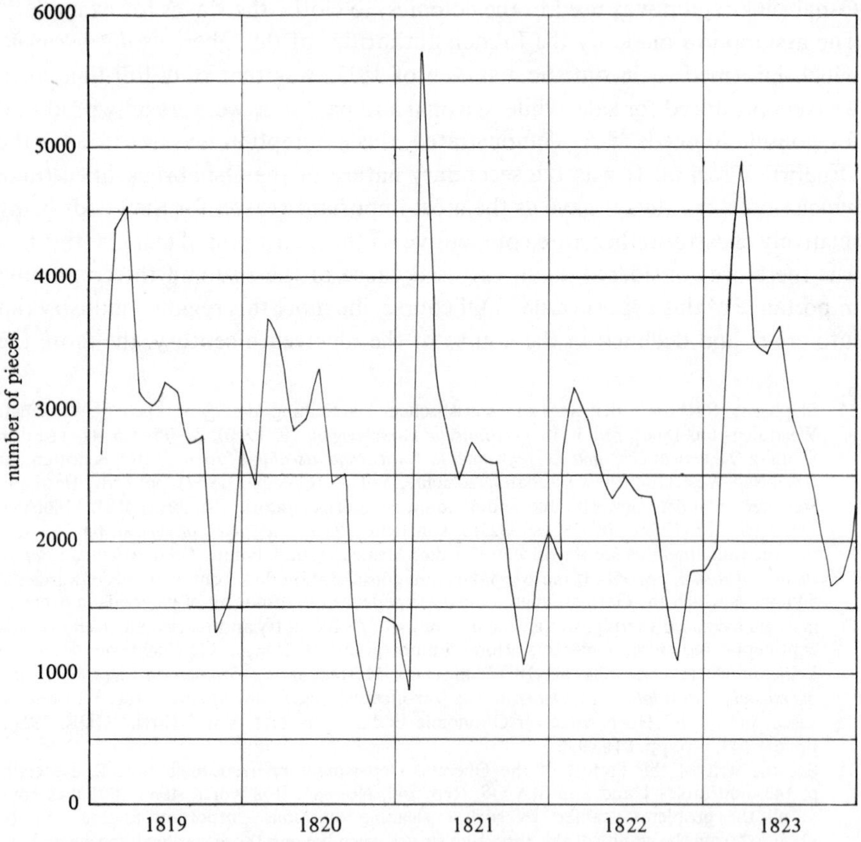

Figure 6.1 Bielefeld *Legge* 1819–23: number of pieces – monthly values

---

37 Wilhelm Roscher, 'Uber die gegenwärtige Produktionskrise des hannoverschen Leinenge-werbes, mit besonderer Rücksicht auf den Absatz in Amerika', in *Göttinger Studien* (Göttingen, 1845), pp. 384–440, quotation p. 410.

mechanised cotton industry – and from the British linen industry – a method of production which was based, not on the specialisation of component workers, but on the seasonal rotation of the worker between various occupations, was seen to be old-fashioned, ineffective and therefore out-of-date.

Our understanding of the seasonal fluctuations of the Osnabrück linen industry may be further clarified by comparison with other regions and other branches of industry. The linen trade in the area surrounding Bielefeld, a geographically adjacent and in many ways a related example, provides one such comparison. Although in the nineteenth century the trip to the *Legge* was less extensively and uniformly enforced in the Prussian county of Ravensberg[38] in comparison to the Osnabrück region, the statistics from the Bielefeld *Legge* should provide an adequate basis for the examination of the *seasonal* fluctuation in production in its area.

The number of pieces of linen brought to the Bielefeld *Legge* can be determined month-for-month for the five years from 1819 to 1823.[39] On the curve of these values (figure 6.1) the annual maxima fall in February (3) or March (2) and the yearly minima in October (4) or January (1), but between these points the curve does not run with the same clear regularity as that for the Osnabrück *Legge* (see figure 3), and the peaks are not equally sharp in all the years. The autocorrelogram for this series (see figure 6.3) does show that there is a distinct 12-month cycle. But the absolute values of these correlation coefficients (-0.42, $+0.64$, -0.40) are not as high as those of the Osnabrück series (see figure 2). The calculation of the mean number of pieces for the individual months (table 3), and the graph of the index to it (figure 6.2), show that the scale of the fluctuation between the average 'strongest' month, in which 160% of the amount of the fictitious 'normal month' came to the Bielefeld *Legge*, and the 'weakest' month, with 46%, is very considerable. However, in comparison with the Osnabrück *Legge* (figure 1), the pyramid representing the distribution of the amount of linen over the individual months is clearly blunter for the Bielefeld *Legge*. Neither do the positions of the maxima and minima correspond with the Osnabrück findings. In Bielefeld the greatest amount of linen was brought to the *Legge* in February and March, when there was practically no traffic at the *Legge* in Osnabrück. The deliveries were then above average until July, and the quieter period started in September and lasted until January. The monthly values which exist for five more years between the mid eighteenth and mid nineteenth centuries

38 Heinz Potthoff, 'Die Leinenleggen in der Grafschaft Ravensberg', in *Jahresbericht des Historischen Vereins für die Grafschaft Ravensberg* (hereafter: *JberHistVRavensberg*), 15 (1901), 1–140, esp. 113ff.
39 Reports of the *Regierung* in Minden: Staatsarchiv Münster (hereafter abbreviated to StA MS), Oberpräsidium, No. 351, Vols. 1–2.

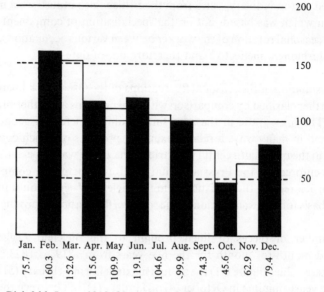

Figure 6.2 Bielefeld *Legge* 1819–23: index of the mean number of pieces per month
(mean annual figure divided by 12 = 100)

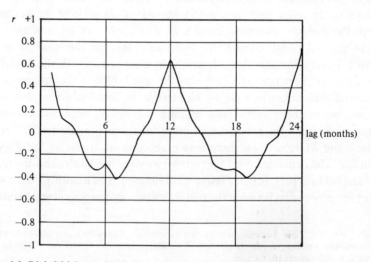

Figure 6.3 Bielefeld *Legge* 1819–23: auto-correlogram of the series 'number of pieces per
month'

Table 3.1: *Bielefeld Legge 1748–1857: number of pieces or mean number of pieces for individual months*

	Jan.	Feb.	Mar.	April	May	June	July	Aug.	Sept.	Oct.	Nov.	Dec.
1748	4911	6167	6965	6402	5053	5843	6111	5842	4426	2442	3378	4384
1770	2333	3851	4887	2878	2755	3347	3654	4317	2636	1344	1596	1726
1794	3178.5	4082	5339.5	6218.5	5502.5	4287.5	4550.5	3912.5	4714.5	2964	1622	2326
1819–23	1956	4143	3943	2986	2841	3078	2704	2581	1919	1178	1626	2053
1840	4617	5877	5073	4426	4070	4307	4344	3389	3283	2641	2491	3778
1857	5327	6262	5556	3808	4543	3771	4144	3325	2406	2231	2516	3050

Table 3.2: *Bielefeld Legge: index of the number of pieces or mean number of pieces for individual months (mean annual figure divided by 12 = 100)*

	Jan.	Feb.	Mar.	April	May	June	July	Aug.	Sept.	Oct.	Nov.	Dec.
1748	95.2	119.5	135.0	124.1	98.0	113.2	118.4	113.2	85.8	47.3	65.5	85.0
1770	79.3	130.8	166.0	97.8	93.6	113.7	124.1	146.7	89.5	45.7	54.2	58.6
1794	78.3	100.6	131.6	153.2	135.6	105.7	112.1	96.4	116.2	73.0	40.0	57.3
1819–23	75.7	160.3	152.6	115.6	109.9	119.1	104.6	99.9	74.3	45.6	62.9	79.4
1840	114.7	146.0	126.0	110.0	101.0	107.0	107.9	84.2	81.6	65.6	61.9	93.9
1857	136.2	160.1	142.0	97.4	116.1	96.4	105.9	85.0	61.5	57.0	64.3	78.0

Sources: see footnotes 39, 40.

(table 3)[40] possibly point to some modification of this seasonal pattern,[41] but confirm the most important finding for the years 1819 to 1823, that here too there is a seasonal rhythm, but one which was by no means as striking as that in Osnabrück.

The causes of these seasonal fluctuations lie, as in Osnabrück, in the socio-economic structure of production. In the county of Ravensberg, just as in Osnabrück, the production of the raw materials (flax planting), spinning and weaving all took place in the same area. But the so-called 'Bielefeld linen', the most important sort at the Bielefeld *Legge*, was very much finer and of higher value than most of the Osnabrück linen.[42] In the area covered by the Bielefeld *Legge* a social division of labour had come to be widely established at the latest by the end of the eighteenth century, a situation which was uncommon in the Osnabrück area even in the mid nineteenth century:

Spinner, weaver, merchant, bleacher[43] and finisher, each runs his own business independently... The flax producer plants the flax on his own account, steeps it in the water, bleaches it on the grass, crushes and breaks it... The spinner buys small quantities of flax in this state from the producer, finishes preparing it and spins it... the spinner sells his yarn in small quantities, generally the result of a week's work, to the weavers or the yarn dealer... The linen-weavers also run their businesses independently with one, two or more looms... In general the weavers buy the yarn from the spinner himself or at the yarn market, weave it, and take the finished fabric, as it comes off the loom, to the town (Bielefeld), where a great number of merchants are prepared to buy the linen as they need it.[44]

In the Ravensberg area there was a division of labour in the various stages of

40 Sources: for 1770, reports of the *Kriegs- und Domänenkammer*, Minden, StA MS, KDK Minden II, 3, Vols. 1–3; for the remaining years, Potthoff, 'Leinenleggen', pp. 136f.
41 Particularly in the instances from the eighteenth century, there seems to be a secondary peak, coming directly before or after the harvest, apart from the main peak at the transition from winter to spring. An interpretation of this would, however, only be worthwhile after an expansion of the data base for the seasonal fluctuations, and only if it were based on a closer examination of the changes in the socio-economic structure of the linen producers.
42 Potthoff, 'Leinenleggen', pp. 43ff., 69ff.; Potthoff, 'Das Ravensberger Leinengewerbe im 17. und 18. Jahrhundert', in *JberHistVRavensberg*, 35 (1921), 27–83, esp. 46ff.; Stephanie Reekers, 'Beiträge zur statistischen Darstellung der gewerblichen Wirtschaft Westfalens um 1800: Teil 2', in *Westfälische Forschungen*, 18 (1965), 75–130, especially 96ff.
43 In contrast to *Löwend* linen, Bielefeld linen was not bleached as yarn, but when woven.
44 *Jahresbericht der Handelskammer Bielefeld für 1849 und 1850* (Bielefeld, 1851) (hereafter: *Handelskammer Bielefeld*), pp. 5ff., quotation p. 5; compare Potthoff, 'Leinengewerbe', esp. pp. 28f., 34, 37f., 47, 66f.; Hans Schmidt, *Vom Leinen zur Seide: die Geschichte der Firma C. A. Delius & Söhne und ihrer Vorgängerinnen und das Wirken ihrer Inhaber für die Entwicklung Bielefelds 1722–1925* (Lemgo, 1926), pp. 22ff.; Emilie Schönfeld, 'Herford als Garn- und Leinenmarkt in zwei Jahrhunderten 1670–1870', in *JberHistVRavensberg*, 43 (1929), 1–172, esp. 27–30, 33–60; Josef Mooser, 'Bäuerliche Gesellschaft im Zeitalter der Revolution 1789–1848: zur Sozialgeschichte des politischen Verhaltens ländlicher Unterschichten im östlichen Westfalen, unpublished doctoral thesis (Bielefeld, 1978), pp. 87ff.

production – flax planting, spinning and weaving – not only between the different households but also between the different areas.[45]

This socio-economic structure of production had its effect on the type and scale of the seasonal fluctuation in the Bielefeld linen trade. The planting of the flax naturally followed the seasonal cycle determined by the weather.[46] There was also a distinct seasonal rhythm for the spinning. 'Spinning is always spare-time work and only occurs in the winter or when there is time left over for it from the agricultural work and there is no possibility of other employment.'[47] It is true that the vast majority of the spinners had no land of their own, but as *Heuerlinge* rented a house and a piece of land from a peasant. They usually did not pay all the rent in cash, but were bound to work on the peasant's land.[48] Even though the amount of labour required from the *Heuerlinge* will have varied depending on the size of the farm, it is clear that in the slack season of agriculture considerably more yarn was produced than otherwise.[49] Although more weavers than spinners had some land of their own, the majority of the weavers in the fine linen district surrounding Bielefeld were also *Heuerlinge*, at least from the early nineteenth century onwards.[50] However, it is said of them, in contrast to the spinners, that 'Among the weavers ... the majority practise the production of

45 'Darstellung der Leinwand-Manufaktur im Distrikte Bielefeld', in *Westfalen unter Hieronymus Napoleon*, ed. Georg Hassel, Karl Murhard, Vol. 1, No. 1, Pt 2 (February, 1812), pp. 14–36, esp. pp. 17, 24; Johann Nepomuk von Schwerz, *Beschreibung der Landwirtschaft in Westfalen und Rheinpreussen*, 2 vols. (Stuttgart, 1836), I, 105, 109; compare Reekers, 'Beiträge: Teil 2', pp. 92ff., 101ff.; Gustav Engel, *Ravensberger Spinnerei AG Bielefeld: Festschrift zum 100jährigen Bestehen* (Bielefeld, 1954), p. 15.

46 Described by von Schwerz, *Beschreibung der Landwirtschaft*, I, 104ff.

47 *Handelskammer Bielefeld*, p. 4.

48 *Ibid.*, also Potthoff, 'Leinengewerbe', pp. 35ff.; Schönfeld, 'Herford', pp. 27ff.

49 Potthoff, 'Leinengewerbe', p. 43, publishes monthly figures for the value (not the quantity) of yarn exported from the Grafschaft Ravensberg into other territories for the years 1770 and 1783 (therefore without taking into account the yarn used for linen weaving within the region). If these values are translated into an index (yearly value divided by 12 = 100), the following result is reached:

	Jan.	Feb.	Mar.	April	May	June	July	Aug.	Sept.	Oct.	Nov.	Dec.
1770	171.1	132.0	166.3	117.4	147.7	70.4	76.3	52.8	41.1	50.9	59.7	114.4
1783	116.7	172.9	177.3	141.0	125.1	88.0	73.0	61.0	44.7	60.6	59.2	80.5

Since contemporaries stressed that spinning was 'fill-in work' in the slack farming season, an even stronger degree of seasonal fluctuation might be expected. It is impossible to decide without a closer examination whether the conditions of traffic and commerce smoothed out an even stronger fluctuation in production, or whether in a considerable number of households several members of the family spent most of the year spinning. This might be true of those *Heuerlinge* who had very little rented land and who were employed by small peasants. Indications of the second alternative are to be found in Gustav Engel, *Bielefelder Webereien AG Bielefeld: Festschrift zur Hundertjahrfeier* (Bielefeld, 1965), pp. 32f., and Mooser, 'Bäuerliche Gesellschaft', pp. 87f.

50 Mooser, 'Bäuerliche Gesellschaft', pp. 88f; compare *Handelskammer Bielefeld*, p. 4.

linen as their trade, and even though less weaving is done at the time of sowing and at harvest-time, a great number of the looms are kept running year in year out.'[51] It can be estimated that in 1798 almost half the weavers in the Bielefeld area wove as their main occupation.[52]

The fact that a lower than average number of pieces of linen was brought to sale between September and January can probably be explained by the fact that even in the district of Bielefeld the weavers did not have equal stocks of yarn at their disposal throughout the year. The seasonal rhythm of raw material production and spinning – which also took place within the county of Ravensberg – had its effect on the weavers. It seems that some of the weaving households also spun some of their own yarn requirement.[53] The widespread, though not complete, distribution of flax planting and preparation, spinning and weaving in different households clearly made it possible for these work processes to run far more concurrently than in the Osnabrück region, where in general all the stages of production were accomplished one after another within the same household. This could be the reason why the greatest amount of linen came to the Bielefeld *Legge* as early as February and March, while in Osnabrück the greatest amount did not come until July. But above all this social division of labour meant that at no time in the year were the weaving looms still, and therefore that the traffic at the *Legge* never ceased.[54]

The seasonal fluctuations (and their underlying socio-economic structures) of the linen industries in the Bielefeld and the Osnabrück regions show both similarities and differences. Industries which had quite different structures offer a stronger contrast. A good example is the woollen industry in the Niederlausitz (part of Prussia since 1815, in the eighteenth century part of the electorate of Saxony), which held an important position in the German woollen industry in the nineteenth century.[55] For this industry there are some series of monthly figures

51 *Handelskammer Bielefeld*, p. 4.
52 Reekers, 'Beiträge: Teil 2'; p. 98; compare p. 95.
53 Potthoff, 'Leinengewerbe, p. 37; Schmidt, *Vom Leinen zur Seide*, p. 24.
54 Information on the degree to which weaving was a seasonal occupation is, of course, a very important addition to the statistics which are based on the number of looms; otherwise it would be easy to draw false conclusions about the relative importance of the textile industry for various regions. E.g., in the interpretation of the statistics and maps concerning the concentration of looms in Reekers, 'Beiträge: Teil 2', pp. 95ff.; *idem*, 'Beiträge: Teil 3', pp. 42ff.; compare *idem*, 'Beiträge: Teil 1', in *Westfälische Forschungen*, 17 (1964), p. 99, her indications as to the nature of weaving as a main or secondary occupation ('Beiträge: Teil 2', p. 93; 'Beiträge: Teil 3', pp. 44f.) must be taken into account.
55 Georg Quandt, *Die Niederlausitzer Schafwollindustrie in ihrer Entwicklung zum Grossbetrieb und zur modernen Technik*, Staats- und sozialwissenschaftliche Forschungen, Vol. 13, No. 3 (Leipzig, 1895); Horst Blumberg, *Die deutsche Textilindustrie in der industriellen Revolution*, Veröffentlichungen des Instituts fur Wirtschaftsgeschichte an der Hochschule fur ökonomie Berlin-Karlshorst, Vol. 3 (Berlin-GDR, 1965), pp. 70f., 200; Hans-Jürgen Teuteberg, 'Das deutsche und britische Wollgewerbe um die Mitte des 19. Jahrhunderts', in *Vom Kleingewerbe zur Grossindustrie*, ed. Harald Winkel, Schriften des Vereins fur Socialpolitik N. F., Vol. 83 (Berlin, 1975), pp. 9–103, 37ff.

Table 4.1: *Production of woollen cloth in several towns of the Niederlausitz: mean number of pieces for individual months*

	Jan.	Feb.	Mar.	April	May	June	July	Aug.	Sept.	Oct.	Nov.	Dec.
Sommerfeld 1816–25	236	276	241	273	232	239	250	237	249	244	246	238
Sommerfeld 1830–47	1210	1111	1292	1095	969	1031	1290	1445	1252	1366	1231	1165
Forst 1819–29	259	330	337	358	309	315	328	364	393	307	355	357
Forst 1837–46	1194	1169	1495	1112	1015	1454	1285	1476	1414	1565	1268	1267
Sorau 1835–44	499	520	537	520	475	492	519	553	547	581	595	563

Table 4.2: *Production of woollen cloth in several towns of the Niederlausitz: index of the mean number of pieces per month (mean annual figure divided by 12 = 100)*

	Jan.	Feb.	Mar.	April	May	June	July	Aug.	Sept.	Oct.	Nov.	Dec.
Sommerfeld 1816–25	95.6	112.0	97.8	110.6	93.9	96.9	101.1	96.2	101.1	99.0	99.6	96.4
Sommerfeld 1830–47	100.5	92.2	107.3	90.9	80.4	85.6	107.0	119.9	103.9	113.4	102.2	96.7
Forst 1819–29	77.4	98.8	100.8	107.0	92.3	94.2	98.2	108.9	117.7	91.9	106.1	106.7
Forst 1837–46	91.2	89.3	114.2	84.9	77.5	111.0	98.1	112.7	108.0	119.5	96.8	96.8
Sorau 1835–44	93.6	97.5	100.7	97.4	89.1	92.2	97.4	103.7	102.6	108.9	111.5	105.5

Source: see footnote 56.

for the cloth produced in the first half of the nineteenth century taken from the fullers' registers.[56] If the mean number of pieces for the individual months and the index for these are calculated from these sources for the continuously documented periods (table 4), differences between the means for the individual months can be found: these, however, are very small compared with those in Onsnabrück and Bielefeld, and probably do not provide much evidence. Nor do the auto-correlograms of these series (that for Forst 1837–1846 is given as an example in figure 7.1) show the regular swing between positive and negative correlation coefficients within a lag of 12 months which is such a striking feature

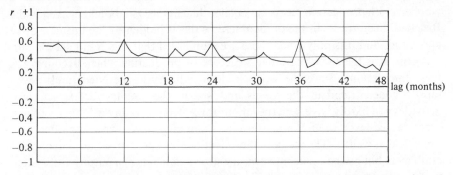

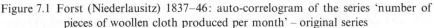

Figure 7.1 Forst (Niederlausitz) 1837–46: auto-correlogram of the series 'number of pieces of woollen cloth produced per month' – original series

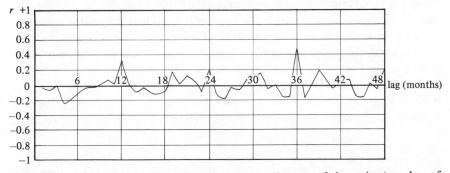

Figure 7.2 Forst (Niederlausitz) 1837–46: auto-correlogram of the series 'number of pieces of woollen cloth produced per month' – residual figures after the elimination of a 12-month moving average

56 Quandt, *Niederlausitzer Schafwollindustrie*, pp. 245–57. Since these figures obviously originate from the fullers' registers (see pp. 251, 258), it must be observed that a proportion of the cloth woven in Sommerfeld and Sorau went through the fulling process either outside these towns, or – in the case of Sommerfeld – in private fullers' mills, and will therefore obviously not be included in the figures (pp. 218, 258). It is possible that the proportion of cloth which went through the fulling process elsewhere was higher at the seasonal peak periods than at other times (see p. 219). Therefore in what follows the series for Forst is given more prominence.

of the Osnabrück and Bielefeld series. It is only when we eliminate the longer-term movements (business cycle and trend) by the calculation of a 12-month moving average, and thus isolate the seasonal component,[57] that the auto-correlogram of the residual series shows more signs of a 12-month cycle (figure 7.2). Here there is a swing between the highest positive correlation coefficients at lags of 12, 24, 36 and 48 months and the lowest negative values of r lying between these points. Even these maximum values of r (between $+0.20$ and $+0.47$ in the correlogram in figure 7.2) lie far behind those of the Osnabrück and Bielefeld series. Also there seem to be fluctuations on a time scale of less than 12 months which play a part.[58] On the whole, the seasonal fluctuation in the Niederlausitz woollen cloth production seems far smaller than in the Osnabrück, or even in the Bielefeld, linen trade. In the original figures this is hidden by the business cycle and trend, and it is only when these are eliminated that this result stands out.

Again, it is the socio-economic structure of production which accounts for these fluctuations. Since the woollen cloth industry in the Niederlausitz was mostly concentrated in the towns and not in the countryside, agricultural activities can hardly have kept the labour force from work in the industry to any great degree (even though a master craftsman may have owned a garden or a small field as well).[59] The method of production was based on a tradition of guild craftsmen, but by the eighteenth century strong elements of a putting-out system had been added to this. During the first half of the nineteenth century some factories were started, especially for spinning, but also for finishing.[60] Thus the Lausitz woollen industry was considered one of the more advanced centres of this trade in Germany in the 1840s.[61] Under these conditions the 'natural' rhythm of the seasons was unable to have a radical effect on the course of production. The raw material, the wool, was of course subject to the seasonal rhythm of sheep shearing, but for the most part it was produced in the Mark Brandenburg, in Silesia and in Saxony, and was the object of an inter-regional or even international trade.[62] For this reason, shortages in the supply of the raw material, which might lead to a limitation in the cloth production, were due less

---

57 Compare Yamane, *Statistik*, I, 318ff.; also Oskar Anderson, *Probleme der statistischen Methodenlehre in den Sozialwissenschaften*, Einzelschriften der Deutschen Statistischen Gesellschaft, 6 (Würzburg, 1962), pp. 180ff. concerning the theoretical and practical problems of such methods. Once again it must be stressed that no elimination of the 'smooth components' was undertaken for the various series from the Osnabrück and Bielefeld regions, and that the respective figures show the auto-correlograms of the original series.

58 The auto-correlograms for the remaining Lausitz series similarly show indications of a 12-month cycle, after the elimination of a 12-part moving average, but also of shorter fluctuations; only for Sommerfeld 1816–25 are there no comparable indications of a cyclic fluctuation.

59 Compare Quandt, *Niederlausitzer Schafwollindustrie*, pp. 263f.

60 *Ibid.*, pp. 19ff., 29ff., 39ff.

61 Blumberg, *Textilindustrie*, p. 200; compare pp. 79f., 107, 109ff., 118, 120f.

62 Quandt, *Niederlausitzer Schafwollindustrie*, pp. 129ff.

to seasons than to business cycles, and were caused by international competition in the demand for the raw material. Even when, in the case of such shortages, the fact that the time of sheep shearing was fixed according to the season led to a worsening of the shortage above all in the first half of the year,[63] this did not produce a dominant seasonal pattern in cloth output. The fulling process was dependent on nature because of the importance of water – great heat in the summer and extreme cold in the winter could hinder the process[64] – but even this did not force a fixed pattern on to the whole of the cloth production. The influences coming from demand and circulation seem to have been at least as important as the seasons in determining fluctuations in cloth production. Since at this period distribution took place mainly at fairs, the dates of the fairs, at Easter, Michelmas (29 September) and New Year, are said to be important causes of the uneven amount of production over the year.[65] But the basic fact remains that with this method of production, in which elements of craftsmanship and industrial capitalism were linked, seasonal fluctuations were of much less importance than business cycles and trends.

It has become clear that the extent and character of seasonal fluctuations were determined by the socio-economic structure of production. But this in turn leads to the question why different structures arose in different regions and industries. Different types of product – such as coarse or fine linen or woollen cloth – obviously required more or less sophisticated techniques as well as different raw materials, which were either easily at hand or available only through the mediation of trade. But why did the villages around Bielefeld turn to the production of fine linen while the Osnabrück region preferred coarse *Löwend* linen? The mercantilist policy of the Prussian authorities is often mentioned in this context. In fact, they took an active interest in the improvement of industrial production much earlier than the Osnabrück government. But this does not provide a sufficient explanation. One might speculate about an earlier and more thorough commercialisation of the agricultural sector in the Bielefeld district. A satisfactory answer, however, will only arise from an investigation of the long-term development of the respective regional economies and societies.

Looking back from the subsequent period of industrial capitalism, it seems tempting to place a structure such as that of the Osnabrück linen trade in the context of a 'traditional', 'pre-industrial' mode of production and way of life, for which, as a general principle, the natural, seasonal rhythm would have been of far

63 *Ibid.*, p. 130.
64 *Ibid.*, pp. 218f.
65 *Ibid.*, pp. 251, 258; compare Blumberg, *Textilindustrie*, p. 183. The fact that, according to the auto-correlograms, fluctuations of a shorter period than 12 months played a role in the production of woollen cloth in Lausitz would be consistent with this.

more basic importance than for a 'modern', 'industrial' society. Agricultural production, as the basic and dominant sector, was deeply influenced by this seasonal rhythm, but the important events of human life, marriage, conception, birth and death, were also to a large extent subject to the changing seasons,[66] and research into folklore has stressed the importance of the seasonal cycle in customs, festivals and beliefs, and in all spheres of everyday life.[67] But the dichotomous juxtaposition of a naturally determined mode of production and way of life of a marked seasonal cyclical nature, and a technical and industrial world, which had freed itself of these things, is probably no more realistic than the idea of a straight and even path of 'modernisation' and 'industrialisation', which led step by step from the old to the new situation. Firstly, even under conditions of advanced industrial capitalism, there are still a number of 'relics': fluctuations in production in different areas of the economy are caused by nature and climate, and by 'artificial' institutional factors, which bring a considerable scale of seasonal fluctuation even to a 'modern' economy.[68] Secondly, even in the period before industrial capitalism, production and way of life were not determined by nature in any simplistic sense. To explain the seasonal rhythm of demographic events, we must account not only for the natural annual cycle of climate, with its possible direct influences on the human body as well as its indirect effect through changing agricultural work and food supply, but also for factors of mentality and society, such as the ecclesiastical year or the seasonal pattern of migration.[69] As has been shown in this essay, seasonal fluctuations in linen production were caused by socio-economic structures which were decisive in determining the extent to which the seasonal rhythm of flax growing influenced the total production process. And there was no unilinear 'progress' from a 'traditional' economy with marked seasonal fluctuations to increasingly 'modern' forms, with fewer and more even fluctuations. Instead, large areas of urban craft work, for the most part working for a local market in a comparatively 'old-fashioned' manner, would hardly have known the scale of seasonal fluctuation to be found in the Osnabrück linen trade, which, like the other linen regions of

66 See Arthur E. Imhof, *Einführung in die historische Demographie* (Munich, 1977), pp. 98ff.: Edward Shorter, *The Making of the Modern Family* (New York, 1975), pp. 248f., 340ff. On the question whether this seasonal birth rhythm was weakened in proto-industrial regions, see Medick, in Kriedte, Medick, Schlumbohm, *Industrialization Before Industrialization*, pp. 91f.
67 See the articles on 'Jahreszeiten' 'Frühling', 'Sommer', 'Herbst', 'Winter', in *Handwörterbuch des deutschen Aberglaubens*, ed. Hanns Bächtold-Stäubli, 10 Vols. (Berlin/Leipzig, 1927–42), or Eugen Fehrle, *Feste und Volksbräuche im Jahreslauf europäischer Völker* (Kassel, 1955).
68 See Hans-Wolfram Finck von Finckenstein, 'Saisonschwankungen', in *Handwörterbuch der Sozialwissenschaften*, 9 (1956), 84f.; closer examination in Simon Kuznets, *Seasonal Variations in Industry and Trade*, Publications of the National Bureau of Economic Research, No. 22 (New York, 1933), a study which is still of interest.
69 Imhof, *Einführung*, pp. 98ff.; see also François Lebrun, 'Démographie et mentalités: le mouvement des conceptions sous l'ancien régime', in *Annales de Démographie Historique* (1974), pp. 45–50.

'proto-industrialisation', owed its rise above all to the emergence of the 'modern world system', to the 'new colonialism' and to the triangular Atlantic economy. The effects of nature and the seasons were mediated by society, and the 'modern' was less sharply divided from the 'traditional' than an undialectical method of observation would assume.

Perhaps the labels of 'modern' and 'archaic' are somewhat misleading with regard to the development of the division of labour as well. In the eighteenth and early nineteenth centuries, contemporaries thought a major competitive advantage of the Osnabrück linen industry was that the rural producers combined it with agriculture. In order to refute any idyllic view of this, it must be said that it was generally need which drove people to take on this work besides agriculture: '... spinning and weaving are the most thankless tasks. It is not easy for anyone to make a living from them', wrote Justus Möser.[70] Theorists of bourgeois society and capitalist economic development such as Adam Smith and Arthur Young came to look at the growing division of labour as a major vehicle of progress.[71] In fact, in the period of capitalist industrialisation, the Osnabrück region suffered the fate of de-industrialisation as far as textiles were concerned, whereas Bielefeld, after a sharp crisis in mid nineteenth century, was transformed into a centre of textile factories. In our day, however, some revisionist economists and historians take up views held by contemporary opponents of Adam Smith and Arthur Young. They point to the fact that growing division of labour is not so much a question of technological efficiency as one of control of labour by capital. These revisionists recommend technologies based on less division of labour (including a rotation of people between different tasks, which reminds one of the Osnabrück linen industry) as an aim of future development.[72] It seems to be somewhat difficult to distinguish the 'modern' from the 'archaic', since even the ideas of what is progressive and what is backward do not develop in a unilinear way.

70   Justus Möser, 'Abhandlung von dem Verfall des osnabrückischen Linnenhandels und den Mitteln, solchen wieder aufzuhelfen', in *Sämtliche Werke. Historisch-kritische Ausgabe*, Vol. 8, ed. Ludwig Schirmeyer (Oldenburg/Hamburg, 1956), pp. 27–46, esp. p. 37. Cf. above references in note 36.

71   Adam Smith, *An Inquiry into the Nature and Causes of the Wealth of Nations*, Book 1, Chapter 1, in *The Glasgow Edition of the Works and Correspondence of Adam Smith*, Part 2, ed. R. H. Campbell *et al.*, 2 vols. (Oxford, 1976), I, 13ff.; Arthur Young, *Travels During the Years 1787, 1788 and 1789 .. of the Kingdom of France*, 2 vols. (London, 1792), I, 503–11, particularly 505; cf. *idem*, *A Tour in Ireland*, 2 vols. (London, 1780), II, 303–9; cf. above reference in note 37.

72   Honoré-Gabriel Riquetti, Comte de Mirabeau, *De la monarchie prussienne sous Frédéric le Grand*, 7 vols. (London, 1788), III, 109; John Quincy Adams, *Letters on Silesia, Written During a Tour Through that Country in the Years 1800, 1801* (London, 1804), pp. 15–17, 60–1; Stephen A. Marglin, 'What Do Bosses Do? The Origins and Functions of Hierarchy in Capitalist Production', in *The Division of Labour*, ed. André Gorz (Brighton, 1976), pp. 13–54; Thomas Kuby, *Vom Handwerksinstrument zum Maschinensystem*, Bildung und Gesellschaft, Vol. 5 (Berlin, 1980).

5

From manor to mill: the West Riding in transition

PAT HUDSON

There has been a strong tendency in recent literature to generalise about the nature of rural domestic industry, its emergence and its 'role' in the transition to industrialisation.[1] The purpose of this essay is to examine the structure of the rural textile industry in the West Riding of Yorkshire. This region was one of the key areas of Britian's Industrial Revolution, more important than Lancashire until the late eighteenth century and second only to its neighbour as the centre of factory textiles by the second half of the nineteenth century.[2] The different organisational forms of the rural textile industry in this region were intimately related to their agrarian setting and promoted very different types of transition to centralised production. The case of the West Riding thus demonstrates something of the difficulty and danger of presenting the phenomenon of proto-industry in terms of a general economic model.

Rural production in Western Europe by the seventeenth and eighteenth centuries encapsulated a vast variety of organisational forms, some arising directly from technological dictates, others not. At one pole were *Kaufsystems* of independent artisan households working on their own raw materials and

---

1 See F. F. Mendels: 'Industrialisation and Population Pressure in 18th Century Flanders', unpublished dissertation (University of Wisconsin, 1969), 'Proto-industrialization: The First Phase of the Industrialization Process', *Journal of Economic History.* 32 (1972); 'Recent Research in European Historical Demography', *American Historical Review*, 75 (1970); 'Agriculture and Peasant Industry in 18th Century Flanders', in W. N. Parker and E. L. Jones (eds.), *European Peasants and their Markets* (Princeton, 1975); 'Seasons and Regions in Agriculture and Industry', in S. Polland (ed.), *Region und Industrialisierung* (Göttingen, 1980). See also H. Medick, 'The Proto-industrial Family Economy: The Structural Function of Household and Family During the Transition from Peasant Society to Industrial Capitalism', *Social History*, 3 (October 1976).

2 H. Heaton, *The Yorkshire Woollen and Worsted Industries* (Oxford, 1965); E. M. Sigsworth, *Black Dyke Mills: A History* (Liverpool, 1958); D. T. Jenkins, *The West Riding Wool Textile Industry 1770–1835: A Study in Fixed Capital Formation* (Edington, 1975); P. Hudson, 'The Genesis of Industrial Capital in the West Riding Wool Textile Industry 1770–1850', unpublished D.Phil. thesis (University of York, 1981).

producing a saleable product. Usually a small farm and dual occupation were crucial to the viability of these units. At the other extreme were found putting-out or *Verlagsystems*, often incorporating sophisticated division of labour between households. Here the catalyst was the merchant who put out work on various processes to an increasingly dependent, often landless, rural proletariat. Between these poles existed a broad spectrum of organisational forms with their associated mix of agriculture and industry and their different household and property structures.

Clearly, one would expect this spectrum to produce an equally varied 'proto-industrial dynamic', but the tendency of much current theorising has been to regard the variety of proto-industrial forms as representing stages in a linear progression towards sophisticated *Verlagsystems* and the rural proletarianis-ation of labour. The diversity of structures and of their implications is thus subsumed by a supposed universality of change, but inconvenient exceptions to any general pattern abound.

Deyon has argued that, at least in the case of Flanders, models of *Kaufsystem* and *Verlagsystem* do not represent the diversity found in practice. The early-nineteenth-century woollen industry was run on the basis of extensive putting-out networks centred on Roubaix; the linen industry, however, was based on individual enterprise and direct dealing in the market-place. The characteristic producer was a cultivator-weaver who grew his own flax, harvested it in the summer and worked it up in the winter. The cotton industry functioned within yet another permutation, combining concentrated manufactories and dispersed weaving.[3]

The West Riding of Yorkshire presents a further such exception in the shape of two major contrasting sectors of the eighteenth-century rural textile industry. Although the divide was not entirely clear cut, the traditional woollen branch of the region, which had existed since the Middle Ages but expanded notably from the seventeenth century, exhibited the artisanal form or *Kaufsystem*. The newer sector of worsted production which was introduced to the area largely from the eighteenth century, was conducted on a putting-out basis. It has been shown elsewhere that this division is not capable of a simple explanation in terms purely of technology, capital requirements or market imperatives.[4] The spatial distribution of the two branches indicates that the major influence on proto-industrial forms lay in the agrarian, social and institutional structure of the regions in which they were found.

As illustrated in the accompanying map and demonstrated in an earlier

3 P. Deyon, 'La Diffusion rurale des industries textiles en Flandre francaise à la fin de l'Ancien Régime et au début du XIXième siècle', *Revue du Nord*, 240 (1979).
4 P. Hudson, 'Proto-industrialisation: The Case of the West Riding Textile Industry, *c.* 1700–1830', *History Workshop Journal*, 12 (October 1981).

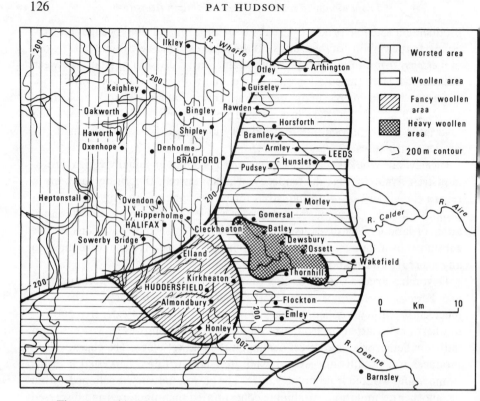

The geographical location of the woollen and worsted sectors *c.* 1780–1830

paper,[5] the *Verlagsystem* of the worsted industry spread rapidly in the eighteenth century, supplanting woollen production in areas of high ground and poor soils in the north and west of the textile region. These areas to the west of Halifax, Bradford and Keighley were characterised by early enclosure and enfranchisement and the emergence of a large landless wage-dependent cottager class. These areas also saw the earlier decline of traditional manorial forms. The artisanal structure of the woollen branch prevailed into the nineteenth century in areas of generally better soils, where much land was held in leasehold and copyhold farms of a size suitable for the dual economy, and where the decline of manorialism was generally more retarded.

The purpose of the first part of this essay is to ask in a little more detail how it was that these contrasting environmental conditions supported such different systems of manufacturing production. It will then be demonstrated that the *Kaufsystem* and the *Verlagsystem* had very different influences on the nature and speed of the transition to centralised production. Their agrarian links had

5 *Ibid.*

important implications for the finance of factory construction and for the emergence of factory employers and waged workers. Elements of custom and agrarian culture were particularly influential in creating an unusual form of transition in the shape of the company mill of the woollen branch. This is an interesting finding, as *Kaufsystems* have been studied so little in recent literature on the dynamics of rural production.

I

Fifty years ago, in analysing the emergence of the textile industry in Lancashire, Wadsworth and Mann were moved to comment: 'The two movements, industrial and agrarian, went on side by side, and it is hard to say how far the breakdown of the medieval economy turned men to industry, and how far industrial opportunities hastened the making of new farms at the expense of old grazing rights on the common wastes.'[6] This observation also contains some relevant clues to understanding the process of change on the eastern slopes of the Pennines.

In eighteenth-century topographical surveys of the West Riding several farming areas are discernible, but two major agricultural zones are apparent. The first, covering over a third of the Riding, and almost contiguous with the worsted area, was one of upland and pasture with little arable cultivation. This area included immense tracts of upland waste, some used as common pasturage. Farms were generally small, the majority under fifteen acres.[7] The second zone comprised the lands of the river valleys and intervening hills in the east of the region. Here soils were generally better and small mixed farms were common. By the eighteenth century most of the small farms – under twenty acres – were held by woollen clothiers.[8]

The impact of these agrarian environments upon patterns of manufacture was mediated by institutional developments, particularly by the differential decline of manorialism and its effects on landholding and inheritance practices. It is difficult to analyse the manorial history of such a vast area as the West Riding. From the fourteenth century, if not earlier, a large amount of subinfeudation took place, resulting in a complex plurality of manorial rights and estate ownerships:

6   A. P. Wadsworth and J. de L. Mann, *The Cotton Trade and Industrial Lancashire, 1600–1780* (Manchester, 1931), p. 26.
7   W. Marshall, *Rural Economy of Yorkshire* (London, 1778); Messrs Rennie, Brown and Shirreff, *A General View of the Agriculture of the West Riding of Yorkshire* (London 1800); J. Bigland, *A Topographical and Historical Description of the County of York* (London, 1812); W. Harwood Long, 'Regional Farming in 17th Century Yorkshire', *Agricultural History Review*, 4 (1956); W. B. Crump, 'The Wool Textile Industry of the Pennines in its Physical Setting', *Journal of the Textile Institute*, 36 (1935).
8   *Ibid.*

very numerous manors anciently arose without any express grant from the paramount lord; but those persons who held large tenures and subgranted their possessions to numerous tenants, either in base or free tenure, found it necessary to hold courts for the better government of these tenants and the internal management of their estates; and thus by slow degrees, manorial rights were obtained in the localities comprised in the great tenures.[9]

In the western areas, and especially in the sub-manor of Halifax and in those of Bradford, Keighley and the Craven area, manorial controls were historically weaker than in the eastern zone.[10] As on the Lancashire side of the Pennines; 'field systems were irregular and in the hilly parts the common fields were of secondary importance, as from the 13th century settlement had been going on by the taking in of the waste in the form of scattered homesteads outside the field systems'.[11] Alongside the enclousure of waste and of most of the open fields went the growth of leasehold and freehold rather than customary tenure, and considerable subinfeudation. These developments helped to forward the evolution of an open market in land and formed the backcloth of the primary accumulation process.

The seventeenth century saw a marked acceleration in the break-up of large feudal estates through the decay and impoverishment of their owners and the sequestrations of the Civil War period. Many manors in the western area were sold by the Crown to raise finance in the pre-war decades. In this way the Manor of Bradford was passed via a syndicate of London merchants to a group of yeoman freeholders who then compounded for the conversion of all copyholds into freeholds in 1631.[12]

The seventeenth century also witnessed a further great movement of enclosure of the commons in the western upland areas and, as in Lancashire

The course of the enclosure movement ... tended not so much to drive workers into the towns as to help the spread of industry in the country. The process was not catastrophic but constructive, and consisted in the bringing into use of common pasture and large tracts of moorland ...

Along with the increase in the number of farms following the enclosure of the waste

9   J. James, *History of Bradford* (Bradford, 1841), p. 355.
10 There is a vast secondary literature on this: e.g. M. J. Ellis, 'A Study of the Manorial History of Halifax Parish in the 16th and Early 17th Centuries', *Yorks. Archaeological Journal*, 40 (1962), 250–420; M. E. François, *The Social and Economic Development of Halifax 1558–1640* (Leeds, 1966); D. F. E. Sykes, *The History of Huddersfield and the Valleys of the Colne, the Holme and the Dearne* (Huddersfield, 1898); A. G. Foster, *The Manor of Leeds* (ND); R. Thoresby, *Ducatus Leodiensis* (Leeds, 1715); C. Stephenson, *The Ramsdens and Their Estate in Huddersfield* (Almondbury, 1972). Primary source material is also extant: e.g. enfranchisment and leasing agreements, Halifax Manor CAL 73 TN MSS, Calderdale Archives; Wakefield Manor Court Rolls, Yorks. Archaeological Society; various Manorial Rolls and Surveys, Leeds City Archives.
11 Wadsworth and Mann. *Cotton Trade*, p. 26.
12 James, *Bradford*, pp. 115ff.

went the tendency towards smaller holdings. Master manufacturers bought farms and let them out to their weavers much as the factory owners built cottages for their operatives.[13]

However, by 1632 an investigation in Halifax manor revealed that a large amount of waste land had been enclosed since 1608 by several leading citizens 'to ye great wrong and annoyance of ye inhabitants'.[14] Clearly the independent smallholders were losing out, their plots were becoming unviable without the supplement of the commons, and a trend to landlessness was increasingly apparent.

At the same time enfranchisement was common and was often a very lucrative business for the manorial lord. In the sub-manor of Halifax enfranchisement proceeded apace after 1606 when Arthur Ingram bought the lordship. Eighty-five enfranchisement deeds have survived for the period 1609–41 alone. These gave some 91 copyholders their freedom for payments ranging up to £80.[15] By the Civil War fewer than one-third of the landholders of this area remained as copyholders.[16]

The enclosure of commons reduced the need for close regulation by the manorial courts, while the multiplication of freeholds created influential groups of yeomen freeholders at one pole and a landless class at the other. This tendency to social polarisation was further encouraged by partible inheritance. This was 'much more widely practised in highland than in lowland Britain, associated with pastoral regions not firmly held together by manorial controls and where the family remained as the most powerful agent of social control and discipline'.[17] Partible inheritance was further encouraged by the ability of households to earn a living outside of the agricultural sector and appears to have been particularly characteristic of the putting-out areas.

In Halifax in the early seventeenth century partible inheritance was the norm.[18] Baumber has shown that, in Keighley manor, well over half of the wills made in the seventeenth and early eighteenth centuries stipulated the division of land between male heirs.[19] By 1740, for example, the Heaton family, who were extensively involved in the worsted putting-out trade, owned farms in many parts of the Worth valley. Each was owned by a different branch of the family, ownership having been dispersed through previous generations of partible inheritance.[20]

---

13 Wadsworth and Mann, *Cotton Trade*, pp. 320–1.
14 Quoted by Ellis, 'Manorial History of Halifax Parish', pp. 425–6.
15 *Ibid.* p. 419 – extant in TN MSS, Calderdale Archives.
16 Ellis, 'Manorial History of Halifax Parish', p. 265.
17 J. Thirsk (ed.), *The Agrarian History of England and Wales 1500–1640*, IV (Cambridge, 1967), 9.
18 François, *Development of Halifax*, p. 252.
19 M. L. Baumber, *A Pennine Community on the Eve of the Industrial Revolution* (Keighley, 1977), p. 112.
20 *Ibid.*

Enclosure, enfranchisement and partible inheritance together contributed further to the declining size of agricultural holdings and to the emergence of an increasing landless element of the population. The average valuation of holdings detailed in wills of the Keighley area declined from £49 3s in the period 1689–1710 to £35 12s by 1731–50.[21] In Halifax manor the majority of holdings were 5–15 acres as early as the 1630s.[22] These seventeenth-century characteristics of what were to become the main worsted areas of the eighteenth century reflected changes in land distribution and a degree of social polarisation found much less commonly in the east of the textile region. By the early seventeenth century in Halifax manor 'The average clothier's will included leasehold more often than freehold land, and sometimes the land in question was large enough only for a house and garden.'[23] It was these lowly clothiers, dependent on the precariousness of international cloth markets for woollen stuffs, who in the eighteenth century were to become the employees of the larger yeomen clothiers organising worsted production on a putting-out basis.

The existence of a landless rural proletariat and a precariously placed clothier group being absorbed from the early eighteenth century by putting-out capitalists is evidenced particularly from the occupations listed in parish registers. The proportion of persons described as clothiers declined, whilst that of weavers, combers and labourers increased.[24] These rural employees were dependent on the market for their basic necessities, and virtually all of the foodstuffs required in the region were supplied from the farms of the East Riding.[25] The landless proletariat was divorced from agricultural involvement, as employment in manufacture was usually more easily available and more lucrative. This was much to the consternation of those local landowners requiring harvest labour. The spinners of Bradford manor came particularly under fire from the Court Leet in 1687, not only for neglecting agricultural work, but also for asserting their sexual and social independence: 'Whereas many young women, healthful and strong combine and agree to cot and live together without government, and refuse to work in time of harvest and give great occasion for lewdness, therefore it is ordered that no person receive such into his house as cotter or tabler without the consent in writing of the church wardens upon pain of 39s 11d.'[26]

Thus early enfranchisement and enclosure, together with a decline in manorial controls over the land, encouraged the accumulation of capital in the hands of a

---

21   *Ibid.*, p. 35.
22   François, *Development of Halifax*, p. 238.
23   *Ibid.*, p. 239.
24   See A. Betteridge, 'A Study of Halifax Administrative Records, 1588–1762', unpublished Ph.D. thesis (University of Leeds, 1979); P. Hudson, 'Proto-industrialisation', diagram 1.
25   Rennie, Brown and Shirreff, *Agriculture of the West Riding*, p. 25.
26   Quoted in James, *Bradford*, p. 121.

few and the growth of wage dependency on the part of the others. In retrospect this can be seen to have paved the way for the extensive putting-out systems of worsted production.

When one turns to the woollen-producing area it appears that the *Kaufsystem* was supported by more fertile and larger agricultural holdings[27] with a greater seasonality of agricultural work.[28] These areas, apart from the city of Leeds, were also historically more dominated by traditional manorial controls over land tenure, retained more copyhold land and had to await the late eighteenth century before experiencing the most fundamental enclosure of common land.[29] John Houseman, on his tour of the area in 1800, noted that the recently enclosed corn farms held in large holdings in the Aire valley contrasted markedly with the small grass farms of the Bradford area, owned by manufacturers.[30]

Although, as in the westerly areas, freehold land was common, copyhold land was equally prevalent in the woollen region in the eighteenth century, and much of it was strictly held at will. The Ramsden, the Savile and the Dartmouth families, the most powerful manorial authorities in the region from the seventeenth century, all eschewed proper leasehold development in favour of short lets and peasant insecurity.[31]

From the early eighteenth century, if not before, manorial lords and other large estate owners saw considerable advantage in fostering the joint occupation of farming and cloth making in short leases, as a way of increasing the revenues from their lands.[32] Both here and in parts of Lancashire agricultural rents were high because of the income derived from manufacture in the dual occupation, and on many estates the land was consciously divided into small farm plots or closes suitable for clothiers' needs.[33]

Although rents were high, clothiers turning over their own capital had the possibility of accumulation and could achieve independence by buying up freehold land and surrendering copyhold.[34] It was less easy for them to subdivide

27 Evidence for this is available in clothiers' inventories and wills. For extensive comment and analysis of these, see M. J. Dickenson, 'The West Riding Woollen and Worsted Industries, 1689–1770: An Analysis of Probate Inventories and Assurance Policies', unpublished Ph.D. thesis (University of Nottingham, 1974). For a summary of his findings, see P. Hudson, 'Proto-industrialisation', tables.
28 Implied in Dickenson, 'West Riding Woollen and Worsted Industries'.
29 Enclosure awards survive in great number for the woollen area in the late eighteenth and nineteenth centuries. They are held in the County Record Office, Wakefield, in Leeds City Archives and in the other repositories of the region.
30 J. Houseman, *A Topographical Description of Cumberland, Westmorland, Lancashire and a Part of the West Riding of Yorkshire* (Carlisle, 1800), p. 171.
31 See Dartmouth Estate Terriers, the Estate Office, Slaithwaite; Sykes, *Huddersfield*; Savile Estate Records, Dewsbury Public Library and Nottingham Record Office.
32 There are many examples of this. Some are examined in Hudson, 'Genesis of Industrial Capital', Ch. 4.
33 Wadsworth and Mann, *Cotton Trade*, p. 316. Also, see below, pp. 142–3.
34 See Hudson, 'Genesis of Industrial Capital', Ch. 4.

their copyholds between heirs. Tight control over land transfers was maintained, particularly in areas where leasehold remained undeveloped – and these were many. A topographical survey of 1794 remarked that much of the land of the mid West Riding was let without lease, tenants being removable at six months' warning.[35] Another contemporary agricultural tract describes in detail the common process of tenant removal which usually occurred on Lady Day when rents fell due.[36]

Sykes, the Huddersfield historian writing in the early twentieth century, noted that some of the Dartmouth estates in Slaithwaite were even then still held in precarious tenancy[37] and, until the copyhold agitation and court cases of the mid nineteenth century, the enormous Ramsden manors around Huddersfield were controlled to such an extent that 'supposed transfers were altogether ineffectual'.[38] The annual Ramsden rent audit as late as 1846 had a feudal atmosphere,[39] and it was not until 1920 that the town of Huddersfield managed to buy itself free of the Ramsden possessions.[40] The Court Leet records of the manor of Wakefield indicate just how communal the system of agriculture was in the late seventeenth century, and copyhold land remained ubiquitous in the wapentake of Agbrigg (which covered the south of the West Riding) until the twentieth century.[41]

Thus, although much research remains to be done, particularly on the manorial history and tenurial arrangements of the manors of the lower Aire valley, it appears that the contrast between the two major agricultural and industrial zones in terms of their agrarian and institutional development was marked. Variations in topography, in soil and in the resultant agricultural possibilities were instrumental in influencing the form and emergence of rural industry, but the effect of these variations was clearly mediated by the institutional framework which either promoted or retarded enclosures and enfranchisement and thus influenced primary accumulation. The direction of manorial development from the sixteenth and seventeenth centuries appears to have been related to the perceived ways in which the maximum revenue could be gained from estates with different agricultural and manufacturing potentials.

The mediation of the institutional structure is particularly apparent in the case of the manors of Huddersfield, Almondbury and those to the west along the

35 Rennie, Brown and Shirreff, *Agriculture of the West Riding*, p. 12.
36 Marshall, *Rural Economy*, p. 40.
37 Sykes, *Huddersfield*, p. 43.
38 Quote from Lord Chancellor in court case of 1866, cited by Sykes, *ibid.*, p. 43.
39 Described by Isaac Horden, Ramsden estate agent, 1846, in 'Notes Relating to the Ramsden Estate and Huddersfield', manuscript notebook, Leeds City Library.
40 Stephenson, *The Ramsdens*, describes this.
41 S. H. Waters, *Wakefield in the Seventeenth Century: A Social History of the Town and Neighbourhood, 1550–1710* (Wakefield, 1933), Ch. 1.

upper Colne valley. Huddersfield and Almondbury were bought by the Ramsden family from the Crown in 1599 and 1627 respectively. The Ramsdens originated from a prosperous yeoman clothier family in Elland and achieved upward social mobility within a few generations by careful acquisition and exploitation of their estates.[42] For reasons both of prestige and of perceived maximisation of revenue, the Ramsdens held on to manorial privileges and controls, especially with respect to land tenure, long after their demise elsewhere in the West Riding. The manors of the upper Colne – Marsden, Slaithwaite, Whitely and Saddleworth – were similarly administered until the late eighteenth century,[43] which may go some way to explaining why these were the only upland, pastoral areas to retain the *Kaufsystem* into the nineteenth century.

Thus it appears that the agrarian and institutional setting was of crucial importance in influencing the emergence and nature of rural production. Any theory seeking to establish an understanding of industrialisation, particularly in a regional context, must incorporate such social and institutional variations and explore their implications.

II

Given the importance of the agrarian environment for the emergence of rural domestic industry, it is necessary to examine the extent to which the transition to factory production was influenced by these same variables. Although technological and commercial factors did much to dictate the pace and nature of the transition to factory production, some of the contrasting features of factory ownership and finance, which affected the potential for growth and change, were intimately related to the history and the agrarian environment of industrial regions.

One interesting feature of the early factory woollen industry – but not of the worsted branches – was the prevalence of the company mill form of organisation and finance. Company mills were, in effect, joint-stock concerns organised through the legal facility of a trust deed. They were found as early as the 1780s and continued as an important feature of the woollen branch until the second half of the nineteenth century. Processing materials on commission, these mills became a vital element of the proto-industrial structure, supporting the continued viability of the artisanal concerns who were their main shareholders and customers.

The company mill is an interesting organisational form to study because, apart from a few corn mills in other parts of the country, it seems to have been an institution unique (in England) to Yorkshire in the period before 1844. It was

42 Stephenson, *The Ramsdens.*
43 Sykes, *Huddersfield*; Edward Baines, *Baines' Yorkshire*, 2 vols. (Leeds, 1822), I, descriptive accounts of villages and townships.

linked to the peculiarly artisanal structure of proto-industrial production and gave rise to a form of co-operative capitalism rather different from the norm.

As early as the first decade of the nineteenth century company mills were numerous in the woollen area.[44] In the second quarter of the century their number appears to have expanded apace and, as a manufacturer wrote to the House of Lords in 1843, their prominence was undeniable:

From the first introduction of machinery the clothiers united to build mills in shares. At first a few and on a small scale as experiments by the more enterprising, then more extensively as the success of their neighbours and the increase of trade naturally and gradually led to the extension of the system up to the present time. The numerous woollen mills scattered throughout the populous clothing villages of the West Riding are principally owned and occupied by clothiers in shares.[45]

Some company mills were built, and others rented, by partnerships of clothiers and merchants; others were entirely financed by consortia of clothiers. Some stipulated that individuals had to be clothiers in order to buy shares; others insisted that shareholder-clothiers had to live and work within a certain radius of the mill so that their custom would be guaranteed.[46] Such were the mills described by Baker, the Factory Inspector in the early 1840s:

The history of Joint Stock Company Woollen Mills exhibits a singular instance of energy amongst the smaller capitalists of the manufacturing districts... the clothiers of certain country districts, such as Farsley, Idle, Eccleshill, Batley, Dewsbury etc., put their heads together and subsequently their purses... by erecting mills at home to scribble their own wool and full their own cloth... In the formation of a company mill a number of clothiers (for they must be clothiers to be partners) of small capital meet together and determine to become a company of so many partners, from 10 to 50, in shares generally of £25 each, each person taking as many shares as his capital will enable him... With this subscribed capital deeds of partnership are drawn, land is bought, a mill erected and machinery put up.[47]

The 1844 House of Lords Report on West Riding Joint Stock Mills discussed the financial arrangements in more detail:

Where the shareholders are more numerous – say 40 (they seldom exceed but often amount to that number) they will subscribe £50 per share in the first instance. They then

44   The author has a card index of mills established before 1850. It is derived from insurance records, business papers, *Parliamentary Papers*.
45   Letter from John Nussey, woollen manufacturer, 9 August 1843, quoted in *Parliamentary Papers*, 1844 (119), VII, 366.
46   John Goodchild has done much to isolate the various types of company mill: see his 'The Ossett Mill Company', *Textile History*, Vol. 1, No. 1 (1968). The Ossett Mill Company Records (John Goodchild MSS, Wakefield City Archives) are a mine of information. Another mill established in 1825 stipulated that partners must reside within one and a half miles: *Parliamentary Papers*, 1844 (119), VII, 366.
47   Factory Inspector's Letter, 1843, quoted by E. Lipson, *History of the Woollen and Worsted Industries* (London, 1921), pp. 177–9.

buy the land and proceed with the building. They next borrow on mortgage the largest amount which they can gain credit for which will generally pay for the building and steam engine; the machinery is obtained on credit.[48]

The use of the mortgage to secure loans for mill construction appears to have been particularly important in the case of company mills. The Ossett Mill Company trustees were empowered to borrow £3000 on mortgage in 1786 and raised part of this sum – £1200 – from the Leeds Cloth Hall.[49] When Kellett, Brown and Company were establishing their mill they raised £10 000 on security of mortgages.[50]

Kellett, Brown and Company of Calverley near Leeds is perhaps a good example of a fairly typical company mill launched in the second quarter of the nineteenth century, from which period the vast majority of such mills appear to date. Apart from the funds raised by mortgage, the other major source of finance was of course the shareholders. There were forty-three when the company was launched in 1834, and each held between two and eight shares at £25 per share. The average amount invested per shareholder in 1834 was £62. Each year from 1838 to 1843 an additional call of £10 per share was made. The majority of shareholders appear to have been local clothiers, although a handful are identifiable as merchants and tradesmen from Leeds.[51] The establishment of the Gill Royds Mill Company of Morley in 1835 involved similar shareholdings and borrowing from the local capital market, much done on security of land and property.[52]

Many of the company mills launched in the 1830s and 1840s seem to have continued in existence until well into the second half of the nineteenth century. The Rawden Low Mill Company, founded in 1844, is a typical example. Comparing a surviving share book for the 1860s with the initial record of the fifteen founder-subscribers shows a remarkable continuity of involvement of the local clothier families.[53] How did these small clothier dynasties and their communal mills manage to survive?

The financial symbiosis between the company mill and the artisan clothier is of crucial importance in understanding the latter's continued existence, alongside the factory, well into the second half of the nineteenth century. The company mill performed the fulling, scribbling, carding and slubbing processes; some included dyeing and some of the later ones also did rag grinding and spinning on

48   *Parliamentary Papers*, 1844 (119), VII, 366.
49   J. Goodchild 'The Ossett Mill Company', p. 50.
50   Kellett, Brown and Company, Item 1, Brotherton Library, University of Leeds.
51   *Ibid.*, and Commercial Directories, Leeds City Library.
52   Minute Book of the Gill Royds Mill Company, 1835–61, John Hartley and Sons, Item 3, Leeds City Archives.
53   Rawden Low Mill Company, Committee Minute Book, 1843–51, Articles of Partnership 1847, Share Book 1860s: FW2, Calderdale Archives.

commission. The other more labour-intensive processes of weaving, and the bulk of the spinning, continued to be carried on in workshops attached to the workers' homes. Of great importance in assessing the role of the company mill is the way in which work done by the mill on commission was charged and paid for. Shareholders were usually committed to send their work to their mill for processing; some mills even insisted that shareholders promised a certain amount of work per year.[54] Most clothiers involved in the finance of company mills were probably only too pleased to send their work there; for the majority the promise of rapid and efficient service was the main motivation for becoming a shareholder in the first place. One can reasonably expect that company mill shareholders benefited from the lower prices charged. The traditional fulling mills had often held a monopoly position which was reflected in their pricing and, as company mills spread, it appears that commission fulling and scribbling in all mills became more competitive, to the benefit of the clothier in terms both of cost and of speed. Furthermore it was not unknown in periods of bad trade conditions for company mills to waive some of their charges for a while to enable their proprietors to weather the storms of commercial life. In December 1844, for example, the Rawden Low Mill Company resolved that 'there be nothing charged for scouring for the next three months'.[55]

Perhaps the most important advantage for the clothier deriving from the company mill was the credit allowed to customers, especially to shareholders. Pay-days when accounts were settled were usually held half-yearly or quarterly, giving average credit periods of 2–3 months. Accounts were often overdue for longer than this but were not normally penalised or charged interest until after two pay-days had passed. Credit terms of this sort were of considerable importance to the small clothier concern whose biggest cost after wool purchase was the payment for commission processing of his materials. Long credit made it possible for the clothier to make and sell his cloths before laying out the full cost of their production. Such flexible credit terms were crucial at a time when the most common form of business failure was liquidity problems.

All company mills got round the legislation against joint-stock companies by organising under a trust deed, but there were problems arising from this legal form. They could neither sue nor be sued, and they did not have the power to proceed at law against a member of the partnership. Partners had 'no security on each other'[56] for the money which they advanced and no legal redress if, for example, a book-keeper or treasurer absconded with the cash-in-hand. They

---

54 See for example, Rawden Low Mill Articles of Partnership 10 April 1847, Minute Book, 1843–51: FW2, Calderdale Archives.

55 Minute Book, 30 December 1844: FW2, Calderdale Archives.

56 Letter from Mr Baker, Factory Inspector, 1843, quoted in *Parliamentary Papers*, 1844 (119), VII, 366.

could not even compel the sale of a share if the shareholder's account was long overdue. Much of the success of these ventures thus depended on the mutual trust and co-operation within the clothier communities.

Perhaps the most interesting aspect of company mill history is the way in which it ties in very closely with the agrarian and institutional factors described earlier. It is difficult to reconstruct a complete record of company mill development, as insurance data and other records upon which one has to rely usually list ownership under the trustees' names without designating them as such and it is difficult to distinguish these from a partnership. Thirty-one company mills have been identified in the period to 1850.[57] Though far from a complete record, we can assume that these mills are a fairly random sample as far as their location is concerned, and it is immediately apparent that they were concentrated in specific geographical areas. First there was a clustering to the south of the Aire valley between Leeds and Bradford, and the second concentration existed in the Calder valley to the west of Wakefield. It may be worth enquiring what these areas had in common, if anything, which made them fertile ground for the development of company mills.

Although any conclusions here must remain tentative, it appears that the clue to the spatial distribution of different types of organisational unit seems to lie in the agrarian environment, and specifically in the emergence of the proto-industrial artisanal unit. These were both areas where land was generally held in larger plots by both freeholders and copyholders. The river valleys were more fertile than the nearby highland zones and the two areas where company mills later grew had emerged as the main areas of the production of mixed cloths in the eighteenth century. Mixed cloth production was generally the province of the more substantial clothier with a reasonable-sized farming plot and a fairly viable dual occupational structure which cushioned him against years of bad trade and supported the accumulation of capital. It was this type of clothier who was obviously most able to contemplate the joint finance of mill construction or renting and who could afford to invest in two or three shares at £50, which appears to have been the average price of company mill shares. Such clothiers were also in a position to offer land and property as security for loans raised by the mills. Thus the agrarian environment appears to have been a significant influence in the growth of a mutually supportive co-operative form of early centralised production within the close-knit clothier communities.

The implications of the agrarian environment and of the different organisational structures of rural manufacture which it supported spread much wider than the instance of the company mill. This was particularly so in the general field

57   Card index of mills, formed from insurance data (Sun and Royal Exchange) collected by Dr
      D. T. Jenkins, Parliamentary Papers, business records, rate valuations, and other primary and
      secondary sources.

of mill finance in the first half of the nineteenth century. In the transition to the factory system the woollen and worsted branches drew upon very different sources for the supply of capital. This was particularly so where finance from landed and mercantile sources was concerned.

There were three main ways in which capital finance could flow from the land into early industrial enterprise: by direct investment, by indirect investment through the local capital market and, finally, by the mortgaging of farms and fields to raise funds for manufacturing.[58] The extent of direct investment in industrial enterprises by landed families and estate owners appears to have been of only minor importance for the Yorkshire textile sector as a whole. A survey of mills built before 1850 indicated that less than 6% were owned by estate owners.[59] However, if the investigation is confined to woollen mills, particularly those built before 1820, the extent of direct construction, or purchase and ownership, by landowners of industrial premises for hire appears much more significant. If other textile premises, such as clothiers' dwellings and workshops, warehouses and dyehouses, are included the importance of direct landed finance to the woollen sector appears even greater.

This important contribution of landed capital to the early centralising woollen sector resulted from the historically close ties between estate ownership and the traditional trade of the West Riding. From their introduction in the thirteenth century, fulling mills had been a manorial monopoly. These monopolies continued to be enforced in the seventeenth and early eighteenth centuries, when the mills were generally hired out to fullers for a fixed annual rental.[60] With the mechanisation of scribbling and carding in the 1770s and 1780s old fulling mills were extended and new ones built to accommodate the three processes. It is thus not surprising that landowners played an important role in mill building and finance at this time. It merely represented an extension of their traditional involvement. Only with the expansion of company mill construction and the mechanisation of spinning in the second quarter of the nineteenth century did the role of direct landed investment cease to be of major importance to the woollen sector.

Landowners in the woollen area in the eighteenth century were also involved in providing artisan clothiers' dwellings and small farms for hire. This appears to have been particularly prominent in the Aire valley, with notable developments on the estates of Sir Walter Calverley, Walter Spencer-Stanhope and Sir James Graham.[61] This practice also occurred, though to a lesser extent, on the estates of

---

58   For a full discussion of these three channels, see Hudson, 'Genesis of Industrial Capital', Ch. 4.
59   Card index.
60   See, for example, A. F. Upton, *Sir Arthur Ingram* (Oxford, 1961), p. 49.
61   Heaton, *Yorkshire Woollen and Worsted Industries*, pp. 290–1; M. F. Ward, 'Industrial Development and Location in Leeds, North of the River Aire 1775–1914', unpublished Ph.D. thesis (University of Leeds, 1972), p. 158; *Parliamentary Papers* (1806), pp. 444–7.

Lord Dartmouth and the Savile family to the south.[62] By fostering the dual occupation of farming and weaving, improving landlords could considerably raise the rental of their estates. This was particularly so in the areas where short leases predominated, and these often coincided with areas of strong and traditional forms of landed control. In the woollen area, where land was generally more fertile than in the worsted region, estate owners, on the whole, were more actively interested in estate improvements, including the building and modernisation of both clothiers' premises and mills for hire as well as the improvement of agricultural land.

Lord Dartmouth alone owned nineteen mills in 1805, in addition to numerous workshops and clothiers' premises.[63] Although it appears that he was unusually active as an industrial financier, the Savile family owned nine mills at this time and Sir James Graham owned four.[64] All the main examples of mills owned and largely financed by landowners are woollen mills. There appears to have been no significant direct participation by landowners in the ownership and finance of worsted factories.[65] The latter were built in the less fertile worsted area, where there were fewer improving estate owners, more leasing and greater absenteeism. The worsted industry had fewer historical links with landownership, as it only developed in Yorkshire from the eighteenth century and employed no powered processes until the mechanisation of spinning from the 1820s. Many of the early mills were thus steam powered, and a high proportion were built in towns away from rural sites and landed influence.

The role of landowners in the finance of the textile industry through the mechanism of the local capital market appears to have been relatively unimportant for both the woollen and worsted sectors at least before the era of blind investment and deposit banking. It would appear that the mortgaging and sale of land by industrialists to raise finance was, however, very significant. In the case of the woollen sector, with its capital dispersed so widely among landowning craftsmen, this was particularly true.

As early as 1703 the West Riding Registry of Deeds was established as one of only five in the country. The statute preamble, written at a time before worsted production was widespread in the area, outlined the importance of the Register for the woollen clothiers in particular:

The West Riding of the country of York is the principal place in the north for the cloth manufacture and most of the traders therein are freeholders and have frequent occasion to

---

62 Savile Survey and Valuation Book, 1809, Dewsbury Public Library, and Dartmouth Estate Terriers, Dartmouth Estate Office, Slaithwaite.
63 Register, Survey and Rental of the Earl of Dartmouth's Estate in the West Riding of the County of York, 1805, Dartmouth Estate Terriers.
64 Savile Survey (1809) and Title Deeds of Estates in Kirkstall, Leeds City Archives.
65 Card index.

borrow money upon their estates for managing their said trade, but for the want of a register find it difficult to give security to the satisfaction of the money lender (although the security they offer be really good) by means whereby the said trade is very much obstructed and many families ruined.[66]

The extent to which company mills raised cash by mortgaging land and property has already been mentioned and has been confirmed by a recent study of the land transactions of Ossett clothiers in the first half of the nineteenth century.[67] It appears that a great deal of *de facto* mortgaging of copyhold as well as of freehold land was a feature of the woollen textile communities.[68] Although the mortgaging of land to raise industrial finance was not unknown in the worsted area, the greater separation between agriculture, landowning and industry appears to have limited this type of activity in favour of other sources of funds.

Apart from differences in the importance of landed finance, it is also possible to link the structure of rural production in the woollen and worsted sectors with a marked contrast in the way in which finance from mercantile and credit sources was available as a spur to the transition to factory production.

In an earlier paper it was argued that the role of merchants in the direct finance and construction of woollen mills was relatively minor.[69] This confirmed the conclusion of Wilson's detailed study of Leeds merchants.[70] Only rarely were the mercantile elite of Leeds prepared to risk their liquidity position by heavy investment in fixed capital. Most of the early woollen mills were financed and occupied by small manufacturers who had emerged as the more successful artisans of the domestic system. They were aided in this by the relatively small size of a competitive mill until well into the nineteenth century, by the company mill form and by the ubiquity of cheap multiple tenancies.[71]

The emergence of factory manufacturers from the ranks of the domestic producers was also connected with this sector's position within the credit matrix of the industry in the eighteenth century. The artisan producer was generally able to gain credit from wool staplers, from other suppliers and from his family workforce to a much greater extent than he was forced to extend credit to merchants. This was particularly so whilst weekly sales in the cloth halls remained the dominant form of marketing. The turnover time of production as well as trade was more rapid in the woollen than in the worsted sector. In the

66   W. E. Tate, 'The Five English District Statutory Registries of Deeds', *Bulletin of the Institute of Historical Research*, 20 (1943–5), 98.
67   See Hudson, 'Genesis of Industrial Capital', Ch. 4.
68   It appears that copyhold land was almost as good a mortgageable security as freehold. For Wakefield manor all transactions were carefully recorded in the Manor Court Rolls (Yorkshire Archaeological Society, Leeds).
69   Hudson, 'Proto-industrialisation'.
70   R. G. Wilson, *Gentlemen Merchants: The Merchant Community in Leeds, 1700–1830* (Manchester, 1971).
71   For full discussion of these points see Hudson, 'Genesis of Industrial Capital', Chs. 2 and 3.

latter, fleeces were oiled for up to twelve months, there were more processes and separate households involved in production, and the market was much more overwhelmingly an export market than was the case in the woollen sector. In the latter the net credit gained by the manufacturer could, and generally did, cover the time of production and circulation. This provided an environment for capital accumulation which facilitated the gradual evolution of larger centralised concerns.[72]

In the worsted sector the transition to a fully mechanised factory system occurred much more rapidly but only accelerated from the 1820s.[73] The key figures in early factory finance appear to have been the putting-out merchants, but factory masters from outside of the domestic industry, particularly from the cotton trade and wool stapling, were common.[74] Rapid centralisation and technological change, together with consignment marketing, from the 1820s ensured that the threshold of entry into the trade was relatively high and that there were far fewer possibilities of upward mobility for the small domestic producer.

Credit availability also played a part in the very different transition to the factory in the worsted branch. The *Verlagger* of the eighteenth century usually bought his wool direct from the grower or his agent on short or no credit. This continued to be the case until the 1830s and 1840s as the worsted sector used largely English long-stapled wool whilst the use of imported wools in the woollen branch implied an important role for the broker and stapler. Worsted cloths were sold at three or four months' credit at least, the cloth hall system with sales for cash never gaining the prominence which it held in the traditional woollen sector.[75] This may well have been a major factor, together with the longer turnover time in production, which ensured that the worsted sector was dominated by concerns of larger capital than the woollen branch. These relatively large putting-out concerns in the eighteenth century were mercantile in their nature, employed little fixed capital and were as involved in merchanting as in manufacture. This, together with the disarray of worsted markets in the early nineteenth century, may account for the very slow build up of fixed capital in the industry before the 1820s. The credit matrix, together with the slow turnover time of production and sale of worsted piece-goods, may also have stimulated the vertical distintegration which was becoming a marked feature of the trade from the 1820s and which was virtually unknown in the woollen branch.

Thus it is possible that before the 1820s the credit matrix favoured capital accumulation in the woollen rather than the worsted branch of the industry, with

72   Hudson discusses this in detail, *ibid.*, Ch. 8. and Part VI.
73   Jenkins, *The West Riding Wool Textile Industry*, pp. 171–2, 176.
74   Card index.
75   See Hudson, 'Genesis of Industrial Capital', Chs. 5–7.

a large role being played by staplers, wool importers and fulling and scribbling mills. On the demand side the traditional possibilities of selling for cash or on short credit remained. From the 1820s, mechanical innovation in worsted spinning, and the accelerated trend to vertical disintegration, increased the turnover speed of capital in that branch at a time when the period of realisation was also shortening because of transportation, mercantile and financial improvements. In the climate of generally reducing open or book credit after the mid 1820s it would seem that the firms best placed to take advantage were those capable of reducing turnover speeds by mechanical or organisational innovation. It was then that the worsted sector came into its own. With fewer of the customary, familial and community restraints, and divorced from the artisan tradition, the disappearance of the rural domestic sector was relatively rapid and the factory became dominant.

In the woollen sector the domestic system in alliance with the company mill remained fully viable until the 1850s and 1860s. The volatility of the trade cycle, which particularly affected the production and export of cheap coarse cloths, was felt relatively harder by factory producers with their high overheads than it was by the traditional domestic sector. But its survival also owed much to family cohesion and attitudes, to the customary web of credit and to community ties, affiliations and loyalties. These insulated the traditional sector from the play of purely market forces.

It is these aspects of the traditional sector which require most additional study. Contemporaries were well aware of the flexibility of wage costs in domestic manufacture. The artisan income was a conglomerate derived from the agricultural holding, sidelines such as jobbing and carting and what was left of the common rights of gaming and gleaning, as well as from the textile trade itself. Sidelines could provide an essential subsidy to artisanal wage costs, and it is perhaps therefore not irrelevant to note that the major wave of enclosure of common and waste land in the woollen region did not occur until the Napoleonic War period.[76] In addition the artisan household, working as a production unit, could be called upon to work longer hours than those endured in the factories.[77] Small masters were known to give support to factory workers' demands for higher wages because the resistance of wage labour opened up the possibility of survival of the family-based unit whose loyalty and effort were conditioned by factors outside of the monetary reward.[78]

The survival of the artisan unit was also endorsed by the greater tendency to impartible inheritance found in the woollen area. The leasehold and copyhold

76　Evidence from Enclosure Awards.
77　See, for example, evidence of Law Atkinson, clothier and merchant of Bradley Mills, near Huddersfield: *Parliamentary Papers*, 1802–3 (71), V, 380.
78　Diary of Thomas Cook, Dewsbury Mills, 14 February 1820.

CAMBRIDGE
UNIVERSITY PRESS

have pleasure in sending for review a copy of:

BERG ET AL. Manufacture in Town and Country
    Before the Factory.
Price.£22.50 B H/c (0 521 24820 5)

Publication Date. 24th November 1983

It is requested that no review should appear before this date.

May we ask you to let us have a copy of any review published
or, if you send a copy of your journal, to indicate the pages on
which a review appears?

The Edinburgh Building, Shaftesbury Road, Cambridge CB2 2RU
Telephone (0223) 312393

land of the clothier was a vital element in the continued viability of the traditional structure. It could be used as collateral for loans and was a mark of prestige and standing in the local community which was essential in gaining a foothold in the chain of credit. Acceptance by the local clothier group was also a function of the long period of training and work in the household which, long after the decline of formal apprenticeship, usually preceded setting up on one's own account.[79]

The network of interpersonal relationships in the woollen textile communities was perhaps most important in its effects on credit extension and on the availability of loan finance. A study of Ossett clothiers' mortgages has shown that the vast majority of transactions appear to have occurred between clothiers living in the area and personally known to each other.[80] This was the case even where attorneys were involved, and the extent to which these intermediaries themselves gave interest-free small loans within the locality further endorses the importance of non-pecuniary relationships based on the localised capital market and local knowledge and influence.[81]

The collective and communitarian spirit embodied in financial and credit relationships and, *par excellence*, in the organisation of company mills, was also manifest in the formation, community support for, and lending policies of the early West Riding banks, but this is a separate story which has, to some extent, already been documented.[82]

One of the most fundamental forces undermining the influence of custom and community was the declining rate of profit which characterised the coarser end of the industry in particular from the 1840s. Whilst the problem of competition remained purely one of comparative costs, the artisan sector could compete. This ability was sustained by increasing use of recycled wool and by a reduction in living standards. However, as production increased and markets became periodically overstocked, profit rates fell, and low rates of profit could only be compensated for by mass production.

It has only been possible in this short essay to cover a few of the implications of different proto-industrial structures for the transition to centralised production. Research is beginning to indicate that the demographic dynamics of natural increase and inmigration were also very largely determined by the peculiar nature of domestic and early factory production in the West Riding.[83] The central concern of this essay has been to indicate that the contrasting proto-industrial

---

79 *Parliamentary Papers*, 1802–3, 1806, *passim*.
80 Hudson, 'Genesis of Industrial Capital', Ch. 4.
81 *Ibid.*, Ch. 9; M. Miles, 'The Money Market in the Early Industrial Revolution: The Evidence from West Riding Attorneys 1750–1800', *Business History* (1982).
82 Hudson, 'Genesis of Industrial Capital', Ch. 10.
83 Work in progress and P. Hudson, 'The Environment and the Dynamic of Proto-industry', unpublished paper circulated at the Eighth International Economic History Congress, Budapest, August 1982.

structures of the West Riding, emerging from different agrarian environments, conditioned to a large extent the pace and nature of the transition to factory production. This was particularly so via their effects on mill finance – on the contribution of landed wealth, merchant capital and credit. It has also been suggested that the survival of the artisan sector was closely conditioned by many aspects of co-operation, custom and community which were in part the legacy of the older agrarian order.

PART II

'Work' and 'wages'

6

Work and wages in Paris in the eighteenth century*

MICHAEL SONENSCHER

The terms 'work' and 'wages' seem to belong together. Like a number of other associated terms, they form a natural couplet, stretching back into the mists of time. Unlike work on the land or in the household, it has been usual to think of work in urban trades as work for wages.[1] In many of the urban trades of the eighteenth century, however, the relationship between work and wages was mediated by a variety of non-monetary customs and rights.[2] This fact is relatively well known, although its implications have still to be developed. This essay is an examination of the meaning of the wage in such a context, formed in this case by the often-disputed range of rights and customary arrangements which existed within the trades of eighteenth-century Paris. Its aim is to suggest a perspective upon the structure and internal mechanisms of artisanal production in which non-monetary forms of power are given their due weight.

* Research for this essay was made possible by grants from the S.S.R.C. and the British Academy as part of a wider study of certain aspects of manufacture in eighteenth-century France. I would also like to thank Colin Jones, David Garrioch, Pat Hudson and Maxine Berg for their very helpful criticisms of previous drafts.
The following abbreviations have been used in the notes: A. N. – Archives Nationales; B. N. – Bibliothèque Nationale; A. V. P. – Archives de la Ville de Paris; B.H.V.P. – Bibliothèque Historique de la Ville de Paris; B.A. – Bibliothèque de l'Arsenal; A. P. P. – Archives de la Préfecture de Police.

1 See, for example, B. Geremek, *Le Salariat dans l'artisanat parisien aux XIII–XVe siècles* (Paris, 1968); E. H. Phelps Brown and S. V. Hopkins, 'Seven Centuries of Building Wages', *Economica*, 22 (1955), 195–206; for a more nuanced discussion – in which credit is discussed alongside of wage payments – see R. A. Goldthwaite, *The Building of Renaissance Florence* (Baltimore, 1980), ch. 6.

2 See T. S. Ashton, *An Economic History of England: The Eighteenth Century* (London, 1955), Ch. 7; J. G. Rule, *The Experience of Labour in Eighteenth Century Industry*, Chs. 5 and 8; R. W. Malcolmson, *Life and Labour in England 1700–1780* (London, 1981), pp. 54–5. The fullest and the most thoughtful discussion of these matters is to be found in P. Linebaugh, 'Tyburn: A Study of Crime and the Labouring Poor in London During the First Half of the Eighteenth Century', unpublished Ph.D. thesis (University of Warwick, 1975). Readers of this work will immediately recognise the degree of my own intellectual indebtedness to its methods and preoccupations.

It has been usual to think of the rights and customs of the world of workshop production of the eighteenth century within a framework of analysis informed either by notions of 'the popular culture' of the 'pre-industrial world' or by a perspective centred upon the idiom of corporate organisation and its attendant cultural and political implications.[3] The objective here is to resituate custom and right within the organisation of the workshop itself. The present emphasis upon popular culture or the idiom of corporate organisation as explanatory principles of custom and right has occurred because it has been usual to assume that the workshop was merely a unit of production. One of the aims of this essay is to begin to go beyond this procedure by situating custom and right within a context in which a great deal more than production in any conventional sense took place within eighteenth-century workshops.[4] For the structure of workshop organisation extended beyond the production of vendible commodities to include a variety of different arrangements concerned with the acquisition of materials, the subcontracting of work, the sale of goods, the negotiation of credit, the hiring of journeymen and the creation and preservation of co-operation between masters and journeymen, men and women, adults and children over the course of time. The imbrication of life and work, the varying imperatives of a substantial number of different time schedules, intersecting with one another and calling for an extended repertoire of modes of negotiation, co-operation or conflict, meant that work itself existed within a context which was not always and not exclusively defined in a monetary way. Thus if money was only one of the terms mediating the relationship between work and wages, many aspects of 'the language of labour' of the eighteenth century, and much of the broader eighteenth-century discourse centred upon the relationship between wealth, manufacture, 'luxury' and 'progress', are likely to be more intelligible in terms of the non-monetarised transactions which endowed the world of urban manufacture with its specific texture, substance and culture.[5] The purpose of this essay is to bring together the concerns of social historians with custom and convention and the older concerns

3 See, for example, A. Farge, *Vivre dans la rue à Paris au XVIIIe siècle* (Paris, 1979), where artisanal culture is situated within the social geography of the public and the private, and W. Sewell, *Work and Revolution in France* (Cambridge, 1980), where the attitudes of artisans are defined primarily in relation to the public discourse of the corporations of the eighteenth century.

4 In this, I have learnt much from P. Bourdieu, *Esquisse d'une théorie de la pratique* (Geneva, 1972), and D. Bertaux and I. Bertaux-Wiame, 'Artisanal Bakery in France: How it Lives and Why it Survives', in F. Bechhofer and B. Elliott (eds.), *The Petite Bourgeoisie* (London, 1981), pp. 155–81.

5 The phrase 'the language of labour' has, of course, been borrowed from Sewell, *Work and Revolution in France*. On the problem of 'luxury' in the eighteenth century, see E. Ross, 'The Debate on Luxury in Eighteenth Century France: A Study in the Language of Opposition to Change', unpublished Ph.D. thesis (University of Chicago, 1975); A. O. Hirschman, *The Passions and the Interests* (Princeton, 1977); J. J. Spengler, *The French Predecessors of Malthus* (Durham, 1942).

of economic historians and historians of the French Revolution with wages and consumption, in order to suggest a way of understanding workshop organisation in the eighteenth century in its own terms, with its own particular logic, imperatives and politics. For if wages and consumption were mediated by custom and convention, then it may be that the well-attested 'stickiness' of eighteenth-century wage rates and their relative unresponsiveness to price movements can be approached from a different direction. It may be that what was 'fluid' in the eighteenth century was not so much the wage rate itself as the nebula of other transactions, carried out in the interstices of production, whose existence was intrinsic to the maintenance and cohesion of workshop organisation.

I

Fifty years have passed since the publication of C. E. Labrousse's monumental *Esquisse du mouvement des prix et des revenus en France au XVIIIᵉ siècle*.[6] Its examination of the relationship between price movements and the distribution of income in eighteenth-century France has made it possible to define many of the forces shaping the development of French society before the Revolution. Nowhere in that great work, however, was Labrousse more prudent and more tentative than in his discussion of the wage. The series which he presented were, 'et de beaucoup, les moins sûres de toutes celles dont nous avions usé'.[7] They made it possible, he wrote, 'de calculer, très approximativement, le salaire moyen des grandes périodes 1726–1741 et 1771–1789'.[8] Consequently, 'les résultats obtenus sont faiblement significatifs', and were retained, 'simplement à titre provisoire'.[9] The same tone of caution prevailed in Labrousse's brief discussion of wage movements in the more recent *Histoire économique et sociale de la France*.[10]

Others however, have subsequently been more confident. 'The journeyman ... found his prospects of advancement declining at a time when wage increases were failing to keep pace with the cost of living', writes Norman Hampson.[11] 'Pour autant qu'on en puisse juger', reports Michel Vovelle, 'l'accroissement médiocre du salaire nominal ... ne couvre pas la montée séculaire du prix des denrées'.[12]

6 C. E. Labrousse, *Esquisse du mouvement des prix et des revenus en France au XVIIIᵉ siècle* (Paris, 1933).
7 *Ibid.*, p. 466 ('by far the least certain of all those that have been used').
8 *Ibid.*, p. 485 ('to calculate, very approximately, average wage rates during the two long periods 1726–41 and 1771–1789').
9 *Ibid.*, p. 486 ('the results are of limited significance' and were retained 'only provisionally').
10 C. E. Labrousse and F. Braudel, *Histoire économique et sociale de la France*, II (Paris, 1970), 487–97.
11 N. Hampson, *A Social History of the French Revolution* (London, 1963), p. 20.
12 M. Vovelle, *La Chute de la monarchie* (Paris, 1972), pp. 61–2 ('For as much as can be judged, the feeble increase in the nominal wage did not match the secular rise in the price of foodstuffs').

'The two closing decades of the ancien régime were marked ... by a rise of 65 per cent in the price of grain set against wage increases of a mere 22 per cent', states Olwen Hufton.[13] 'Quant aux salariés, pas de problème: ils furent perdants au XVIIIe siècle', concludes Michel Morineau. 'Les salaires nominaux ne progressèrent, en effet, que de 22%, incapables de rattraper les prix de sorte que les salaires réels chutèrent d'environ 25%.'[14] Over the years, the prudence of the great economic historian has given way to an assured and rather misleading precision which, as we have been reminded recently, is not based upon any new research. 'So little is known about wages and output among early modern workers', Robert Darnton has written, that comparisons between the earnings of workers employed by the Société Typographique of Neuchâtel, which he has studied, and those of printing workers in France are impossible: 'The labor history of the Old Régime remains too underdeveloped to provide comparisons with the rich material in Neuchatel.'[15]

It is thus worth recalling the tone of prudence and caution which Labrousse adopted in presenting the results of his research. For the *meaning* of the figures which he collected over fifty years ago remains far from clear. Since the nineteenth century it has been usual to think of the wage as the monetary equivalent of 'the necessities and conveniences' of life required by workers to, as Ricardo put it, 'subsist and perpetuate their race'.[16] The size of the wage and the amount of money earned over a given period has been used to calculate how much workers were able to spend on food, drink, clothing, housing and other articles of consumption. This is the perspective underlying the comments of the historians cited above. In the eighteenth century, however, a moralising discourse, centred upon the relationship between wage rates and the 'luxury' and 'debauchery' of working people, allowed for little discussion of the relationship between income and expenditure measured in purely monetary terms. Restif de la Bretonne's remark about the destructive effects of 'la chèreté de la main d'oeuvre' upon a Parisian population which, 'si elle peut gagner son nécessaire en trois jours, elle ne travaille que trois jours, et se débauche les quatre autres',[17] echoes a long tradition of mercantilist discourse and reiterates one of the commonplaces

13 O. Hufton, *The Poor of Eighteenth Century France: 1750–1789* (London, 1974), p. 16.
14 M. Morineau, 'Trois contributions au Colloque de Göttingen', in E. Hinrichs *et al.*, *Vom Ancien Régime zur Französischen Revolution* (Göttingen, 1978), p. 377 ('As regards wage-earners, there is no problem: they lost out during the eighteenth century. Nominal wages rose by a mere 22% and were thus unable to keep up with prices, so that real wages fell by about 25%').
15 R. C. Darnton, *The Business of Enlightenment* (Princeton, 1979), p. 219.
16 D. Ricardo, *The Principles of Political Economy and Taxation* (Pelican edn, 1971), p. 115.
17 N. E. Restif de la Bretonne, *Les Nuits de Paris* (U. G. E. edn, Paris, 1963), p. 127 ('I contemplated the terrible inconveniences arising from the dearness of labour' for a populace which, 'if it can earn what it needs in three days, only works for three days and spends the other four in debauchery').

of the complaints made by Parisian master artisans in disputes with their journeymen.[18] The persistence of such comment in the eighteenth century seems somewhat paradoxical in the light of the findings of Labrousse and the statements by his successors. This essay is an attempt to understand that paradox.

One way of doing so would be to invert the terms of the paradox and initiate a debate upon 'the standard of living' in the eighteenth century. This is most emphatically not what is at issue in this essay. Instead its purpose is to suggest that the assumption that *wages* were the means of acquiring 'the necessities and conveniences' of life has had rather anachronistic consequences. The most obvious has been the procedure customarily followed by historians in computing real wages by multiplying nominal wage rates by a notional number of days worked and setting the result against the price of a certain bundle of goods. For a number of reasons, it is likely that some of 'the necessities and conveniences' of life existed in forms which were either non-monetised or were only indirectly related to the rhythms of productive work in eighteenth-century Paris. Money wages paid for work done or time spent working were not the only means available for the acquisition of 'the necessities and conveniences' of life. It may thus be possible to understand the paradox between the eighteenth-century concern with *débauche* and the twentieth-century discovery of falling real wages, once it is recognised that eating, drinking, housing and other forms of consumption were not exclusively predicated upon the wage. The moralising discourse of the eighteenth century may mean rather more if the money wage is taken out of the context of necessity in which it was placed by Ricardo in the early nineteenth century. It may indeed have fitted into an economy of, for want of a better term, 'luxury', in so far as 'necessity' was, to varying and conflictual degrees, provided for by other means.

II

The largest concentration of waged workers in eighteenth-century France inhabited Paris. If, as the author of a *Tableau général du commerce* published in 1789 put it, the capital, 'considéré comme ville de fabrique... ne peut soutenir aucune comparaison avec Lyon, Rouen etc.', the sheer size of the city meant that it housed a labouring population of between 200 000 and 400 000 men, women

18 On this mercantilist tradition, see E. A. Furniss, *The Position of the Laborer in a System of Nationalism* (New York, 1919) and P. Mathias, *The Transformation of England* (London, 1979), Ch. 8. On its counterpart in the rhetoric of the Parisian corporations, see S. Kaplan, 'Réflexions sur la police du monde du travail', *Revue Historique*, 529 (1979), 17–77. Turgot's abolition of the corporations in 1776 gave rise to a flood of *mémoires* from the guilds couched in this vein: see B. N. MS Joly de Fleury 462, *passim*.

and children.[19] Employment was either of the seasonal, labouring sort or was to be found in the many trades whose products were, in large measure, consumed by the inhabitants of the Marais, Saint-Germain-des-Prés and the expanding *faubourgs* beyond the Chaussée d'Antin. Paris was not a great exporter of manufactured commodities, as were some of the great provincial centres. Its economy was grounded upon the expenditure of its noble and bourgeois *rentier* population on the one hand, and upon the general demand for housing, clothing, transport, fuel and food on the other. Together they provided work for one of the largest concentrations of waged workers in eighteenth-century Europe.

The rates at which this great mass of people was paid are not difficult to find. The figures can be retrieved from the scattered surviving wage books housed in the Archives de la Ville de Paris or from the surviving accounts of hospitals or one or other of the *manufactures royales*.[20] Thus, towards the end of the *ancien régime*, a skilled mason was paid between 40 and 50 *sous* a day, as were stonecutters, carpenters and quarrymen, while builders' labourers worked for between 20 and 35 *sous* a day.[21] The examples could be multiplied and some rough estimate of earnings could be calculated, as Labrousse did in 1933.

Journeymen themselves, however, could be remarkably vague when asked to state how much they were paid. An engraver on wood, who was arrested on suspicion of theft in 1788 and, since he was found to have over 30 *livres* in coin in his possession, was asked how much he was paid, replied

qu'il ne sait pas combien il gagne, que le Sr Nique entrepreneur des batiments de la Reine à Saint-Cloud (his employer) luy donne tantôt douze francs, tantôt un louis, et que hier il luy a donné deux louis qu'il a demandés, sur quoi il a donné douze francs à sa femme avec laquelle il est parti de Saint-Cloud aujourd'hui.[22]

There were a number of reasons why this vagueness should have been caused by more than an urgent need to explain possession of a relatively large sum of money to a police official. Together they suggest a perspective upon the money wage rate which implies that its relationship to earnings was more complex than is customarily assumed.

19   J. Kaplow, *The Names of Kings* (New York, 1972); S. Kaplan, 'Réflexions sur la police': the best-documented estimates of the working population of eighteenth-century Paris remain L. Cahen, 'La Population ouvrière de Paris au milieu du XVIIIᵉ siècle', *Revue de Paris* (1 September 1919) and F. Braesch, 'Essai de statistique de la population ouvrière de Paris vers 1791', *La Révolution française*, 63 (1912), 289–321.
20   A.V.P.D⁵B⁶, *dossiers des faillites*. See also Y. Durand, 'Recherches sur les salaires des maçons à Paris au XVIIIᵉ siècle', *Revue d'Histoire Economique et Sociale*, 44 (1966), 468–80; C. Pris, *La Manufacture des glaces de Saint-Gobain, 1665–1830* (Lille, 1975).
21   Kaplow, *Names of Kings*, p. 53. For other examples, see the works cited in the previous note.
22   A. N. Y 11 283 (26-2-1788) ('that he does not know how much he earns, that Sr Nique, building contractor to the Queen at Saint-Cloud, sometimes gives him twelve *francs*, sometimes one *louis*, and that yesterday he gave him two *louis* as he had requested. He gave twelve *francs* of this to his wife, with whom he has left Saint-Cloud today').

The money rate has an intrinsic clarity. It suggests a transaction: the payment of an agreed amount for a certain quantity of time spent working or, in the case of piece-rates, of things produced. It suggests too that the transaction in question was one involving two figures: the journeyman or labourer and the master. Closer examination, however, reveals a more elaborately structured transaction, in which other figures make their appearance alongside those of master and journeyman. On the journeyman's side can be found the often under-recorded presence of members of the family or less skilled assistants and mates. In 1741 the *maîtres imprimeurs en taille douce* prohibited their journeymen from taking on apprentices, since 'par la même supercherie ces mêmes compagnons fassent travailler de la même profession leurs femmes, filles et celles d'autres personnes'.[23] Since printers on copper plate were usually paid by the piece, the practice was probably a means of increasing earnings by printing more engravings. In other cases additional workers were employed on the journeyman's own account. In the building trades, builders' labourers were usually engaged by journeymen at the Place de Grève and depended upon them for their wage.[24] Women employed in the hatting trade were also paid by the journeymen with whom they worked.[25] Apprentices too worked alongside of those who had served their time and, in certain trades, could be a source of additional income for the journeymen concerned. According to the printer Nicolas Contat, many apprentice printers were discouraged from remaining in the trade because of the hostility shown to them by journeymen. Those who managed to succeed, 'se mettent à la presse en intéressant un ouvrier avec qui ils travaillent et à qui ils donnent tant par jour'.[26]

These examples suggest that it may be instructive to think of the wage within a context similar to that described by Chayanov in his *Theory of Peasant Economy*.[27] The size and distribution of earnings would then have varied in terms of the position of journeymen within a familial cycle. At the least, it is clear that age had some bearing upon earnings. Its importance was apparent in the

23 A. N. AD XI 19 (23-10-1741) ('in a similar spirit of presumption, these same journeymen give work to their wives, daughters and those of other individuals').
24 A. N. Y 15 775 (29-9-1740); Y 15 842 (13-5-1770); 0'487, fol. 758 (17-10-1776).
25 J. A. Nollet, *L'Art de faire des chapeaux* (Paris, 1765), p. 12.
26 G. Barber (ed.), *Anecdotes typographiques* (1762), Oxford Bibliographical Society (1980), p. 37 ('begin work at the press by involving one of the workers, to whom they give so much a day').
27 A. Y. Chayanov, *Theory of Peasant Economy* (Irwin, 1966). This, of course, would imply a household economy based upon the income of men, women and children at different stages in the family cycle, and a variety of modes of living and negotiating these stages. The question has not been investigated very fully, but see N. Z. Davis, 'Women in the *Arts Mécaniques* in Sixteenth Century Lyon', in *Lyon et l'Europe: mélanges d'histoire offerts à Richard Gascon* (Lyons, 1980), pp. 139–67; O. Hufton, 'Women in the Family Economy in 18th Century France', *French Historical Studies*, 9 (1975), 1–22; *idem*, 'Women, Work and Marriage in 18th Century France', in R. B. Outhwaite (ed.), *Marriage and Society: Studies in the Social History of Marriage* (London, 1981).

divisions which arose among journeymen locksmiths during a dispute with their masters in 1746. Several hundred journeymen met on three occasions in the late summer of that year to discuss whether to organise a general stoppage of work as part of a campaign against an *arrêt* of the Parlement of Paris obtained by their masters to force journeymen to register at the corporation's *bureau* before finding work. Those in favour of the stoppage were the younger, usually single, men, while those opposed to it were older and often married. 'Il y a encore esté question ... de ne point travailler de la semaine', one witness stated, describing an assembly at the Petit Charonne:

Ce qui a été contre le sentiment ... d'une vingtaine qui étoient des anciens compagnons, à quoy les jeunes leur disoient ... que c'étoit à cause qu'ils avoient de bonnes boutiques qu'ils ne vouloient pas qu'on cessât.[28]

One of the older men who did stop work, a 43-year-old journeyman named Louis Chevalier, stated that he had stopped because his employer had refused to give his, Chevalier's, son the customary *pâté de veille* offered to journeymen when the nights began to draw in and working by candlelight became necessary. According to Chevalier, the right was worth 30 *sous* and was one to which both he and his son, with whom he worked, were entitled.[29]

By definition – if not in fact – the condition of a journeyman was a transitory one, an interval between apprenticeship and the formal independence associated with full membership of a guild. Although it is unlikely that many journeymen were able to become masters, it is still probable that a complex series of co-operative and initiatory arrangements co-existed with the practicalities of work itself. There was an interdependence between the mechanisms of production and the cycle of familial reproduction which varied according to the particular circumstances of individual journeymen and the different opportunities for making the transition from apprentice to master provided by the micro-society of each familial network. Thus the relationship between individual wage rates and aggregate earnings was mediated by relations between men and women, husbands and wives, fathers and children at different moments in the family cycle.[30]

---

28 A. N. Y 13 751 (13-9-1746) ('It was again a question of not working ... This was contrary to the sentiment of two dozen who were *anciens compagnons*, to whom the young ones replied ... that it was because they had good shops that they did not want there to be a stoppage').

29 The custom is described in the early nineteenth century by the former *compagnon menuisier* Agricol Perdiguier, *Mémoires d'un compagnon*, ed. Alain Faure (Paris, 1977), p. 252. According to Perdiguier, the custom was still observed in Chartres, but had been replaced by a payment of 3 *francs* in Bordeaux, as presumably it had already been in Paris during the eighteenth century.

30 See the works cited above (note 27). Some sense of the complexities of this relatively invisible world is to be found in Balzac's novels *César Birotteau* and *La Maison du Chat-qui-Pelote*. See also R. Phillips, *Family Breakdown in Late Eighteenth Century France* (Oxford and London, 1980), pp. 96–101.

It is also likely that the figure of the isolated master craftsman is equally misleading. Much has been made of the dispersed and artisanal character of manufacture in eighteenth-century Paris. The multitude of small workshops, the generally small number of journeymen employed by each master, the implied intimacy of relationships between journeymen and their masters, all suggest a certain particularity, a myriad tiny worlds in which bargains would be struck and agreements made.[31] Too frequently, however, these conclusions have been produced by simple arithmetic, by dividing the number of journeymen by the number of masters recorded in the administrative records of the Revolutionary period.[32] Consequently, far too little attention has been paid to the manner in which the technical division of labour cut across these apparently self-contained units of production. After the collapse of a small hatting enterprise in 1775, one of the partners visited their various workshops to make a final inventory. He visited six establishments – on the Rue du Grand Heurleur, the Rue Saint-Martin, the Rue des Grenetiers and the Rue Philippeaux – each responsible for one of the stages in the division of labour involved in hatting.[33] The business of coach making, which involved carpenters, joiners, wheelwrights, locksmiths, painters and decorators, or braidmaking – with its weavers, gold-wire drawers, embroiderers and seamstresses – provides sufficient indication of the manner in which the apparent fragmentation of units of production fails to reflect the essential unity of the product as it passed through an elaborately structured division of labour organised around the subcontracting of particular processes.

Far too little is known about the circuits through which primary materials passed before becoming manufactured commodities for any statement about the material structure of manufacture in eighteenth-century Paris to carry much weight. In those branches of manufacture in which the costs of raw materials required a substantial outlay, the fragmentation of production was undoubtedly complemented by a centralised structure of ownership. One large gauze maker in 1790, for example, employed 2II *ouvriers*, 135 *dévideuses* and *ourdisseuses* and 84 *découpeuses* and *brodeuses* scattered all over Paris.[34] Even in trades with

31 See, for example, A. Soboul, *Les Sans-Culottes parisiens en l'An II*, 2nd edn (Paris, 1962), pp. 433–9; G. Rudé, *The Crowd in the French Revolution* (London, 1959), Ch. 11. The same somewhat limited perspective is to be found in R. Monnier, *Le Faubourg Saint-Antoine (1789–1815)* (Paris, 1981) and H. Burstim, 'Conflitti sul lavoro e protesta annonaria a Parigi alla fine dell' Ancien Régime', *Studi Storici*, 19 (1978), 735–75.

32 The practice goes back to the classic study by F. Braesch, ('Essai de statistique'). The only historians to have attempted to discover something of the internal organisation of the Parisian trades have been historians of furniture. See P. Verlet, *L'Art du meuble à Paris au XVIIIᵉ siècle* (Paris, 1968); S. Erikson, *Louis Delanois, menuisier en sièges (1731–1792)* (Paris, 1968); *idem*, *Early Neo-Classicism in France* (London, 1974), and the papers presented to the conference on 'Möbelskunst und Lüxusmarkt im 18. Jahrhundert', Nuremberg, 1981.

33 AVP D⁵B⁶ 3664. The classic discussion of the organisation of manufacture is K. Marx, *Capital*, Vol. I, Ch. 14.

34 A. N. F³⁰ 137 d. Dumas Descombes (I am grateful to M. Claude Maire for this reference).

relatively limited costs, masters and journeymen could be physically separated, so that the attendant fragmentation of units of production may have concealed less visible networks of ownership and subcontracted work. In the tailoring and shoemaking trades, much work was carried out in *chambrées* dispersed all over the capital.[35] The role of the *marchands merciers* in the organisation of subcontracted work awaits its historian.

The elaborate networks of subcontracted work involved in building, transport and the clothing trades cut across corporate boundaries and meant that it is likely that many masters were drawn into more or less extended chains of extra-economic activity which ensured the supply of raw materials, credit, banking functions (for the discounting of paper for cash was carried out by a wide variety of individuals with access to funds: *notaires, marchands de vin*, the *jurés* of the corporations, as well as *négociants*), recommendations, clients and, where necessary, journeymen for particular pieces of work. The rhythms of this substantial mass of para-economic activity were not necessarily the same as those of production, and a master artisan was therefore obliged to contend with a variety of different schedules of activity either directly or indirectly related to production. Unless this fact is borne in mind, it is very difficult to understand the elaborate rituals of *sociabilité* of eighteenth-century artisans. The *fabrique* of the parish, the institutions of the *quartier*, the *confrérie*, the corporation and the *cabaret* were not just the terrain upon which a certain public persona might be established; they were also the basis of *living* a trade, a reservoir of actual or potential opportunities to be maintained or developed, and the context in which work itself was, from a master's point of view, situated.

All this suggests that a degree of caution is required before assuming that small, dispersed units of production implied a correspondingly direct relationship between journeymen and their masters. Instead it is likely that the relationship between masters and journeymen was mediated by an indeterminate number of *clercs, commis, premiers garçons* or – in the case of printing – *prôtes* whose business it was to ensure that materials were distributed, that quantities of finished articles were weighed or inspected and that work was carried out with a degree of regularity and speed. More importantly, masters' wives, daughters or servants were crucial intermediaries between journeymen and their employers. The few surviving autobiographies produced by eighteenth-century Parisian journeymen or former journeymen – Restif de la Bretonne's *Monsieur Nicolas*, Nicolas Contat's *Anecdotes typographiques* and Jacques Ménétra's *Mémoires* – exaggerated and fanciful as they may be, indicate that the re-

---

35   A. N. Y 15 345 (9-6-1745). In the case of the tailoring trade, the practice led to work being given out to *garçons fripiers* and to a strike by journeymen tailors in August 1789: E. Lacroix (ed.), *Actes de la commune de Paris pendant la Révolution* (Paris, 1894–1942), 1st Series, Vol. I, pp. 265–70.

lationship between journeymen and their masters was governed as much by the silent presence of wives and daughters as by that of their husbands and fathers.[36] Their presence formed a zone in which power was translated into an erotic and sexual idiom, where women represented the material possibilities arising from sexual encounters between social unequals within the world of the workshop. The ambivalent relationship between journeymen and the wives and daughters of master artisans was reflected in the variety of *plaintes* made to the *Commissaires* of the Châtelet.[37] It was the product of a situation in which the possibilities of belonging to a trade and becoming a master lay as much within the sphere of personal acquaintance as in the opportunities of the market. In this sense, an extra-productive sphere encroached upon the sphere of production and meant that the contractual relationship represented by the wage was affected by the possibility of other – equally contractual – relationships of a non-monetary sort.

Even in the directly productive sphere, the presence of intermediaries represented an additional element in the relationship between journeymen and their masters. Complaints that *commis* or *premiers garçons* had appropriated money intended as wages were common and suggest something of the underworld of irregular fees and informal payments which coexisted alongside of the wage.[38] In the textile trades, deductions were a common occurrence. In April 1776 a master gauze maker lodged a complaint against a *compagnon gazier* and his wife for failing to repay the sum of 27 *livres* (#) which they had borrowed. He also produced a statement of account indicating that the journeyman owed him money for other reasons: 'je reconois avoir recu ... 6 one et demie d'ouvrage à 14s ... fait 4# 11s, surquoy il me doit 2 mois de place de metié et chaufage ... fait 6# 8s'.[39] The defaulting journeyman had also been employed by another master until the middle of January 1776 and owed him the sum of 10 *livres*. When he left, his new master paid off the debt.

36 N. E. Restif de la Bretonne, *Monsieur Nicolas* (repr. Paris, 1959); for Contat's *Anecdotes*, see note 26; a printed version of the glazier Jacques Ménétra's *Mémoires* (located in the B.H.V.P. MS 678) was published in 1982: see Daniel Roche (ed.), *Jacques-Louis Ménétra, Journal de ma vie* (Paris, 1982). On the role of the wives or daughters of master artisans in the surveillance rather than the organisation of activities in the 'masculine' trades, see N. Z. Davis, 'Women in the *Arts Mécaniques*'. According to L. S. Mercier, *Tableau de Paris*, IX (Paris, 1782–8), 'la femme est l'âme d'une boutique'.

37 Frequently, when master artisans made formal complaints about their journeymen to one of the *Commissaires*, the final – and presumably most damaging charge – was to have 'gravely insulted' their wives. In 1769, for example, a *garçon tourneur* was accused by his master of organising a *cabale* which had left him without any journeymen and of announcing 'que la femme du plaignant etoit une f ... p ... et qu'il l'avoit foutu pour huit sols': A. N. Y 12986ᵃ (23-8-1769). I hope to publish an essay on workshop organisation and the position of masters' wives within that organisation shortly.

38 For one example, in the quarries of Paris, see A. N. Y 13 693 (28-7-1784, 2-8-1784, 16-9-1784); B. N. 4º Fm 35344. See also A. N. Y 11008 (7-3-1767).

39 A. N. Y 11 267ᵃ (13-4-1776) ('I recognise the receipt of 6 and a half *aulnes* of work at 14s ... making 4 # 11s, from which he owes me 2 months on the loom and heating ... making 6 # 8s'). I am grateful to David Garrioch for this reference.

This example suggests that there may have been something of a gap between the sums of money represented by the wage rate and the sums of money actually paid out. Not only might the wage rate serve as a measure against which deductions could be calculated; it was also used to arrive at the amounts paid out in the complicated settling of accounts which occurred on pay-days. Saturdays or, more usually, Sundays were the days on which *la paie ouvrière* took place. Intervals between payments varied, and weekly, fortnightly or monthly payments were all current, often in the same trade. It is clear, however, from the variations in the amounts which journeymen were paid from week to week or fortnight to fortnight, that payments were rarely a simple multiple of the wage rate by the number of days worked or the quantity of things produced.[40] Instead, payments were usually preceded by a preliminary settling of accounts. This transaction occurred because many journeymen expected and received an advance before beginning work. Masters might be required to make a cash advance or to pay off debts due to the journeyman's previous employer. The practice was recognised in the statutes of many corporations, although they usually stipulated a maximum of between 10 and 30 *livres* in order to limit competition between masters for journeymen.[41] The resultant fusion of credit and wage payments was central to the relationship between journeymen and their masters in eighteenth-century Paris. If the

---

40   See, for example, A.V.P. D⁵B⁶ 2804 *rolle des ouvriers pour Fillion maître-charpentier*, 1771–3 (wrongly described in the inventory as a tailor). Between 4 and 31 October 1772 he employed 11 journeymen. They were paid as follows:

	No. of days	Amount (in *livres, sous, deniers*)		
Poitevin	23 1/2	52	17	6
Maillard	23 1/2	32	8	
Langevin	23 1/3	39	3	4
Bourbonnais	23 1/3	37	19	4
Champagne	23 1/3	39	13	4
Lefrère	23	39	2	
Le Gascon	22	37	8	
Condon	18	32	8	
Langevin	17 1/2	29	15	
Langevin La Culotte rouge	17 1/2	29	15	
Beaujolais	12	20	8	

The rate at which these journeymen were paid was 34 *sous* a day; the variations were undoubtedly the results of deductions or advances, since the amount of time spent working has been recorded.

41   Kaplan, 'Réflexions sur la police', p. 54. The statutes of many of the corporations can be found in the series F of the B. N. and the Collection Rondonneau of the A. N.

practice allowed masters the possibility of regulating journeymen's mobility and offered them grounds for legal action if journeymen left before completing their work, it also ensured that the income which journeymen received was made up of irregular amounts and bore little direct relationship to the quantity of work which they carried out.

The apparent stability of wage rates during the eighteenth century is thus somewhat misleading, since the size of the advance was very much more elastic and depended considerably upon the balance of forces between journeymen and their masters. Many of the labour disputes of eighteenth-century Paris turned not upon the wage rate *per se*, but upon the relationship between amounts advanced and the rate at which these sums would be worked off. For if masters had an interest in making advances in order to retain their journeymen, journeymen had an equal interest in exercising as much control as possible over both the size of the advance and the rate at which it was covered by completed work. There was also the possibility, where journeymen were able to find work for themselves, of advances being transferred from master to master. In the summer of 1748, for example, the corporation of hatters complained that their journeymen,

s'étant ingérés depuis quelques tems de se placer les uns les autres et de ne pas souffrir qu'un ouvrier travaille chez un maître ou ils ne l'ont pas placé eux-mêmes. Lorsqu'il arrive qu'un maître blesse quelqu'un de leurs pretendus privilèges et refuse de leur avancer autant d'argent qu'ils en demandent, ils obligent leurs camarades de sortir chez ledit maître et refusent de lui en placer d'autres.[42]

On 8 July all 23 journeymen employed by a master hatter on the Rue Saint-Sauveur had walked out when four of them had been refused an advance of 100 *livres* each, even though the four had worked previously for the same master and had left without completing their month's work. The stoppages spread to most of the workshops in the trade until the exemplary arrest of a number of journeymen.[43]

III

The practice of giving advances meant that it is likely that many journeymen received an income which was only indirectly related to the rhythms of work carried out. This ensured that income was spread over periods in which, for various reasons – seasonal, liturgical or otherwise – work itself was probably irregular. It is often said that earnings in the eighteenth century were limited

42   A. P. P. Fonds Lamoignon 38, fol. 436 ('have recently organised things in such a way as to place each other and will not permit a worker to work for a master unless they have placed him there themselves. If a master should encroach upon any of their so-called privileges and refuse to advance them as much money as they demand, they compel their comrades to walk out and refuse to place any other workers there').

43   *Ibid.*

because of the existence of a large number of days on which no work was done. 'In computing "effective" earnings', writes Rudé, 'allowance has been made for the numerous unpaid Feast Days of the *ancien régime* . . . assumed to number 111 per year.'[44] The mode of wage payment in the eighteenth century suggests that computations of this sort may have very limited significance. Advances, together with the system of settling accounts at relatively regular intervals, indicate that payments were made as much to ensure that work *would* be carried out as in recognition of work that had already been carried out. The wage, in this sense, was a device among a number of others, both monetary and non-monetary, designed to preserve a degree of stability and continuity in the relationship between journeymen and their masters. There is also evidence indicating that journeymen *were* paid for feast days as well as working days. In 1751 a master baker complained that his two *garçons* had ruined his dough by mixing ashes and excrement into it after he had dismissed them for failing to keep regular hours. It transpired, however, that the sabotage had been caused by the master's failure to pay his *garçons* when he had promised to. The *juridiction consulaire* of Paris ordered him to pay one of the two *garçons* 20 *livres* 11 *sous* owed on the sum of 140 *livres* 11 *sous* earned during 35 weeks 2 days' employment at the rate of 4 *livres* a week. Although the rate was low (because the *garçons* were also fed and housed) the amount was calculated on the basis of payments for every day, whether it was a working day or not.[45] Another *garçon boulanger*, arrested in 1751 on suspicion of begging, stated that 'il gagne par jour aux environs de trente sols et que cela suffit pour le nourrir, et qu'il le gagne les jours de feste et dimanches comme les jours ouvriers'.[46]

Bakers were not the only workers in this position. For much of the eighteenth century, journeymen farriers were employed and paid by the month, irrespective of Sundays and holidays. Towards 1770, however, their masters appear to have succeeded in imposing a day rate. This led to a series of disputes, ostensibly over the size of the rate but actually over the question of whether the day rate was sufficient to cover non-working days. In the last of these to occur during the eighteenth century, in 1791, the master farriers still claimed that payments were made for '82 jours de repos, y compris les deux fêtes de Saint-Eloy et sans compter les fêtes de paroisse'.[47]

In some trades too it was the custom for journeymen to receive an income when they were ill or injured. One of the men involved in a dispute with the

---

44   G. Rudé, 'Prices, Wages and Popular Movements in Paris during the French Revolution', in G. Rudé (ed.), *Paris and London in the Eighteenth Century* (London, 1970), p. 167. See also *idem*, *The Crowd in the French Revolution*, p. 21.

45   A. N. Y 12416 (11-1-1751).

46   *Ibid.* (21-1-1751) ('he earns about 30 *sols* a day, which is enough to feed him, and earns it for feast days and Sundays as well as working days').

47   A. N. AD XI 65, *Précis pour les maréchaux de Paris* (4-6-1791).

administrators of the quarries of Paris in 1784 stated that he was paid at the rate of 40 *sous* a day 'pendant qu'il travailloit et moitié pour les jours qu'il étoit malade ou blessé'. Another of the quarrymen stated that the practice applied to all the workers in the trade.[48] Some journeymen also expected to be paid during periods when there was no work, when the term of employment which they had agreed with a master had not yet expired. In 1744 a journeyman wheelwright succeeded in forcing his master to pay 18 *livres* due to him for the period of 8 days' notice at 45 *sous* a day which was customary in the trade before a journeyman could be dismissed. The case was taken up by the officials of the corporation, who argued that the practice was incompatible with the rhythms of production because it would prevent masters from taking on or dismissing journeymen as and when they needed to. Accordingly, the *lieutenant-général de police*, de Marville, overturned the sentence in 1745. His decision provoked an unsuccessful appeal by 60 or 80 *compagnons charrons*, who were then accused of organising a *cabale*.[49]

The practice of payment by a combination of advances and settling of accounts, together with the indications that an indeterminate number of workers received an income even when they were not at work, tends to suggest that the money rates of the eighteenth century meant something rather different from the modern wage. It is well known too that money was frequently only a component of many labourers' and journeymen's incomes, and that non-monetary rights were a recognised, if negotiable, part of the terrain upon which manufacture was situated. A journeyman wheelwright arrested in 1763 with a sack of wood in his possession, informed the *sergeant de la garde* that the pieces were only 'des copeaux'. His employer, a widow, testified that the journeyman 'a emporté de chez elle un soir de la fin d' octobre dernier, comme il est d'usage, plusieurs morceaux de bois et de fer qu'elle lui avoit donné et pour raison de quoi il a été arreté... Elle le connaît pour un honnête homme.'[50] The right to take *copeaux* was something which all those working on wood – carpenters, joiners and wheelwrights – expected and which, despite attempts to replace it by a monetary payment, was exercised throughout the eighteenth century.[51] Labourers responsible for the circulation of primary commodities – wood, coal, wine, corn and flour – enjoyed other material forms of income. Women working at the flour

48 A. N. Y 13 693 (2-8-1784).
49 B. N. MS fr. 8090, fols. 49ff and 282ff.
50 A. N. Y 11 580ᵇ (20 and 27-10-1763) ('one evening, towards the end of last October, carried away, as is the custom, several pieces of wood and iron which she had given him, and for which he has been arrested... She knows him to be an honest man').
51 There was a substantial conflict between master and journeymen carpenters over the question between 1698 and 1700. In 1786 a dispute over the same question indicates that journeymen continued to enjoy their right. See Kaplan, 'Réflexions sur la police', and my forthcoming essay on 'Labour Disputes in 18th Century Paris'.

market 'faisoient le metier de plotteuse, qui est de prendre dans les jalles at même dans les sacs de farine des poignées de farine'.[52] In 1755 coal heavers working on the *quais* and the Place de l'Isle Louvier were prohibited from collecting the charcoal left on barges after they had been unloaded on the grounds that the right had been abused:

Les garçons de la pelle qui ont la faculté de recevoir lesdits fonds des bateaux seulement en payement de la totalité ou de portion de leurs salaires ne sont plus depuis longtemps dans l'habitude d'user de cette faculté, mais les achettent conjointement avec les officiers porteurs de charbons et les regratiers directement de leurs marchands ou de leurs facteurs et en privent ainsy [les] bourgeois et artisans.[53]

Like many labourers, including the *forts de la Halle*, coal heavers worked in gangs or *bandes* and were paid collectively. The money wage which they earned was the basis of elaborate networks of redistribution of a part of the commodities which they handled, involving other members of their *bandes*, officials and members of their own families. Money wages and customary rights complemented one another in a situation in which the line dividing work from the acquisition of supplies for the myriad forms of micro-commerce of the labouring poor was very indistinct.

Many journeymen expected to be fed and housed. Ten journeymen cutlers arrested in November 1748 and accused by their masters of organising a combination or *cabale*, replied by denouncing the officials of the corporation:

Ce sont ceux qui n'ont pas d'ouvrage, qui sont plus souvent dans les tavernes que dans leurs boutiques, lesquels prennent des compagnons non pas pour travailler mais pour garder leurs boutiques, qui les nourrissent mal et les payent encore plus mal. Tous maistres qui travaillent qui payent et nourissent bien leurs compagnons n'en manquent jamais.[54]

A *garçon chartier* arrested in January 1752 stated that he had left his employer 'parce qu'il n'étoit pas content de la nourriture qu'il luy donnoit'.[55] Rights of this sort could become a source of tension in certain trades. In 1751 the nail makers and ironmongers complained that the practice had led to ill-feeling among masters, since

52 A. P. P. Fonds Lamoignon 28, fol. 312 (16-2-1725) (The word 'plotteuse' is untranslatable; the women 'took handfuls of flour from the sacks and bags').
53 *Ibid.* 40, fol. 316 (19-6-1755) ('Those who shovel, who have been given the right to take the aforesaid dregs from the boats solely as payment of a part or all of their wages, have long since ceased to make use of this faculty. Instead, together with the coal heavers and petty traders, they buy them directly from merchants or their factors, thus depriving artisans or householders'). On the great variety of forms of micro-commerce among the labouring poor, see in particular Hufton, *The Poor of Eighteenth Century France*. There is a place for a study of the economy of the *quais* of eighteenth-century Paris.
54 A. N. Y 9533; Y 12151 (12-11-1748) ('They are those who have no work, who are more often in inns than their workshops, who take on journeymen to mind the shop rather than work, who feed them badly and pay them even worse. Any master who works, pays and feeds his journeymen well will never be lacking any').
55 A. N. Y 13 760 (31-1-1752) ('because he was not satisfied with the food that he was given').

la methode prise par chacun maître de ladite communauté de nourrir ou donner à souper seulement à leurs compagnons est un abus prejudiciable à toute la communauté... puisque le leger avantage fournit aux maitres le moyen de s'enlever reciproquement leurs compagnons.[56]

The widespread existence of subcontracted work meant that journeymen might be used by masters other than those with whom they had engaged themselves. In these circumstances, the presence or absence of customary non-monetary rights could affect the willingness of journeymen to remain with a particular master.

It is clear that not all of what was received by right was destined solely for personal consumption. One of the issues involved in a protracted series of disputes between journeymen painters and decorators and the Académie de Saint-Luc between 1760 and 1770 was an attempt to end their customary right to take the gold and silver waste left after decorating coaches or apartments, a practice which, according to the corporation, 'occasionne la ruine des maîtres'.[57] The waste had no domestic use and could only have been collected for subsequent sale. Although pieces of wood could be used for fuel, they could also be sold, as was the charcoal collected up by the *garçons de la pelle* working on the quays. Journeymen in the hatting trade were entitled to the rabbit or beaver pelts left once the fur had been removed, and sold them at the rate of 6 *deniers* a pound 'comme mauvaise bourre à quelques selliers'.[58] Hatters were also given hats as an advance on the wage and were accustomed to sell them.[59] In other cases, the right to a part of the product amounted to a right to a part of the product's price. 'Depuis un tems immemorial', stated the *jurés* of the corporation of *pâtissiers en pain d'épices* in 1751,

l'usage de leur communauté est de donner par mois au plus dix livres à chacun compagnon, de les loger, blanchir et nourrir, et dix sols par ecu de vente des marchandises qu'ils debitteront en cette ville et quinze sols par ecu de vente de celles qu'ils debittent dans les campagnes.[60]

They complained that the journeymen were threatening to walk out unless they were paid 12 *livres* a month and a larger share of the value of the goods sold.

The timing of this episode – in October, as work for the major period of sales

---

56 A. P. P. Fonds Lamoignon 40, fol. 135 (2-11-1751) ('the practice adopted by each master in either feeding or only giving dinner to their journeymen is prejudicial to the whole community... because the slight advantage enables some masters to appropriate each others' journeymen'). Among the grievances of quarrymen in dispute with the administrators of the Parisian quarries in 1784 was the withdrawal of their customary *chopine de vin* and *coup d'eau de vie*: A. N. Y 13 693 (2-8-1784).

57 B.A. MS Bastille 12 369.

58 Nollet, *L'Art de faire les chapeaux*, p. 12.

59 A. N. Y 15 352 (29-10-1753); A. P. P. Fonds Lamoignon 38, fols. 436ff.

60 A. N. Y 14 195 (30-10-1751) ('the custom of their community is to give each journeyman 10 *livres* monthly at the latest, to house them, feed them and pay for their laundry, and give them 10 *sols* for each *écu*'s worth of goods which they sell in town and 15 *sols* per *écu* of goods sold in the country').

in January began – is significant. It suggests a general perspective in which the variety of different forms of income associated with the eighteenth-century 'wage' might be situated. Journeymen received an income made up of three elements which coexisted in varying proportions: weekly, fortnightly or monthly payments for work done at an agreed rate; irregular advances which were subsequently accounted for in terms of a certain number of days worked or articles produced; and the revenue produced by a right to a part, or the price of a part, of the final product. In addition, some journeymen also had the right to be fed and housed, and could also expect to receive a number of other, less frequent, customary payments. The *pâté de veille* given to locksmiths, the product of the *quêtes* carried out by journeymen printers among their masters' clients at the beginning of the year, the collections made by butchers and bakers for the carnival before Lent and the fees paid to journeymen farriers by their masters' clients all coexisted, to a greater or lesser extent, with the wage.[61] This combination of a monetary income and non-monetary rights reflected the intrinsic irregularity of the rhythms of artisanal production. From a master's point of view, it created the possibility of a degree of continuity and stability with a nucleus of relatively regularly employed journeymen, to whom others could be added when circumstances required. From a journeyman's point of view, it provided the possibility of a degree of continuity and stability in acquiring 'the necessities and conveniences' of life when work itself could never be guaranteed. At the same time, however, the existence of customary rights introduced an element of rigidity into the relationship between masters and journeymen which a completely monetised relationship would not have allowed. When demand was slack, credit tight or prices high, the existence of non-monetary rights ensured that monetary wage rates remained relatively less responsive to short-term fluctuations. In this sense, eating and drinking or not eating and drinking, being housed or not being housed and the presence or absence of other customary rights were as fundamental to the relationship between journeymen and their masters as was the amount of the wage rate itself. The clear distinction between work, wages and consumption, which is assumed in any calculation of real wages, did not exist in the eighteenth century because consumption itself was not predicated exclusively upon a monetary income.

The nature of artisanal production and the resultant emphasis which it placed

---

61 At the beginning of January 1770, two journeymen spur makers complained that the journeymen of another master had visited their own master's clients and collected 'les étrennes qu'elles sont dans l'usage de donner aux compagnons': A. N. Y 12057 (2-1-1770). On the custom of the *boeuf gras* among butchers, see A. N. Y 11 302 (7-2-1739) and A. Faure, *Paris Carême-Prenant* (Paris, 1978), pp. 128–31. On the implications of these practices, see Bourdieu, *Esquisse*, and G. M. Sider, 'Christmas Mumming and the New Year in Outport Newfoundland', *Past and Present*, 71 (1976), 102–25 and *idem*, 'The Ties that Bind: Culture and Agriculture, Property and Propriety in the Newfoundland Village Fishery', *Social History*, 5 (1980), 1–39.

upon different kinds of flexibility and calculation for both masters and journeymen explains much about the complexity of the systems of payment which existed in the eighteenth century. Masters had their *pratiques*, which were more or less substantial. The orders which came from their clients were irregular, both temporally and quantitatively. The result was a situation in which mobility from job to job and master to master was not uncommon. For many journeymen, work could be no more than a specific task performed for a particular master for a fee. In any year, the number of journeymen employed by a master could fluctuate dramatically from month to month, if not from week to week.[62] A journeyman tailor accused of assaulting the *jurés* of the corporation as they were inspecting his master's workshop in 1730 stated that he had been with his master, Lafond, for six months: 'Il y a quelque fois chez ledit Lafond quinze garçons, dix, huit et quatre. Sur la fin du mois dernier il n'y avoit que sept ou huit.'[63]

Irregular employment meant recourse to an 'economy of makeshifts' whose boundaries extended well into the ranks of those with apparently fixed occupations and settled trades.[64] A journeyman mason arrested in 1786 for smuggling two parcels of linen through the *barrière* of Saint-Denis readily admitted his offence, explaining

qu'il fait ce metier de fraudeur depuis six ans, que l'été il travaille à son metier de maçon, que l'hyver il gagne sa vie comme il peut, notamment en fraudant comme il nous l'a dit, qu'il sait, comme tout le monde le sait aussi, que du coté de Saint-Denis il y a beaucoup de fraudeurs.[65]

The working population of Paris lived with the permanent problem of maintaining a continuity of income when there was no necessary continuity of work. From their point of view, the business of living was bound up with their capacity to subvert the economy of time embodied by the wage rate and redefine it around their changing economy of needs.

---

62 Fluctuations would obviously have been more marked in trades affected by the seasons. During the year 1772, for example, a *maître-menuisier* recorded payments to between 3 and 21 journeymen or labourers at different times of the year: A. V. P. D⁵B⁶ 5930. The *livre de receptions des ouvrages des ouvriers et leurs payements* of a silk throwster in 1777 indicates a very similar pattern of short-term employment and a high level of turn over: A. V. P. D⁵B⁶ 375. On the mobility of labour in printing, see Robert Darnton, 'A Journeyman's life under the Old Régime', *Princeton Alumni Weekly* (7 Sept. 1981), pp. 13–17.

63 A. N. Y 9532 (9-8-1730).

64 The phrase is from Hufton, *The Poor of Eighteenth Century France*. On the absence of any clear division between the mendicant poor and the stably employed, see A. Farge, 'Le Mendiant, un marginal?...' in *Les Marginaux et les exclus dans l'histoire*, Cahiers Jussieu 5 (U. G. E., Paris, 1979), pp. 312–29.

65 A. N. Y 9535 (27-1-1786) ('that he has been at the trade of defrauding for six years. In summer he works at his trade as a mason; in winter he earns his living as he can, mainly by smuggling as he has said, and that he knows, as much as everyone else does, that there are a great many smugglers in the neighbourhood of Saint-Denis').

IV

Paradoxically this may have meant that the relationship between time and work was more problematic than the wage rate itself. Credit was an essential component of the structure of artisanal production. It mediated the relationship between masters and their suppliers and clients and that between journeymen and their masters. The accumulation of capital was largely a function of the extent to which it was possible to increase the rate at which goods turned over. Thus the way in which time was used determined the frequency with which capital could be turned over. In a situation in which the productivity of labour, in the modern sense, was relatively stable, a great deal of importance was necessarily attached to the length and 'density' of the working day. It is often said, however, that the working day in the age before the factory was largely undefined, a notional *journée* spent at work, rather than a precise quantity of hours: 'ce vieux temps d' artisan, extensible, élastique, fluide comme la lumière, allongé ou reduit suivant les saisons, ce temps du soleil, nonchalant et rêveur'.[66]

In Paris in the eighteenth century however – and probably in any urban trade in which master artisans had to contend with a multiplicity of different schedules of credit – this was not the case. The longer or the more 'dense' the working day, the more rapidly it would be possible to recover advances on wages, be credited with goods produced and endorse promissory notes or bills of exchange to suppliers or other third parties. The morality of industriousness and assiduity which characterised artisanal culture was grounded upon this preoccupation with time and its competing imperatives. Much of the relationship between work and wages was mediated by masters' and journeymen's common recognition of the divergent implications which their respective use of time entailed. Masters could counterpose the virtues of 'travail' and industriousness to the 'friponneries' and idleness of their journeymen; journeymen could counterpose their prowess in a trade to the frequent absence of masters from their *boutiques* in pursuit of clients or credit or both. The morality of industriousness was the medium in which the struggle over the use to which time was put found its expression. As a song circulating among journeymen decorators – 'Sur l'air de Ramponneau' – put it,

> Nous autres compagnons du metier
> qui scavent travailler
> Tous les maistres il faut estimer
> qui scavent nous considerer,
> Mais pour tous les maistres fougeux
> il nous faut mocquer d'eux.[67]

66 Michèle Perrot, *Les Ouvriers en grève* (Paris, 1974), p. 271.
67 A. N. Y 11 345^a (2 and 10-7-1761) ('We journeymen of the trade/who know what work is/esteem

Conflicts over the length of the working day were not, therefore, unusual. In 1720, journeymen curriers were reported to have attempted to impose a reduction of two hours on their day's work.[68] Painters and decorators were expected to work at night and the question of the number of hours involved in this additional *demi-journée* was a source of repeated disputes in the trade.[69] In 1776, journeymen bookbinders stopped work to demand a reduction in the length of the working day from sixteen to fourteen hours when their corporation was merged with the *maîtres papetiers* whose journeymen already enjoyed the shorter day.[70] In what was arguably the first co-ordinated movement among Parisian journeymen, in 1791, masons, carpenters, joiners, *couvreurs* and members of many other trades succeeded in reducing the length of the working day from fourteen to twelve hours, from six in the morning to six in the evening.[71] Time and money were thus closely interrelated. As a journeyman joiner, interrogated for his role in a dispute with the corporation over wage rates, explained in 1749:

ils demandait une égalité dans le payement des ouvrages, c'est à dire il y a de certains ouvrages que les maîtres leur payent ce qu'ils vallent et sur lesquels ils n'ont demandé aucune augmentation, qu'il y en a d'autres qui ne leur sont pas payés ce qu'ils vallent pour le tems qu'ils y employent et sur lesquels ils ont demandé une augmentation.[72]

Yet the relationship between time and money was complicated by the penumbra of customary practices, the variety of subcontracted networks and the irregularity of productive cycles in which both masters and journeymen were imbricated. It is probable therefore that many of the complicated monetary and non-monetary transactions between masters and journeymen were designed to establish forms of labour mobility which responded to the erratic schedules of artisanal production. They formed the ground upon which a degree of co-operation over the competing claims of different time schedules could be established. At the same time, however, the more anonymous processes of capital accumulation and the cycles of different trades called for broader movements of labour of a geographical, seasonal or occupational sort. Much of the history of the relationship between journeymen and their masters in eighteenth-century

all those masters/who know how to respect us/but any hot-tempered master/will have to be mocked'). When the song was actually sung the word 'mocquer' was changed to 'foutre'.
68   A. N. Y 13 350 (27-6-1720).
69   B.A. MS Bastille 12 369; see also my essay on 'Labour Disputes in 18th Century Paris'.
70   B. N. MS fr. 6682, fol. 281; A. N. Y 12 793 (11-10-1776), Y 12 826 (18-10-1776).
71   A. N. AD XI 65 *Requete au roi et mémoire sur la necessité de rétablir les corps de marchands*, Paris 1817.
72   A. N. Y 9223[b] ('they demanded equality for the payment of work, which is to say that there are certain kinds of work for which masters pay their worth and for which they had not demanded any increase, while there are others which are not paid at their worth, given the time which they require, for which they had demanded an increase').

Paris was governed by the problem of trying to resolve the tension between the claims of intimacy as the basis of co-operation at work and the inevitability of anonymity as the basis of the accumulation of wealth. Increased productivity implied additional journeymen and additional journeymen implied the problem of ensuring that strangers would become *bons ouvriers*.

Many of the implications of this problem unfolded in the attempts to impose a printed document – the *livret* – as a bridge between the intimacy of the workshop and the anonymity of the labour market.[73] The *livret* was a sort of impersonal record of the individual qualities which made up the morality of industriousness and assiduousness, presented in a form whose uniformity allowed for the requisite degree of labour mobility. It was thus much more than a simple record of employment. It was designed to transpose the system of interpersonal evaluation and individual assessment which created co-operation within the workshop to the impersonality of the market for labour. From a master artisan's point of view, it made moral qualities – the moral qualities of anonymous journeymen – mobile. A brief outline of its origin and development, and of the very substantial opposition to its application in eighteenth-century Paris, will therefore do much to explain the continuing importance of non-monetary transactions within workshop organisation.

V

The history of the *livret* remains to be written. By the middle of the eighteenth century, however, its function was clear. It was intended to ensure that journeymen passed through a designated place – usually the *bureau* of the corporation of the trade in question – before beginning work. The corporation thus had at its disposal, at least in theory, a register of all the journeymen in a trade and, on the basis of this information, could control the movement of journeymen from master to master and from *boutique* to *boutique*. The institution appears to have been the product of a fusion between seventeenth-century regulations directed at vagrancy and the determination of the guilds to control recruitment into employment. In 1683, for example, journeymen cutlers were forbidden to 'faire aucunes embausches soit des compagnons arrivant en cette ville... que de ceux qui changeront de boutique', and were ordered to register for work at the *bureau* of the corporation. They were to be provided with work by the clerk of the corporation, who was enjoined – in a language which retained overtones of an older system – 'pour faire trouver un maistre à un compagnon, de mener et présenter ledit compagnon aux maistres de ladite

---

73 On the *livret*, see Kaplan, 'Réflexions sur la police'.

communauté chacun à son tour suivant l'ordre de la liste desdits maistres qui se fait tous les ans'.[74]

By the eighteenth century, the injunctions of the regulations governing *placement* had lost this intimacy. Journeymen were required to register with the *bureau* and present a written or printed *billet de congé* (which in slightly more elaborate form became the *livret*) indicating that they had completed their work and were available for new employment. It is likely that the growing use of printed certificates was a development from the body of regulations directed at the itinerant poor of the seventeenth century. An *ordonnance de police* of 1640 ordering journeymen to register at a number of *bureaux d'adresse* within twenty-four hours of their arrival in Paris stipulated that failure to comply would result in their being treated as 'errans, vagabonds et comme tels punis des peines des ordonnances'.[75] Over the following generations this assimilation of journeymen to the ranks of the migrant poor disappeared. The regulations of the eighteenth century reflected the growing concern of the corporations to establish an effective monopoly over the system of *placement*.

Almost nothing is known of the world of work in seventeenth-century Paris. There are indications, however, that control over the distribution of employment by the corporations was only partial in a number of trades. Among the rules of the confraternity of master and journeymen *cartiers* drawn up in 1648 was a provision that 'tous compagnon qui viendront de la campagne et se presenteront pour estre recus en boutique seront obligés de payer pour leur bien venue à la boete de la confrairie la somme de dix livres'.[76] A century later provisions such as these – indicating some formal recognition of journeymen's rights to limit access to work – no longer existed. During the last years of the seventeenth century, journeymen printers and hatters fought long struggles to maintain similar restrictions. Both groups appealed to the Parlement of Paris, the hatters demanding that 'il doit estre deffendu à tous les maistres chapelliers de prendre et se servir des compagnons de dehors appellez compagnons battans la semelle'.[77] In November 1721 the master hatters were still able to complain that 'les compagnons chapelliers fatiguent les maîtres, s'assemblent et caballent... Ils empechent les compagnons qui viennent de province de travailler avec eux et

74 A. P. P. Fonds Lamoignon 17, fol. 84 (12-3-1683) ('to take on any journeymen arriving in this city... or those moving from one boutique to another... To find a master for a journeyman, to lead and present the aforesaid journeyman to each master of the community in turn, following the order in the list of masters drawn up every year').
75 *Ibid.* 12, fol. 4 (4-2-1640).
76 *Ibid.*, fol. 924 (20-3-1648) ('every journeyman coming from the provinces who presents himself for reception into a *boutique* shall be obliged to pay the sum of 10 *livres* as their *bienvenue* to the box of the confraternity').
77 B. N. MS fr. 21 793, fol. 178 (17-9-1699) ('Every master hatter should be prohibited from using journeymen from the outside known as *compagnons battans la semelle*').

lorsqu'un maître prend un compagnon de province tous les autres quittent le travail.'[78]

By the second half of the eighteenth century, however, complaints such as this were no longer heard. It is probable though that many of the rites which accompanied entry to a workshop during the eighteenth century were a displaced continuation of previously recognised practices, of the sort mentioned in the statutes of the confraternity of card makers in 1648. Journeymen printers continued to pay a *bienvenue* when they entered a *boutique* and were entitled to a share in the *bon de chapelle* distributed every year on the *fête de la Saint-Martin* out of the money which was collected in fines which they imposed upon each other.[79] In 1748 journeymen hatters were said to have arrogated the right

de se placer les uns les autres [ce qui] occassionne un découragement considerable appellé devoir qui consiste à boire autant de pintes de vin qu'il y a d'ouvriers dans chaque boutique pour l'entrée et la sortie de chaque ouvrier, ce qui les empêche de travailler plusieurs jours et ce qui leur arrive fort souvent.[80]

As the system of registration was extended, so what may have been practices common to both masters and journeymen before the early eighteenth century became the means by which journeymen alone attempted to retain control over the provision of employment and the organisation of work. The result was a heightened sensitivity to the role of journeymen's associations (both confraternities and, to a lesser extent in Paris, *compagnonnages*) in maintaining systems of finding work independently of the corporations.[81] It is clear, however, that journeymen were able to maintain a degree of autonomous mobility during the eighteenth century. Journeymen locksmiths successfully resisted an order to register with the *bureau* of their corporation in 1746, as did the painters and decorators after 1766.[82] Journeymen saddlers appealed to the Parlement to avoid having to register in 1766 and continued to place themselves when their appeal was rejected.[83] In 1763 a master button maker complained that one of his journeymen, named Louis Cordon,

78 A. N. Y 14932 (10 and 13-11-1721) ('the journeymen hatters are exhausting their masters' patience with their assemblies and cabals... They are preventing journeymen arriving from the provinces from working with them and, when a master takes on a journeyman from the provinces, all the others walk out').
79 Barber (ed.), *Anecdotes*, pp. 65–93.
80 A. P. P. Fonds Lamoignon 38, fol. 436 (31-7-1748) ('to place one another, which has given rise to considerable disruption in the form of a *devoir* or duty, which consists of drinking as many pints of wine as there are workers in the shop on the arrival or departure of each worker. This prevents them from working for several days and occurs very often').
81 Kaplan, 'Réflexions sur la police', pp. 58–65. See also C. Truant, 'Solidarity and Symbolism among Journeymen Artisans: The Case of *Compagnonnage*', *Comparative Studies in Society and History*, 21 (1979).
82 See Sonenscher, 'Labour Disputes in 18th Century Paris'.
83 A. N. Y 9500 (10-2-1768); Y 11 583ᵃ (31-1-1766); B. N. F 26 468, *Statuts des Maîtres Selliers*, Paris, 1770.

depuis environ trois mois ne cesse de le deranger, en allant de boutique en boutique et s'attroupant avec d'autres pour faire sortir et entrer de chez les maîtres les compagnons ... qu'il a été fort surpris lundy dernier lorsque ledit Cordon luy est venu annoncer qu'il alloit sortir et qu'il luy mettroit en place un autre compagnon.[84]

In 1777 a master baker complained that five of his *garçons*, members of a trade with a strong tradition of autonomous mobility centred upon the *auberges* and lodging-houses in which they stayed, had walked out. The five explained that they had left 'sans sujet de mécontentement et seulement à la sollicitation d'autres garçons'.[85] The resurrection of the *livret*, and the long, if unsuccessful, campaign to restore the corporations during the First Empire, are indirect testimony to the continuing capacity of journeymen to move from master to master and from job to job independently of the rhythms of the productive cycle.[86]

VI

There was thus no 'natural' market for labour in eighteenth-century Paris, no mechanism which ensured that it would be *the wage rate* which responded to fluctuations in the demand for labour. The assumption that there *was* has meant that all those concerns which can be placed under the general rubric of 'reproduction' – eating, drinking, housing, marrying, bequeathing or inheriting property or rights to property – have been separated off from work itself and analysed in terms of the extent to which earnings made it possible to acquire more or less of them. This is an anachronistic procedure. In varying degrees all of these concerns were imbricated within the texture of work itself. They made up a part of the environment of non-monetary manoeuvre and symbolic negotiation in which masters and journeymen encountered and dealt with one another. Any discussion of eighteenth-century urban wage systems must begin with this fact. Without it, it is only too easy to produce notional journeymen's budgets and insist upon the erosion of real wages over the eighteenth century without taking any cognisance of the idiom of eighteenth-century discourse. Both the morality of industriousness and the preoccupation with *luxe* and *débauche* were grounded upon the reality of artisanal production. Rather than trying to prove that this was an idiom centred upon the things that money could buy, it is more helpful to situate it in a context in which money was not, as yet, needed to buy all the

84　A. N. Y 15 368 (30-7-1763) ('has not ceased disrupting him for some three months, by going from workshop to workshop and gathering with others in order to make journeymen come and go from their masters ... He had been very surprised last Monday when Cordon came and told him that he was going to leave and would put another journeyman in his place').

85　A. N. Y 12 627 (30-6-1777) ('with no cause for complaint and only at the request of other journeymen').

86　On this campaign, see M. Sibalis, 'The Workers of Napoleonic Paris', unpublished Ph.D. thesis (University of Concordia, 1979). I am grateful to Dr Sibalis for allowing me to read his thesis.

necessities of life. Mercier's remark about the insubordination of the working population, 'visible ... depuis quelques années et surtout dans les métiers', and Restif's complaint that 'les ouvriers de la capitale sont devenus intraitables' are more intelligible from this perspective than from one which insists that 'la masse d'ouvriers ressentait durement l'érosion très sensible de leur pouvoir d'achat'.[87] The wage too has a history, and a history which transcends its reassuringly neutral figurative appearance.

87 Kaplan, Réflexions sur la police', p. 72 ('the mass of workers was substantially affected by the marked erosion of their purchasing power').

7

Embezzlement, industry and the law in England, 1500–1800*

JOHN STYLES

Historians have differed over the precise advantages that putting-out offered the master manufacturer relative to other available methods of organising industrial production, but there is virtual unanimity that the principal disadvantage of putting-out for the employer was the difficulty of supervising the labour force and, in particular, the problem of embezzlement by workers. Indeed it has been argued that the key to the shift to centralised production by some employers in the late eighteenth century was not the technical superiority of factory-based technologies, but rather the extent of embezzlement and associated problems of labour discipline under the putting-out system.[1]

There are dangers of exaggeration here. Just as the factory did not give the employer absolute control over the labour process in general, neither did it abolish at a stroke the illegal appropriation by the workforce of goods in the process of manufacture.[2] Nor, before the coming of the factory, was such appropriation confined to the putting-out sector. The eighteenth-century dockyards, where production was concentrated on single sites, were notorious for their workers' pilfering of wood, ropes, canvas and other naval stores. Similarly coal miners took coal from the pits. Employees in small workshops made similar appropriations. Apprentices were especially suspect.[3]

Though frauds during the process of manufacture were by no means confined

---

* I should like to thank John Langbein, Donald Coleman, Ken Ponting and Joanna Innes for their comments on earlier drafts of this essay, and Maxine Berg and Pat Hudson for their considerable assistance in preparing the final version.
1 E. Lipson, *The History of the Woollen and Worsted Industries* (London, 1921), p. 69, and S. A. Marglin, 'What Do Bosses Do? The Origins and Functions of Hierarchy in Capitalist Production', *Review of Radical Political Economics*, 6 (1974), 46–55.
2 See, for example, D. Jones, *Crime, Protest, Community and Police in Nineteenth-Century Britain* (London, 1982), p. 157.
3 See, for example, R. J. B. Knight, 'Pilfering and Theft from the Dockyards at the Time of the American War of Independence', *The Mariner's Mirror*, 61 (1975), 215–25; and M. Beloff, 'A London Apprentice's Notebook, 1703–5', *History*, 27 (1947), 39.

to industrial organisation of the putting-out type, the character of such frauds under the putting-out system was in two respects distinctive. First, as historians have long recognised, concentration of the ownership of the raw materials, combined with the remoteness of the owner from the point of manufacture, made for special problems of supervision and provided peculiar opportunities for fraud. Second, the status at law of appropriation of the employer's materials by the putting-out worker differed both from that of similar appropriation by workers in centralised manufactures and from that of marketing frauds by independent producers. To study embezzlement and associated frauds in the putting-out industries in the period from the fifteenth to the eighteenth century is, therefore, to study a major arena of conflict between capital and labour over control of the labour process under the putting-out system. In so far as both embezzlement and efforts to control it took place within a distinctive legal framework, to study them is also to study the relationship between a particular form of industrial organisation and the wider institutional framework provided by the early modern state.

The study of embezzlement in the putting-out industries also bears directly upon the much-debated question of the extent to which the criminal law was an instrument of class politics in eighteenth-century England. Some historians have presented the large body of eighteenth-century legislation against such frauds as an instance of what they argue is the critical development in eighteenth-century criminal law – the transformation into criminal offences against property of a large number of infractions that had previously been violations of trust or corporate obligation.[4]

This essay is divided into four sections. The first considers the structure of opportunities offered by the operation of putting-out industries for covert appropriation by outworkers of the employer's property. It illustrates the problems of surveillance faced by the employer who wished to prevent such appropriation, the extent of the loss he might sustain and the uses to which the embezzling employee might put the goods appropriated. Of course in practice the appropriation of goods in the process of manufacture was not necessarily regarded by employers as 'embezzlement'. It was often carried on with their approval. In the second section, therefore, such appropriation is considered as a terrain of both conflict and compromise between employer and employee, within the wider context of industrial relations in the putting-out industries.

The third section is devoted to the law. A comparison of its content and its enforcement is used to challenge the notion that the offence was decisively criminalised in the mid eighteenth century. The final section addresses the

4   E. P. Thompson, *Whigs and Hunters* (London, 1975), p. 207; P. Linebaugh, summary of paper in *Bulletin of the Society for the Study of Labour History*, 25 (1972), 11–15.

relationship of law making and law enforcement to the circumstances of the industries concerned.

I

Almost every industry organised along putting-out lines provided a multitude of opportunities for workpeople to defraud their employer with a good chance of escaping detection, or at least in such a way that it was difficult to verify any suspicions. Under the putting-out system the employee normally undertook to work up a particular volume of materials to a specified standard and to deliver the completed work to the owner-employer within a fixed time. Payment was, at least notionally, on a piece-rate basis, with different rates for different qualities of goods. It was usual for materials to be delivered out by weight and to be reweighed on their return; indeed, this was a statutory requirement in several industries. The criteria by which standards of quality were set and measured varied according to the material.

Outworkers, therefore, could defraud their employers both by appropriating the materials delivered out and by producing work of a quality inferior to that demanded. Once the materials were delivered out, not only was it easy to set some of them aside or to exchange them for materials of lesser quality, but it was also easy to manipulate them in such a way as to conceal any loss of weight or alteration in quality on return and inspection. Moreover, when the numbers employed were large (and they could amount to several thousand in some putting-out concerns),[5] detailed checking for such frauds on redelivery might be prohibitively time-consuming and expensive for the employer, who was usually anxious to achieve a rapid turnover.

An employers' assessment of some of the opportunities for fraud is available from the evidence presented to a 1774 Parliamentary committee by Gloucestershire woollen clothiers seeking more rigorous legislation. One witness described the considerable illicit gains available to outworkers at each stage of production. He claimed that wool pickers could embezzle over 5% of the wool delivered to them and conceal the fact by 'throwing the wool upon wet stones, whereby it impregnates the water, and they bring it home again full weight'. Scribblers could conceal a similar appropriation by adding oil to make up the weight. Spinners could hold back 8% of the yarn and entirely escape detection by steaming the remainder over a boiling pot. By wetting the cloth, weavers could retain 7% to 10% of the yarn delivered them, 'which fraud cannot be discovered, as the cloths are always brought home wet'.[6]

5 See, for example, A. P. Wadsworth and J. de L. Mann, *The Cotton Trade and Industrial Lancashire, 1600–1780* (Manchester, 1965), pp. 211 and 274.
6 *House of Common Journals* (hereafter *C. J.*), 34 (1772–4), 451.

As this final remark indicates, concealment was assisted by the fact that many processes in this and other putting-out industries required some legitimate treatment of the materials with substances like oil and water in order to work them. In addition, manufacture inevitably involved the production of various forms of waste. Such materials remained, at law, the property of the employer, but it was wellnigh impossible to account for all waste, even if the employer demanded it. In some industries a standard weight allowance was made by employers for wastage, although it was possible for workpeople to manipulate this to their advantage.[7]

Other frauds involved tale as well as weight. One of the most commonly complained of frauds in the putting-out textile industries during the seventeenth and eighteenth centuries was that of false and short reeling of yarn. The many different varieties of cloth produced required yarns of a wide range of fineness. The coarser the yarn, the easier it was to spin. Hence coarser spinning commanded a lower piece-rate. The raw material was usually delivered out by weight, to be spun to a standard of fineness which was specified in terms of the length to be produced from each pound weight. It was customary from at least the start of the seventeenth century for the spinner to return the yarn wound on a reel into set lengths, known as hanks or skeins. The length of a hank was expressed as a fixed number of revolutions or coils (known as threads) on a reel of a particular circumference. It became customary for different industries and districts to use reels of different circumferences and hanks of different numbers of threads. In the Yorkshire worsted industry, for example, the reel was usually one yard in circumference and 560 threads (or 560 yards) constituted a hank. The types of yarn required by a Yorkshire manufacturer of shalloons in the late eighteenth century ranged from 18 such hanks to the pound to 36 hanks to the pound. The rate paid for spinning yarn at 24 hanks to the pound was approximately 25% higher than that for 18 hanks to the pound.[8]

False and short reeling involved the use of a reel of a circumference shorter than the customary standard, or the inclusion in each hank of a smaller number of threads than was customary. By these practices spinners were said to be able to conceal frauds involving less work than that paid for, the appropriation of the raw material and the production of yarn inferior in fineness to that demanded. It was claimed to be impractical to check all the hanks for length by unwinding and remeasuring them.[9] A manufacturer on a moderate scale in late-eighteenth-

---

7 For example, in the Nottinghamshire framework knitting industry in the early nineteenth century allowance of $\frac{1}{4}$ ounce was made in each pound of yarn weighed out to take account of wastage during winding: J. D. Chambers, *Nottinghamshire in the Eighteenth Century* (London, 1932), p. 122. For manipulation of the allowance, see Parliamentary Papers (1810–11), III, 603.
8 John James, *History of the Worsted Manufacture in England* (London, 1968), p. 281.
9 See, for example, G. Unwin, *Studies in Economic History: The Collected Papers of George Unwin* (London, 1966), p. 295.

century Yorkshire might have 6000 pounds of yarn or 120 000 hanks passing through his hands in large batches each year.[10] He would almost certainly weigh the wool on delivery and the yarn on its return, but, as has been pointed out, such a check was easily circumvented. It was claimed in 1776 that worsted yarn in Yorkshire was reeled on average 6.5% short, a figure which is confirmed by prosecution evidence.[11] The difficulty of checking the workmanship of huge numbers of individual pieces of work probably facilitated the evasion by workpeople of quality standards in the nail trade too, a large proportion of the nails supplied to customers lacking heads or points.[12]

The absence of direct supervision which characterised the putting-out system provided the opportunity for other types of fraud and for practices which facilitated fraud. For example, it was possible for workers to pawn their employer's materials, often thereby delaying their return in a worked-up form, or entirely preventing it. Workers could take work from a number of masters at the same time, again thereby often delaying its return as well as facilitating the substitution of low-value materials belonging to one master for higher-value materials embezzled from another.[13]

The losses that employers could sustain by these fraudulent practices were considerable. The figures provided by the Gloucestershire clothier to the 1774 Parliamentary committee suggest a cumulative loss of materials in the four stages of production referred to of over 25% on each cloth, and these were not the only production processes where such appropriation could be made. How credible are these claims, given that information presented to Parliament in support of legislation was notoriously biased? The records of embezzlement prosecutions confirm that illegal appropriation was undertaken at almost every stage of the production process in many putting-out industries, but only rarely reveal what proportion of the materials delivered had been embezzled. The limited evidence does suggest that to appropriate amounts slightly greater than those described for each stage of production by the Gloucestershire clothier was a common enough occasion for prosecution, and that many of those prosecuted took far more. In the cases of four Norwich bobbin fillers, convicted between 1750 and 1763 for embezzling yarn, the proportion of the yarn taken is recorded. Three

10 Calculated on the basis of the figures for the early 1770s provided in James, *Worsted Manufacture*, p. 280, and E. M. Sigsworth, 'William Greenwood and Robert Heaton: Two Eighteenth-Century Worsted Manufacturers', *Bradford Textile Society Journal* (1951–2), p. 72.
11 *Leeds Intelligencer*, 12 March 1776; West Yorkshire Record Office, Wakefield, QE 15/1–13, Memoranda of summary convictions, 1778–81, and QSF, Quarter Sessions Files, 1776–81, convictions before Joshua Horton, JP.
12 D. Hey, *The Rural Metalworkers of the Sheffield Region* (Leicester, 1972), pp. 47–8.
13 For an example of pawning see Essex R. O., Colchester, T/A 465/2, Colchester Examination and Recognisance Book, 1646–87, entry for 19 October 1669, case of William Jollybrowne. For an example of taking work from several masters see *Norwich Mercury*, 3 June 1769.

embezzled between 8% and 16% of what they received; the fourth took 33%.[14]
The proportion of yarn embezzled by a Colchester weaver prosecuted in 1672
was between 9% and 15%.[15] Most of those prosecuted between 1667 and 1687 at
Colchester appear to have made depredations of a similar magnitude or slightly
greater. Moreover, the loss sustained by the employer as a result of embezzlement
was not simply a matter of the value of the appropriated materials.
Embezzlement and associated abuses diminished the quality of the final product.
Because they were, by their very nature, largely outside the employer's direct
control, they injected an additional element of unpredictability into a business
environment that was already highly unpredictable. They inhibited both the
accurate computing of the manufacturer's costs and his ability to offer products
of a consistent standard, very necessary when dealing with distant markets.

It is, of course, impossible to know precisely what proportion of workers in
any putting-out industry availed themselves of the opportunities for secretly
appropriating their work materials and similar frauds, and on what scale.
Undoubtedly such practices were very extensive. Petty pilfering by modern
workers is enormous in scale, and putting-out masters believed this was the case
in the seventeenth and eighteenth centuries. Evidence from prosecuted cases
suggests that it was often carried on for months or years on a regular basis. It is
possible to make some assessment of the advantage the employee could secure
through such frauds. This was not necessarily just a material advantage. The
literature on similar activities in modern industries has placed some emphasis on
the 'social rewards' they offer, such as the pleasure to be derived from 'beating the
system'.[16] There is every reason to believe that putting-out workers who
embezzled took as much delight in their activities as their modern equivalents
(after all, resentment towards employers was often equally strong), but there is
virtually no substantial evidence. The material advantage to be derived from
these practices is better documented, especially that available from simple
embezzlement.

Some embezzled materials were put to private use by those who appropriated
them. In 1678 Abigail Russel of Colchester 'put out as much of her ... masters
yarne as did make her husband a pair of stockings and last weeke as much as knitt
a pair of childs stockins and stockt a paire for her selfe'.[17] However, a great deal

14   *Norwich Mercury*, 20 October 1750; 8 March 1760; 9 January 1762; 10 December 1763.
15   Colchester Examination Book, entry for 15 March 1672/3, case of Thomas Whitecake. His
      employer claimed he made away with the equivalent of a whole bay's woof while employed in
      weaving bays for a period of three months. Percentages calculated on the basis of figures given in
      K. H. Burley, 'The Economic Development of Essex in the Later Seventeenth and Early
      Eighteenth Centuries', unpublished Ph.D thesis (University of London, 1957), p. 133, suggesting
      that a Colchester bay took between eight and twelve days to manufacture.
16   S. Henry, *The Hidden Economy* (London, 1978), pp. 94–102.
17   Colchester Examination Book, entry for 14 July 1678, case of Abigail Russel.

of embezzlement was for sale. It is depredations of this sort that are best documented, because great emphasis was placed on the prosecution of receivers. Embezzlement for sale could be conducted with a reasonable chance of remaining undetected only if secure opportunities were readily available for realising the value of the embezzled materials. Such opportunities were legion. Workers constantly borrowed, bartered and sold small quantities of materials among themselves.[18] Moreover in the textile and other industries there was an extensive legitimate trade in waste materials of every kind. The boundaries between legitimate dealing of this kind, receiving embezzled goods and even receiving goods stolen by outsiders from workshops and warehouses were not always well defined and were disregarded by many. Buying cheap embezzled materials was widely believed to be a very common route of entry into manufacturing for men with little capital. Larger manufacturers were sometimes implicated.[19] Identification of textile materials by owner was notoriously difficult, especially before they were woven or dyed. It could, therefore, be very hard to establish a case against a receiver who had a legitimate textile trade, other than on the basis of evidence direct from the embezzler.

The records of convictions for receiving embezzled goods at Norwich between 1749 and 1778 illustrate some of the opportunities available for disposing of embezzled materials by sale. The approximately one hundred reported cases involved the purchase of wool from journeymen wool combers, of yarn from warpers, bobbin fillers and journeymen weavers, and of remnants of cloth and cloths made from embezzled yarn from journeymen hotpressers and weavers.[20] The occupations of those prosecuted for receiving included many in the textile industry and a number in retailing. Some of those convicted were both wealthy and respectable, like Mr John Langton, a stuff buyer, convicted in 1754, and Mr Ellis Paston, 'an eminent shopkeeper in this City and reputed very rich', convicted in 1750.[21] A third of those convicted were women. Embezzled materials could pass through extensive local networks of workpeople and small dealers. One group of large-scale dealers during the mid 1770s developed a regular market in Spitalfields, London, for work materials embezzled and otherwise stolen from Norwich, secretly employing the drivers of the London waggons to deliver them.[22]

It would be misleading to draw very firm conclusions from a detailed occupational breakdown of receiving convictions. Occupational data survive for only two-thirds of reported offenders (the occupations of single women and the

18 *Ibid.*, 30 March 1655.
19 Wadsworth and Mann, *Cotton Trade*, p. 399; J. de L. Mann, *The Cloth Industry of the West of England from 1640 to 1880* (Oxford, 1971), p. 230.
20 *Norwich Mercury*, 1749 to 1778, *passim*. See Appendix 1 for the use of this source.
21 *Norwich Mercury*, 2 March 1754; 22 December 1750.
22 *Norwich Mercury*, 30 September 1752; 17 June 1775; 23 November 1776.

husbands of married women are consistently under-reported) and it is probable that prosecution was disproportionately concentrated on particular occupational groups. However, the available occupational profile does display a number of striking features. Thirty-nine of the fifty-nine whose occupations, or whose husbands' occupations, are recorded were involved in the textile industry, and two textile occupations were especially prominent. First, those described as worsted weavers – small independent producers who played a subordinate role in an industry dominated by large merchant-manufacturers. Many appear to have passed backwards and forwards between independence and the status of putting-out employee. Second, those described as duffelmakers. Duffel was a cheap, coarse cloth, unlike most of the products of the Norwich woollen textile industry, which were the highest value worsteds and worsted–silk mixes. Indeed duffel production at Norwich may have existed primarily to use the by-products of the town's high-quality manufactures. Duffel makers, like worsted weavers, were relatively small producers. Between them they accounted for 64% of those convicted who were involved in the textile industry. This suggests that receiving, or at least the attention of the committee of large manufacturers who prosecuted it, was concentrated among those producers with small capital to whom cheap materials offered a means of sustaining their precarious existence in the interstices of the putting-out system.

Twenty of the fifty-nine receivers were recorded as having non-textile occupations, although a number of these may have had subsidiary occupations which included a textile trade (shopkeepers often acted as putters-out for the manufacturers). Retailers were prominent here, with alehouse keepers and their wives accounting for nine of the twenty. In these cases receiving may have involved pawning, or payment for shop goods and beer in embezzled materials. Alehouse keepers were at the centre of local credit networks, operated as pawnbrokers and were notorious as harbourers of thieves and general receivers of stolen goods.

If Norwich offered a multitude of opportunities for the outworker to sell embezzled materials, the men and women who provided those opportunities could drive a hard bargain. Embezzled goods commanded only a proportion of the prices paid for their equivalents on the open market. The *Norwich Mercury* reported cases where embezzled wool worth 10d per pound sold for 2d, where six skeins of yarn worth 14d sold for 4d and where remnants of fine satin worth 7 shillings sold for 3 shillings.[23] The newspaper probably singled out for comment exceptionally low prices, but at Colchester in the late seventeenth century embezzled yarn appears in most cases to have fetched only half its open market value. Elsewhere there were instances of black market prices much closer to the

23   *Norwich Mercury*, 26 December 1772; 16 December 1752.

legitimate price.[24] However, the attempt of a Colchester man accused of receiving yarn in 1687 to establish a defence by claiming that he had bought it at the market price, suggests that it was usual for black market prices to be noticeably lower than their open market equivalents.[25]

By how much could embezzlement for sale supplement an outworker's wages? Given the lack of very extensive evidence either for wages or for the sums paid for embezzled goods, any answer to this question is necessarily highly speculative. Nevertheless, it is possible to indicate broad magnitudes (see Appendix 2 for the basis of calculation of the following estimates). A conservative estimate of the return from such depredations suggests that they could considerably enhance earnings. If it is assumed that embezzled goods generally fetched about half their market value, then the embezzling spinner described in the 1774 Gloucestershire Parliamentary evidence could, by selling the materials embezzled, supplement her wages by approximately 20%. On the same basis of calculation, a Gloucestershire weaver could supplement his gross money earnings by at least the same proportion.

The Spanish wool used in Gloucestershire in the eighteenth century was on average over four times as expensive as the English long-staple wool used in the worsted industry. However, embezzlement could provide a valuable supplement to wages there too. Assuming that short reeling in Yorkshire in the 1770s was undertaken purely as a cover for embezzlement and that the embezzled materials were sold as yarn on the black market at half the legitimate price, the fraud could provide a supplement to the spinner's earnings of approximately 6%, at what was considered the average rate of appropriation.[26] Frauds other than simple embezzlement could also increase the effective wages of outworkers by reducing the amount of work they were obliged to undertake for a specific payment. Moreover, the supplement to money wages secured by means of embezzlement was not an occasional windfall. For many workers, embezzlement probably provided a regular addition to income, the size of which was, within limits, subject to their direct control, unlike work-loads, money wage rates, or the prices of consumables.

II

The foregoing discussion of embezzlement and associated frauds presents them as practices that were both illegal and actively condemned by employers. However, though almost all the practices discussed so far provided the employer

24 Lancashire R. O., Preston, QSP, Quarter Sessions Petitions, 1766; Preston House of Correction Calender, 15 July 1766, case of Mathias Tattersall.
25 Colchester Examination Book, entry for 17 December 1687, case of Abraham Degrate.
26 See above, note 11.

with grounds for legal proceedings against the offending employee, employers' attitudes were not necessarily uniform or consistent.

In order to understand the attitudes of employers and employees to these frauds, it is necessary to consider such practices in the wider context of the wage relationship characteristic of the putting-out system. It is important to emphasise that the money piece-rates under which most work of a putting-out character was arranged bore only an indirect relationship to the actual payment received by the employee for a particular volume of work. This is not to suggest that the wage was entirely divorced from the piece-rate. The piece-rate still provided a standard on the basis of which the employer arrived at a final settlement of his obligation to the employee. The difference between the nominal rate for the work undertaken and that final settlement depended on the various adjustments to which the piece-rate for a particular task was subjected.

The most straightforward of these adjustments took the form of what were known on the one hand as allowances and on the other variously as fines, stoppages, abatements or deductions. The former were payments for tasks performed by the worker in addition to those customarily included in the piece-rate price. For example, in the Gloucestershire woollen industry in the mid eighteenth century allowance was paid for 'stopping' (repairing or edging) cloth.[27] The latter took several forms. Standard deductions were frequently made from the appropriate payment for a certain volume of work on account of the employer's charges for renting premises or a loom, for providing necessary equipment, such as candles, or for preparing the raw materials. These might involve charges at approximately the market rate for the facility provided, but there was much complaint in, for example, the west of England cloth industry and the East Midlands framework knitting industry, that such deductions were made at extortionate rates, or imposed irrespective of whether the facility was actually used by the employee.[28] Outworkers in many industries were also subject to abatements for poor-quality work, or returning work underweight. It was claimed that, especially in periods of bad trade, employers imposed artificially stringent quality standards, or invented faults.[29] Another form of deduction, extensively practised in the worsted industry of the East Midlands and East Anglia in the late eighteenth century, involved the regular withholding

27 See W. Minchinton, 'The Petitions of the Weavers and Clothiers of Gloucestershire in 1756', *Bristol and Gloucestershire Archaeological Society Transactions*, 73 (1954), 219.
28 Anon., 'An Essay on Riots', *The Gentleman's Magazine*, 9 (1739), 9; F. A. Wells, *The British Hosiery and Knitwear Industry: Its History and Organisation* (Newton Abbot, 1972), p. 65. Also see K. H. Burley, 'A Note on a Labour Dispute in Early Eighteenth-Century Colchester', *Bulletin of the Institute of Historical Research*, 29 (1956), 224.
29 See, for examples, the late-seventeenth-century poem, 'The Clothiers' Delight', reprinted in P. Mantoux, *The Industrial Revolution in the Eighteenth Century* (London, 1961), pp. 75–7 and *C. J.*, 36 (1776–8), 289.

of up to a third of the customary payment for work. This practice had grown up ostensibly on account of the high price of wool and the dullness of trade. The rate of deduction was said to fluctuate with the demand for yarn.[30]

Employers also made adjustments to nominal piece-rates by altering the volume of work to be undertaken for a given price. Such alterations sometimes involved a legitimate addition to the weight or volume of materials delivered out in order to take account of wastage, but, like deductions, adjustments of this kind were often imposed unfairly. In early-eighteenth-century Wiltshire some clothiers were said to give out work to weavers using weights containing seventeen ounces to the pound and to lengthen warping bars so that the weaver was obliged to weave three or four yards more than was customary for no extra payment.[31] Similar practices were widespread in almost all the putting-out industries in the eighteenth century, especially during periods of bad trade. However, if employers by these methods frequently imposed extra work on their employees for no extra pay, they could also obtain what was regarded as an unfair advantage by manipulating work-loads in the opposite direction. At Colchester during the trade depression of 1715 the weavers complained that their masters gave out smaller quantities of yarn than were required to weave a standard piece and then made deductions from their pay for lack of weight when they redelivered the yarn woven up into cloths.[32]

Another set of practices which intervened between the nominal piece-rate and the actual wage received by the employee revolved around the manner in which payment was made. Rather than pay for each piece of work on its delivery, employers would often pay cash in advance or in arrears. The former could work to the short-term advantage of the employee, but the extension of such debts over a period of time could place him in thrall to the employer. Payment in arrears could similarly bind the worker to a particular employer and force him to live on credit.[33] Employers also manipulated payments by offering tokens, notes of hand, or counterfeit coin (especially counterfeit coppers) instead of cash. Often these were negotiable only at a discount, or with specific local retailers.[34] In the latter case, a form of truck was usually involved.

Truck is, of course, the best known and was probably the most common method of manipulating wages. It involved either the substitution of inferior

30 John Kirby, *A Letter to a Member of Parliament Stating the Necessity of an Amendment in the Laws Relating to the Woollen Manufactory so far as Respect the Wages of the Spinners* (Ipswich, 1787), pp. 10, 16–17.
31 J. de L. Mann, 'Clothiers and Weavers in Wiltshire During Eighteenth Century', in L. S. Presnall (ed.), *Studies in the Industrial Revolution* (Oxford, 1960), p. 68.
32 PRO, P. C. 1/4 no. 101, Privy Council Office, Unbound Papers, Riot at Colchester, 1715, minutes of Privy Council meeting of 20 April 1715.
33 For payment in advance see Colchester Examination Book, entry for 18 December 1667, case of Nicholas Harrison. For payment in arrears see Burley, 'Labour Dispute', p. 225.
34 Mann, 'Clothiers and Weavers', p. 68.

goods for all or part of the money wage, or the imposition on employees of an obligation to spend their money wages with the employer or his agent on overvalued goods.

It is most important to emphasise that not all renumeration in kind operated to the employee's disadvantage. In many putting-out industries the employee enjoyed a recognised, customary right to perquisites. In the textile industries these often consisted of waste materials. For example, weavers at Bocking and Braintree in Essex were, before 1759, allowed to retain the ends and thrums of each piece of cloth they had woven.[35] A perquisite of this kind bore a different relationship to the piece-rate from truck, in that it was not computed in terms of the money rate at all. Masters sometimes tried to buy out such perquisites by adding to the piece-rate a sum that they considered a fair equivalent to the value of the materials concerned. Given the manipulations to which employers subjected the piece-rate and the changes they sometimes made in the rate it is hardly surprising that workers resisted these attempts. This kind of perquisite was a component of their effective wage which was immune to such adjustment and therefore highly prized, even if its money value did not represent a very large proportion of the piece-rate price (perhaps 2% to 3% on average at Bocking and Braintree if the masters' cash offer was a fair one). Moreover, as employers were at pains to point out, such perquisites provided an encouragement to and a cover for frauds, especially the creation of excessive waste.

The reasons both for the existence of many of the practices which mediated between the piece-rate and the effective wage and for their manipulation to alter effective wages are not well understood. It is especially difficult to explain why it was of advantage to the employer to use such practices in this way rather than to make straightforward adjustments in the money rate. It has been suggested that the key consideration here was the successful resistance of workers to changes in money piece-rates that enjoyed customary status.[36] Though the inelasticity of piece-rates over several decades is certainly a striking feature of a number of putting-out industries during the eighteenth century, this explanation is not altogether satisfactory.[37] The imposition or intensification of truck, false weights and associated practices was as often an accompaniment as an alternative to cuts in piece-rates.[38]

Whether or not workers preferred the imposition of practices such as truck or

---

35 *Ipswich Journal*, 25 November and 2 December 1758.
36 See G. W. Hilton, *The Truck System* (Cambridge, 1960), pp. 40–60, for a discussion of this interpretation as applied to truck. Several of the other essays in the present volume address aspects of this issue.
37 For examples of the inelasticity of piece-rates see Mann, 'Clothiers and weavers', p. 93; J. Rule, *The Experience of Labour in Eighteenth-Century Industry* (London, 1981), p. 61 and A. Smith, *The Wealth of Nations* (London,1970), p. 177.
38 See, for example, Mann, 'Clothiers and Weavers', p. 68.

false weights to outright cuts in piece-rates, there is little doubt that these practices were the object of considerable resentment, especially when employed in what was perceived as a deceitful or illegal manner. Indeed they were key grievances in many eighteenth-century labour disputes.[39] Faced with such deceits, the secret embezzlement of part of the work materials was a highly appropriate response on the part of the employee. Not only did it restore the worker's cut in income, but it did so in a manner that was, like the object of resentment, underhand. That there was a connection between the two phenomena was a matter of contemporary comment.[40] The kind of attitude towards embezzlement that the imposition of such practices could generate among workers is suggested by a statement of a Colchester weaver in 1673. Having admitted an offence, he commented that 'his master was an honest man and it was a pity he should be wronged'.[41]

Yet, as this example indicates, though an employer's fairness might call forth an expression of regret from an embezzling workman, it did not necessarily protect him from embezzlement. As is so often the case when attempting to reconstruct popular attitudes to illegal activities, it is difficult to disentangle individual behaviour, collective beliefs, public utterances and the views of patrician commentators. The latter were often of the opinion that workpeople were generally predisposed to such frauds and indiscriminately regarded them as legitimate.[42] There is certainly ample evidence of collective opposition to the enforcement of penalties against those convicted of such frauds in the eighteenth century. For example, at Manchester in 1750, at Norwich in 1753 and at Stockport in 1772 there were riots against the whipping of embezzlement offenders. However, it is not certain whether these were manifestations of mass support for embezzlement in general, or of opposition to the particular punishments inflicted and the particular circumstances of the prosecutions.[43]

The public utterances, especially in the newspapers, of workpeople or their representatives were neither consistent nor necessarily representative. Workers were prepared to argue their right to previously recognised perquisites against attempts by employers to redefine them as frauds, but public justifications for

---

39 For example, in the Colchester worsted industry in 1715, in the Wiltshire woollen industry in 1726 and 1738, in the Gloucestershire woollen industry in 1756 and in the Manchester smallware industry in 1758.

40 See, for example, *C. J.*, 23 (1737–41), 89.

41 Colchester Examination Book, entry for 15 March 1672/3, case of James Whitecake.

42 See, for examples, *Norwich Mercury*, 30 September 1752; anon., *The Chronicle of the Camp at Rackheath* (Norwich, 1753), *passim; Leeds Intelligencer*, 10 and 24 September 1776; Samuel Finney, 'History of Wilmslow Parish', in T. Worthington Barlow (ed.), *The Cheshire and Lancashire Historical Collector* (Manchester, 1853), vol. 1, no. 11, p. 122 (which refers to the high incidence of false reeling in the parish).

43 For Manchester and Stockport see Wadsworth and Mann, *Cotton Trade*, p. 398; for Norwich see *Norwich Mercury*, January and February 1753, *passim*.

covert embezzlement were, hardly surprisingly, conspicuous by their absence.[44] On some occasions workpeople collectively disavowed embezzlement and even promised to inform against offenders, in particular when they were concerned to promote their position in conflicts with employers over money wages or conditions of employment.[45] Of course, the adoption under these circumstances of public stances hostile to embezzlement does not mean that these attitudes were sincerely or widely held. However, such public statements do confirm that embezzlement was regarded as intimately linked with other aspects of the relationship between employer and employee, and was negotiable in that context.

Problematic though it is, the available evidence does, on balance, suggest that embezzlement was widely condoned by workers, who often regarded it as a legitimate perquisite, irrespective of their employers' attitudes.[46] As studies of modern pilfering indicate, collective support for such activity need not necessarily rest on a clearly articulated general legitimating notion, of the 'moral economy' type.[47] Almost certainly there was a wide range of personal and collective justifications for the unauthorised appropriation of work materials. However, those notions of equity in terms of which workers judged the employment relationship and against which many employers offended by their manipulation of practices such as truck, could provide one source of legitimacy for such appropriation. Another lay in the inconsistent attitudes and behaviour of employers.

The appropriation by outworkers of goods in the process of manufacture intervened, like practices such as truck and false weights, between the money piece-rate and the effective wage. Unlike most of those practices, the employer did not enjoy direct control over the incidence or character of such appropriation, even where it took the form of perquisites which he explicitly countenanced. Nevertheless, a number of indirect methods of control, ranging from abatements through dismissal to prosecution, were available to him. By varying the application and intensity of such controls the employer could manipulate the effective wage in a manner equivalent to that achieved by means of the manipulation of truck or false weights.

In so far as employers did behave in this way, it appears that the incidence and intensity of their controls often varied according to the fortunes of an industry,

---

44 See, for an example of a defence of perquisites, *Ipswich Journal*, 2 December 1758.
45 See, for examples, Wadsworth and Mann, *Cotton Trade*, pp. 347 and 363; *Norwich Gazette*, 11 February 1748/9; *Norwich Mercury*, 11 August 1753.
46 The proliferation of trade terms for embezzlement, such as 'heyhoe yarn' in the Norwich worsted industry and 'bugging' in the hat industry, suggests that it was a routine aspect of working life in many industries. For comment linking the multiplicity of such terms to workers' support for such appropriation, see *Norwich Mercury*, 7 October 1752.
47 See J. Ditton, *Part Time Crime* (London 1977), Chapter 6.

just like their manipulation of truck and false weights. As short-term fluctuations occurred in the state of the labour market and the need to control costs, employers' responses to the appropriation of work materials could shift to and fro across a spectrum which extended from public recognition of such appropriation as a perquisite through tacit approval and passive hostility to active repression. Thus, in hard times, employers might treat appropriation of work materials with greater severity, even attempting to transform into 'embezzlement' types of appropriation that they had previously recognised as perquisites, as was the case in the Essex worsted industry in the depression of 1757 and its aftermath.[48] In good times, recognised perquisites might be extended and control generally relaxed, as occurred in the spinning branch of the Yorkshire worsted industry in the prosperous year of 1776.[49] Under this second set of circumstances, workers had good grounds to believe that even those forms of appropriation that were never publicly recognised as perquisites by their employers were in fact tacitly condoned by them. The experience of such tolerance towards the offence by their employers could provide workers with an additional justification for continuing to embezzle when faced with periodic crack-downs.

If employers' attitudes and responses to embezzlement fluctuated in this way, to analyse the relationship between industrial conditions, the incidence of embezzlement and the incidence of control becomes an extremely complex task. Any attempt to gauge changes in the incidence of 'embezzlement' is rendered problematic, because individual acts of appropriation were not necessarily regarded by their victims in the same light, or subject to the same response, under different conditions of industrial prosperity. Even if each instance of what was technically embezzlement is regarded as comparable across time, it is difficult to know whether there might be more such instances in booms, when control was relaxed, or in slumps, when workers were impoverished, perhaps resentful of employers' increased use of truck and associated practices, but subject to fiercer control. It is striking that contemporary commentators on the matter were able to argue either way.[50] Certainly there is no reason to believe that there was any direct relationship between the incidence of prosecutions and the incidence of individual acts of embezzlement, particularly as prosecution was only one of a number of disciplinary options, the relative attractions of which to employers varied with the state of the trade.

48 *Ipswich Journal*, 12 November 1757, and 23 November and 2 December 1758.
49 *Leeds Intelligencer*, 10 and 24 September 1776.
50 For the view that frauds increased in times of boom and high wages see [W. Temple], 'Remarks on the Essay on Riots', *Gentleman's Magazine*, 9 (1739), 234–5. For the view that frauds were associated with low wages see PRO, SP 12/244, fols. 222–9, State Papers, Elizabeth I, draft act for the amendment of spinners' and weavers' wages, etc. (1593), and Kirby, *Letter to a Member of Parliament*, p. 21.

To assess the significance in practice of inconsistencies of attitude among employers, it is necessary to examine the experience of specific industries. Because embezzlement was liable to prosecution and therefore usually conducted with some secrecy, evidence about it survives in any quantity only in the records of prosecutions. In order to interpret that evidence, it is first necessary to consider the changing character of the laws on which prosecutions were founded.

III

The word 'embezzlement' is today employed to describe the violation of a private financial trust. As the foregoing discussion has indicated, before the nineteenth century it usually meant the unauthorised appropriation of an employer's goods by his employee. The status at law of such appropriation, in so far as it was undertaken by outworkers, was, from the late Middle Ages until at least the end of the eighteenth century, fundamentally different from that of most theft. The unauthorised taking of goods from another's possession constituted larceny. It was a general rule of common law that larceny could not be committed by persons to whom possession of the goods in question had been legally transferred by their owner. This doctrine was subject both to changes of interpretation and to statutory amendment during the period under consideration, but the unauthorised appropriation of work materials by outworkers appears never to have come to be regarded at law as larceny, and was not, therefore, normally the occasion of a trial on indictment at Quarter Sessions or the Crown side of Assizes like most thefts. This was because a worker under the putting-out system came into possession of the materials with their owner's consent. The worker who appropriated work materials on his employer's premises was, however, liable to prosecution for larceny, for as long as the materials were on the premises, they remained notionally in the employer's possession.[51]

---

51 See J. Hall, *Theft, Law and Society* (Boston, Mass., 1935), pp. 3–7, although, curiously, Hall hardly mentions the offences under discussion here. The two principal modifications to the doctrine that larceny could not be committed by persons to whom possession of the goods in question had been transferred by their owner were *The Carrier's Case* (1473) and an act of 1529 (21 Hen. VIII, c. 7). Neither appears to have applied to embezzlement by putting-out workers. In *The Carrier's Case* it was determined that a carrier who converted *part* of the goods delivered to him in way of trade was guilty of larceny. 'Breaking bulk' was held to terminate the bailment and the subsequent appropriation constituted a taking. This doctrine does not appear to have applied to embezzlement by outworkers (at least before the end of the eighteenth century), because, while prosecutions under the summary embezzlement laws for taking *part* of the employer's materials were frequent, I have not come across any indictments for larceny in such cases. The 1529 act made it felony for servants to appropriate goods valued in excess of forty shillings, possession of which had been transferred to them by their master. Most individual acts of embezzlement by outworkers involved materials worth well under forty shillings. However, it is far from certain that outworkers were 'servants' within the terms of the act. Receivers of embezzled materials worth over forty shillings were often prosecuted under summary statutes, but do not appear to have been indicted as accessories in felony.

This is not to say, however, that the putting-out employer was without legal redress against the embezzling outworker. Throughout the period under consideration, he could bring an action for damages in the civil courts.[52] In addition, a succession of statutes, especially in the eighteenth century, enabled the case between an embezzling outworker and his employer to be submitted to the summary jurisdiction of one or more Justices of the Peace (see Appendix 3 for a list of the relevant statutes and the industries to which they applied). It is around the eighteenth-century statutes, which progressively embraced an ever-widening range of industries organised along putting-out lines (or turning to the putting-out system), that historians have focussed their discussion of embezzlement. They have been most interested in changes in legislation which increased the worker's liability if the case was found against him and in the apparent transformation of the legal status of embezzlement wrought by the act of 1749 (22 Geo. II, c. 27): for T. S. Ashton, 'what had previously been treated as a breach of contract was made a criminal offence'.[53] 'The earlier acts had retained the principle that the relation between worker and employer was purely contractual: the person working up the material should make good the losses suffered by the owner. The act of 1749 put the worker in the position of a criminal, by substituting for damages immediate imprisonment for fourteen days with hard labour and a public whipping.'[54] In the words of Edward Thompson, 'what was now to be punished was not an offence between men ... but an offence against property'.[55]

Some historians have interpreted this legislation and its apparent criminalisation of embezzlement as a response to increasing problems of control faced by employers in the putting-out industries as their markets and consequently the size of firms grew during the eighteenth century.[56] The legislation and its changing character are presented as the outcome of intense pressure on Parliament by manufacturing interests seeking a remedy for growing problems of industrial discipline.[57]

Others present the same legislative developments as part of a general attack on traditional and customary perquisites, designed to intensify the exploitation of labour and to rationalise costs of production. Thus, 'one of the main tasks of eighteenth-century capitalist development', involved 'the transformation of the wage from a form in which non-monetary payment constituted a substantial part of the wage to one based exclusively on a money payment'. The extension of the

---

52 See Wadsworth and Mann, *Cotton Trade*, p. 53 for an example of this sort of action.
53 T. S. Ashton, *An Economic History of England: The Eighteenth Century* (London, 1955), p. 210.
54 Wadsworth and Mann, *Cotton Trade*, p. 396.
55 Thompson, *Whigs and Hunters*, p. 207.
56 S. Pollard, *The Genesis of Modern Management* (London, 1968), pp. 42–6.
57 Wadsworth and Mann, *Cotton Trade*, p. 395.

criminal sanction was not restricted to embezzlement in the putting-out industries. It also involved the use of the law to redefine as crimes against property agrarian use rights and other practices which had previously been violations of trust or community obligation. Such developments were 'an integral aspect of the organisation and creation of a "free", mobile labour force'.[58] What is at issue here, therefore, is not a narrow response to specific industrial problems, but one element in a broad transformation of the wage relationship during the late seventeenth and eighteenth centuries, achieved by extending the scope of the criminal law. This was associated with a transformation during the same period in attitudes to property among the English ruling class. A new and peculiarly absolute conception of property reflected both the personal interests of the members of that ruling class and the general requirements of a developing capitalism. It was articulated through a distinctive legislative sensibility after the Glorious Revolution of 1689.[59]

Neither of these interpretations of the connection between developments in the putting-out industries and changes in the legal framework provides an adequate explanation of the content, chronology and implementation of embezzlement legislation. Their primary weakness is their emphasis on a decisive eighteenth-century criminalisation. It is doubtful whether to identify a shift in the legal status of the offence from a category 'contract' to a category 'crime', by reference to changes in the offender's liability on conviction, is consistent with the ambiguities of pre-nineteenth-century law. It is not altogether clear that the relationship between an outworker and his employer was in this or other respects a contractual one, although the word was sometimes used to describe it.[60] The word 'crime' was widely current during the eighteenth century, but it did not have a very precise meaning in law, especially where summary offences were concerned. In fact, since many of the pre-1749 acts subjected the offender to summary jurisdiction and automatic corporal or custodial punishment in case of failure to make restitution, they might be deemed to have rendered the offence 'criminal' already.

The chronology of changes also begs many questions. Many of the acts passed before 1749 already subjected the offender to an immediate, usually financial, penalty rather than to restitution.[61] Although the act of 1749 gave magistrates the

---

58 P. Linebaugh, summary of paper in *Bulletin of the Society for the Study of Labour History*, 25 (1972), p. 13.
59 Thompson, *Whigs and Hunters*, pp. 197, 206–7.
60 For example, in clause ten of 14 and 15 Car. II, c. 15 (1662) and in the Gloucestershire clothiers' petition of 1756 (see Minchinton, 'Petitions of the Weavers and Clothiers', p. 223).
61 The first such act was that of 1512 (3 Hen. VIII. c. 6), which rendered a convicted employee liable to automatic punishment in the pillory (if a man), or the cucking stool (if a woman). The act of 1703 (1 Anne St. 2, c. 18) required a convicted offender to forfeit a sum of money double the damages, and treated this as a fine to be paid into public funds. The act of 1740 (13 Geo II, c. 8) required half the double damages to go to the aggrieved party and half into public funds. The act

power to subject those convicted of embezzlement to an immediate custodial and corporal punishment, it did not remove previous provision for restitution, particularly in certain named industries.[62] Neither did it set in motion an irreversible trend towards punishment for all simple embezzlement offenders.[63] Moreover, after 1749, receivers remained liable to a financial forfeiture rather than to automatic punishment. The forfeiture, at a minimum of £20, was divided between the aggrieved party and the parish poor fund.

There was, therefore, never a once-and-for-all transition *at law* from restitution to punishment. However, it remains possible that there was a change in the implementation of the law. There might have been a criminalisation in the loose sense of a general shift in practice from financial forfeiture to physical punishment.

The 1749 act was generally applied in such a way as to subject convicted offenders to automatic punishment, but this does not necessarily imply there was a marked change from earlier practice. The earlier legislation had provided for payment of a forfeiture in the first instance, but for corporal and custodial punishment if the offender could not pay. If the vast majority of those convicted before 1749 were unable to pay, then the 1749 act would have made little practical difference. Unfortunately, the evidence to test this hypothesis is very difficult to find. It was only after 1750 that magistrates were required to return conviction certificates to the Quarter Sessions for filing. The appearance of newspaper reports of convictions after the same date can probably be accounted for by the general expansion of local news reporting in provincial newspapers after the War of the Austrian Succession. However, two seventeenth-century borough court books have survived which tell us something of convictions under the act of 1610 in the woollen textile industries at Colchester in Essex and Hadleigh in Suffolk.[64]

The Colchester book records seven people who were adjudged to have

---

of 1726 (13 Geo. I, c. 23) treated those gathering or receiving ends of yarn in the woollen manufacture as incorrigible rogues, liable to a whipping or confinement in the House of Correction.

62   Clause ten of the act stated explicitly that it did not repeal the silk acts of 1662, 1668 and 1697.

63   The 1774 wool act (24 Geo. III, c. 25) and the 1777 general act (17 Geo. III, c. 56) made custodial punishment mandatory for simple embezzlers in the industries concerned. However, the watch making industry act of 1754 (27 Geo. II, c. 7) provided for a financial forfeiture in the first instance, out of which satisfaction was to be made to the aggrieved party, and the false reeling act of 1774 (24 Geo. III, c. 44) provided for the payment of a small financial forfeiture to the aggrieved party. The worsted committee acts of 1777, 1784, 1785 and 1791 altered the destination of the financial forfeiture under the 1774 false reeling act as far as that industry was concerned in the counties where committees were established. The forfeiture was made payable into public funds.

64   Colchester Examination Book, *passim*; E. G. Beeton, 'Life in a Seventeenth-Century Weaving Town, as Illustrated by Hadleigh's Book of the Sessions of Peace, 1619–24', *The History Teacher's Miscellany* vol. 3, no. 10 (1925), pp. 162–5.

embezzled their employers' materials between 1667 and 1687. Five of these were unable to make satisfaction and were put in the stocks. Two were given a short time to pay, with the threat of a whipping if they failed. The outcome is not recorded. At Hadleigh both men adjudged to have embezzled materials between 1619 and 1624 received corporal punishment. The experience of receivers was very different. At Colchester over the same period only one out of six people adjudged to have received embezzled materials was deemed unable to make satisfaction, and she was a second (and notorious) offender. The one man adjudged a receiver at Hadleigh was put in the stocks.

What emerges in these seventeenth-century East Anglian textile towns, then, is that a large majority of those convicted of simple embezzlement were unable to make satisfaction and were subjected to corporal punishment, while a large majority of receivers exercised the option of a restitutive payment. If this is representative of the pattern of convictions elsewhere under pre-1749 legislation, the operation of the 1749 act did not bring about a drastic change in practice for the vast majority of those convicted of simple embezzlement. It merely took away the option of payment from that small minority of offenders (probably a very small minority after the 1703 act, which prescribed payment of double the damages) who were able to take advantage of it. That the 1610 act worked in this way is hardly surprising. Its express purpose was to provide punishment for that majority of offenders who could not make satisfaction. Its preamble commented that 'the parties who commit the offences aforesaid [are] poor, and altogether unable to make recompense for the trespasses, deceits and abuses aforesaid'. The distinction made explicit in the 1749 act between punishment of a custodial and corporal character for the convicted embezzler and a forfeit, with the threat of such punishment, for the convicted receiver merely codified a distinction which already existed in practice under the earlier laws and which itself reflected differences in the social background of the two types of offender.[65]

Even if the notion of a decisive eighteenth-century criminalisation of embezzlement must be rejected, it remains necessary to evaluate the changes that undoubtedly did occur in the content and scope of these laws. To do so is not a simple task. This body of legislation was not conceived as a systematic set of general regulations for industrial embezzlement (although by the end of the eighteenth century it covered most of the major putting-out industries). Rather it was the accumulated legacy of a multiplicity of local legislative initiatives, some

---

65 The 1749 act had originally been intended by its promoters to subject both embezzler and receiver to an automatic corporal and custodial punishment. However, during its passage through Parliament, the option of a forfeit was restored to receivers, because it was against normal legislative practice to subject people who might be of some substance to immediate corporal penalties. (British Library, Add. MS 35590, Hardwicke MS, fols 267–8, Horatio Walpole to Earl of Hardwicke, 25 March 1749).

of which were intended to amend or replace previous legislation, but many of which were not. A Scottish commentator in 1809, for whom these acts represented an unwarranted and typically confused English intrusion into Scottish law (after 1707 many of the acts were applied to Great Britain as a whole), remarked on 'their multiple differences in minute particulars, which do not appear to be governed by general rules... this part of the statute book wears such an aspect as if each particular enactment, like a private act, had been passed *periculo petentis*, without any sufficient examination of general principles or former enactments'.[66]

As this is undoubtedly an accurate assessment, it makes little sense to explore the relationship between changes in the content of these acts and problems of industrial discipline or economic rationalisation without an examination of the circumstances that produced each act and under which each act was applied. In section four some of the acts are examined in this way. Unfortunately the evidence regarding their provenance is, with a few exceptions, poor. It therefore remains useful to consider changes in the embezzlement laws in aggregate, if only to point out that considerable caution is necessary regarding the magnitude and significance of such changes. What may appear in isolation to be changes of major importance for the interpretations already discussed often lose their significance when viewed against the background of general developments in the law, in the process of legislating and in the putting-out industries themselves across the three centuries under discussion. For convenience, the major changes in the corpus of embezzlement legislation can be grouped into three broad categories – the offender's liability on conviction, provisions to facilitate detection and conviction, and the number of industries included within the scope of the legislation.

If the vast majority of those convicted of simple embezzlement under the earlier summary embezzlement acts were unable to pay the forfeiture, it was changes in the punishments prescribed by these as well as by the later acts that most affected this category of offender. The prescribed punishment underwent a distinct harshening. The three acts passed before the mid 1660s provided for public and corporal punishment (whipping, stocks, pillory, cucking stool) only.[67] After the mid 1660s a short period of imprisonment, usually in the House of Correction, was imposed in addition to a whipping. As the eighteenth century progressed, longer sentences were made available.

The available evidence suggests that this legislative shift towards harsher punishments was only partially reflected in the decisions of convicting magis-

---

66 G. Hutcheson, *Treatise on the Offices of Justice of Peace... in Scotland*, 2nd edn, 4 vols. (Edinburgh, 1809), II, 185–6.
67 However, an imprecise act of 1464 (4 Edw. IV, c. 1), which may have covered embezzlement in the woollen industry, did provide for imprisonment.

trates. At Colchester and Hadleigh the usual punishment for those convicted of simple embezzlement on the 1610 act was the stocks, though the act also made a public whipping available.[68] Under the acts passed after the mid 1660s the penalty normally applied became fourteen days' hard labour in the House of Correction along with a public whipping. The longer sentences made available in the eighteenth-century legislation were, however, not often used.

It would appear, therefore, that there was a harshening of punishments both at law and in practice during the second half of the seventeenth century. But it is unlikely that this was simply the outcome of a direct demand from the industries concerned for new kinds of punishment designed to confront intensified problems of control or to eliminate customary perquisites. Provision for short periods of incarceration in the House of Correction was an innovatory feature of many post-Restoration penal laws, not all of which were concerned either with industrial discipline, or with the customary perquisites of the poor (industrial or otherwise).[69] It is doubtful that such a general change in penalties can adequately be explained in terms of the experience of individual industries, or even as part of a broad attack on popular custom.

Other changes in the offender's liability on conviction, in particular those concerned with false reeling and receiving, did not mirror broad legislative developments. Yet they reveal no consistent tendency towards a harshening of penalties for embezzlement offenders. False reeling was, by the last quarter of the eighteenth century, the most prosecuted of all the embezzlement offences. Before 1774 it was treated like simple embezzlement, but in that year the offender's liability was reduced to a small financial forfeiture (as low as five shillings for the first offence), with physical punishment only in case of non-payment. Thereafter all but a few of those convicted avoided the corporal and custodial punishment which had previously been automatic and widely used. The penalties for receiving, in contrast, became, both in law and in practice, much harsher during the eighteenth century. The requirement after 1749 that receivers pay an enormous forfeiture of £20 or more, as opposed to their previous liability for a sum equivalent to damages or double damages, involved a massive increase in the sums they were usually required to pay. Nevertheless, the vast majority continued to be able to pay.[70]

The second major area of change was the inclusion in the acts of provisions

---

68   It is possible that offenders were imprisoned for the few days between conviction and their appearance in the stocks.

69   Thus 15 Car. II, c. 2 (1663) dealt with wood stealing, which might be interpreted as a customary perquisite of the poor, but 14 Car. II, c. 1 (1662) dealt with Quakers. To what extent the whole history of the Houses of Correction should be interpreted as a project of intensified discipline for the poor is a much broader issue, which cannot be resolved here.

70   These conclusions are based on the evidence from late-seventeenth-century Colchester and late-eighteenth-century Norwich and Yorkshire.

designed to overcome problems of detection and conviction. Working practices which facilitated embezzlement were one area of concern here. The 1749 and 1777 acts obliged workers to return waste materials on pain of being punished as embezzlers, first within twenty-one days, then within eight. A common perquisite could thus be redefined as an offence. Yet the only real difference made by these two acts was to specify a time limit within which waste should be returned, for the embezzlement acts from 1515 onwards had allowed prosecution for detaining waste. Other eighteenth-century acts (1722, 1749 and the 1777 general act) provided for prosecution of workers who took work from one master before completing work for another. But this only reiterated the terms of the Statute of Artificers of 1563, which may already have applied to a number of the industries concerned.

Another obstacle to detection was the difficulty of identifying embezzled materials. The 1749 act, the 1774 wool act and the 1777 general act created a range of catch-all offences out of mere possession of suspicious materials. The burden of proof was placed on the accused, reversing the normal relationship between prosecutor and defendant in later-eighteenth-century English law. Yet this type of innovation was, once again, not confined to the embezzlement laws.[71] Moreover, it is unlikely that unexplained possession provisions of this kind brought about major changes in practice. It appears probable that they simply provided statutory authority for long-established practice – statutory authority that became necessary only because of the increasingly scrupulous legal climate of the later eighteenth century.[72] Previously a loose interpretation of Elizabethan and Jacobean legislation regulating Houses of Correction was widely used by magistrates to subject those merely suspected of petty offences to short periods of confinement. At Norwich in 1704 it was possible to be confined in Bridewell as 'a wicked, lewd person justly suspected of filching and stealing'.[73] As the eighteenth century progressed, such procedures became unacceptable.

The other measure taken to facilitate detection and conviction was the

71 Examples of non-embezzlement acts incorporating similar provisions are the 1742 act concerned with cloth stolen from tenters (15 Geo. II, c. 26), the 1757 act concerned with various metals (29 Geo. II. c. 30) and the 1766 act concerned with underwood (6 Geo. III, c. 48).

72 A shift towards greater punctiliousness among those who administered the judicial system with regard to statutory justification for their powers was evident across the legal spectrum, from summary jurisdiction to the Assize courts. John Langbein has argued persuasively that at the Assizes and their equivalents the appearance of defence lawyers in criminal cases during the 1730s and 1740s led to a challenge to established legal practices and stimulated the development of the law of evidence: see J. H. Langbein, 'The Criminal Trial Before the Lawyers', *The University of Chicago Law Review*, vol. 45, no. 2 (1978), pp. 263–316. Whether lawyers were as important in bringing about changes in the exercise of summary jurisdiction is not clear. For my remarks on summary imprisonment I am indebted to the unpublished work of Joanna Innes.

73 Norwich and Norfolk Record Office; Norwich City Records, 12 d (1), Calendars of Prisoners, 1703–1749; Bridewell Calendar for 15 January 1704.

introduction of an industrial police force to detect and prosecute false reeling in the worsted industry. Between 1777 and 1791 four committees of worsted manufacturers were established by statute to supervise and pay inspectors of worsted yarn in twelve countries. These inspectors had power of entry into the premises of putting-out agents in order to check the yarn.[74] Though there were precedents for industrial inspectorates,[75] the establishment by statute of a salaried inspectorate of this sort, paid via public funds out of what amounted to a compulsory subscription on manufacturers and licensed by Quarter Sessions, was a genuine innovation. It brought about an enormous leap in the number of convictions in many of the counties concerned. In Cheshire, where records of convictions are good, there were only eight convictions recorded for false reeling of worsted yarn between 1770 and 1774, but for the five years between 1778 and 1782, when a statutory inspector was operating, there was an *annual* average of fifty-six.[76] Hence the reduction in the severity of penalties for false reeling in 1774 was balanced, in the one industry where false reeling continued to be a major problem, by a vastly more efficient system for detection and prosecution.

The third set of changes in the embezzlement laws comprised the extension of this legislation to a growing number of industries. This was predominantly a phenomenon of the late seventeenth and eighteenth centuries, when a spate of new acts progressively incorporated virtually all the major putting-out industries (see Appendix 3). However, it would be wrong to interpret this legislative chronology as the product of a *general* increase in problems of labour discipline, or in employers' efforts to intensify discipline, that was confined to the later part of the period 1500 to 1800. Most of the industries named for the first time in the later Acts turned to the putting-out system on any scale only during the seventeenth or the early eighteenth century (for example, hatting, silk and cotton). The late date of the acts which extended summary process to these industries broadly reflects this fact. The woollen textile industries, some of which had been organised along putting-out lines since the fifteenth century, were incorporated within such legislation much earlier (as early as 1464, if 4 Edw. IV, c. 1 encompassed embezzlement, as is likely).

The increase in the number of embezzlement acts after 1689 must also be

---

74 The 1777 general embezzlement act gave all employers powers to enter their workpeople's premises to inspect their property.

75 For example, the inspectors employed by non-statutory committees of manufacturers to detect embezzlers, the statutory inspectors employed in the woollen cloth industry to regulate quality standards, and the searchers employed by guilds and industrial corporations in the sixteenth and seventeenth centuries.

76 Cheshire Record Office, Chester, Cheshire Quarter Sessions Files, 1770 to 1783, House of Correction Calendars and conviction certificates; Manchester Central Library Archives Department, MS 338.4 W 1, 'An account of frauds and offences committed by the spinners and others employed in the worsted manufactory'. The reduction of penalties under the 1774 false reeling act also appears to have facilitated more precautions.

understood as part of a general proliferation of legislation after the Glorious Revolution, when the availability of Parliament for legislative initiatives was dramatically enhanced. The new pattern of annual Parliamentary sittings, with progressively longer sessions, made legislation a more accessible and predictable process, especially for those distant from the capital. This removed obstacles to legislation like that faced by East Anglian worsted manufacturers in 1621, when they attempted to obtain an act against embezzlement and false reeling. It was 'well approved of by the whole House of Parliament, yet by reason of the sudden dissolution of the said session, nothing was done therein'.[77] Parliament met during only four of the subsequent eighteen years and provisions of the kind the manufacturers sought were not enacted until 1703.

The increased availability of Parliament after 1689 coincided with the decline of practices and institutions which may have provided alternatives to summary embezzlement legislation. It has already been pointed out that there was, in some respects, a less scrupulous attitude towards statutory authorisation for the exercise of legal authority before the early eighteenth century. It is probable that, during this earlier period, simple embezzlers were dealt with in some localities by summary committal to the House of Correction.[78] Such cases may also have been prosecuted sporadically on indictment at Quarter Sessions, either as petty larceny or as some kind of common law cheat.[79]

Before the early eighteenth century, the ordinances of various municipal companies and industrial corporations also offered employers powers for controlling embezzlement. Ordinances against embezzlement were common wherever a putting-out form of organisation was found within a corporate setting, though these ordinances were far from uniform. However, it remains doubtful whether such ordinances represented a genuine alternative to summary embezzlement legislation. Only very rarely did they include the threat of corporal or custodial punishment.[80] At Colchester in the late seventeenth century there were repeated prosecutions on the 1610 embezzlement statute despite the existence of the very active Dutch Bay Hall Corporation. At any rate, the

77 PRO, SP 14/140, fol. 82, State Papers James I, 1622, petition of worsted makers, etc. in Norfolk, Suffolk and Essex to the Commissioners for Trade, n.d. [1622–3].
78 At Norwich in 1704 a man was committed to a period of confinement in Bridewell for being 'a loose and disorderly person who embezzled and sold another person's goods': Norwich and Norfolk Record Office; Norwich City Records, 12 d (1), Calendars of Prisoners, 1703–1749, Bridewell Calendar for 29 April 1704.
79 See, for example, F. G. Emmison, *Elizabethan Life: Disorder* (Chelmsford, 1970), p. 298.
80 Physical punishment for embezzlement does appear to be implied by the Coventry municipal order for the true making of cloth of 1518, but was not included in the London Weavers' Company ordinances of 1492, the Bristol Weavers' Company ordinances of 1602, or the regulations of the Bury St Edmunds Corporation of Clothiers of 1609: see M. D. Harris, *The Coventry Leet Book* (London, 1909), II, 658; F. Consit, *The London Weavers' Company* (Oxford, 1932), pp. 294–5; Bristol Record Office, Weavers' Company ordinances of 1602; Suffolk Record Office, Bury, D 9/1/b, Copy of regulations for the Corporation of Clothiers, etc.

significance of such regulations faded with the decline of municipal companies and industrial corporations during the early eighteenth century.

Employers were, then, increasingly obliged to resort to Parliament. Yet though Parliament became more accessible after 1689, the manufacturers could not use it just as they pleased.

The embezzlement statutes of the late seventeenth and eighteenth centuries had local origins and grew in a piecemeal fashion. Though all were public acts, several were so narrowly conceived that they employed technical vocabulary from local industries that was unknown outside the industry concerned.[81] Many incorporated a wide range of industries, because they amended existing statutes and because additional industries included themselves as the bills progressed through Parliament. Embezzlement provisions were often combined with other regulations for an industry, in particular penalties against workers' combination and truck. Most of the more significant later-eighteenth-century acts (the general acts of 1749 and 1777, the 1774 false reeling act and the 1791 manufacturers' committee act) appear to have originated in one city – Norwich – where employers in the staple worsted industry were well organised, dominated the city corporation and were served by a succession of influential MPs, like Horatio Walpole and Edward Bacon, who were extremely solicitous towards their interests.[82]

Many legislative initiatives failed before they reached Parliament,[83] and there was no certainty about the passage of a bill once legislation had been embarked upon. The bill would usually be committed to the care of an MP from the locality of the industry concerned, but even the best-connected member could not guarantee enactment. As Horatio Walpole MP commented to the Lord Chancellor when managing the 1749 act through the House of Commons, 'care should be taken while endeavours are used to make it effectual, to make it so unexceptional as not to hazard the passing of it'.[84] Both the 1749 and 1777 general acts were amended during their passage through Parliament in such a way as to alter the original objectives of those who framed the bills and, in some

81 For example, the wool act of 1774, which was promoted by employers in the West Country woollen cloth industry, used words like 'chain' and 'abb' that were unknown in the Yorkshire branch of that industry, to which it also notionally applied.

82 This interpretation of the provenance of the statutes listed is based on the identity of the MPs who managed the bills through Parliament, as indicated by the *Commons Journals*, supplemented by BL, Add. MS 35590, Hardwicke MS, fols. 267–8, Horatio Walpole to Earl of Hardwicke 25 March 1749; and PRO, KB 1/20 part 1, King's Bench Affidavits, Easter 17 Geo. III, part 1, no. 1, *Rex* v. *Thompson*, affidavit of N. Thompson. For the MPs' close relations with the manufacturers, see *Norwich Mercury*, 12 March 1768 and 18 April 1772.

83 For example, the proposal to secure a statutory worsted committee for Essex in 1784 (see *Chelmsford Chronicle*, 16 January 1784: I am grateful to Peter King for supplying this reference).

84 Walpole to Hardwicke, 25 March 1749.

respects, to render them less severe.[85] Embezzlement proposals were known to fizzle out in Parliament.[86] At least one bill was lost on a division.[87]

The absence of substantial evidence about the drawing up of embezzlement bills and their history in Parliament makes it impossible to undertake an exhaustive analysis of the constraints on the content and progress of such legislation. It is clear that, to succeed, these bills had to conform to general legislative conventions (as we have seen, the content of successful bills often reflected broad shifts in legislative practice). They also had to accommodate the sometimes antagonistic interests and prejudices of other groups of manufacturers and of local gentry.[88] Nor were what were perceived as the interests of the labouring poor wholly ignored. During the early eighteenth century especially, Parliament appears to have regarded anti-embezzlement and anti-truck provisions as balancing one another, the latter representing a response to the grievances of workpeople.[89] Indeed, in 1711, it was not the anti-embezzlement clauses of the expired 1703 act that secured its revival, but the desire of West Midlands gentry to have its anti-truck provisions reinstated, in order to meet the riotous complaints of the labouring poor in the Black Country.[90]

All this is not to suggest that Parliament was neutral, let alone hostile, towards the wishes of manufacturers. Parliament and successive administrations had long been concerned to further what were perceived to be the interests of industry in general and of the woollen textile industry in particular, though there was no unanimity over methods. By comparison with their workpeople, manufacturers enjoyed privileged access to the legislature through MPs for industrial towns and counties, who were usually extremely anxious to accommodate their wishes. Even when opposed in Parliament by powerful competing interests, manufacturers were often triumphant, as, for example, in their repeated contests with agricultural interests over the export of wool during the eighteenth century. There was no such powerful body of sustained Parliamentary opposition to the manufacturers' embezzlement legislation. However, Parliamentary support for the interests of manufacturers in this and other fields was not unqualified. Groups of manufacturers could and did use their undoubted access to Parliament to further their particular collective interests in this area, but the outcome was never a foregone conclusion.

85 See, for example, note 65.
86 For example, the proposed bill of 1785 for preventing frauds in the linen manufacture in Yorkshire and County Durham: see *C. J.*, 40 (1784–5), 553.
87 The bill of 1702 for the more effectual prevention of frauds in the woollen, linen and cotton manufactures: see *C. J.*, 13 (1700–2), 737, 752 and 781.
88 Most of these considerations had some bearing on the passage of the 1749 act: see Walpole to Hardwicke, 25 March 1749 and Guildhall Library, Manuscripts, MS 4655/12, London Weavers' Company, Court Book, 1737–50, fols. 317–19 and 327.
89 As suggested by the report of the 1702 committee on the Taunton serge weavers' petition: *C.J.*, 14 (1702–5), 67–8.
90 *C. J.*, 16 (1708–11), 519.

IV

In evaluating the industrial and legal dimensions of embezzlement, two perspectives on the connections between control of the offence and the histories of the putting-out industries have been presented. The first concerned the relationship between fluctuations in employers' propensity to control embezzlement and short-term changes in the fortunes of an industry; the second the relationship between changes in the content and enforcement of the legislation and long-term intensification of either problems of control or pressures for the elimination of perquisites. It is the purpose of this final section to provide an assessment of these perspectives by examining the enactment and enforcement of the émbezzlement laws in relation to the circumstances of the industries concerned.

Unfortunately evidence about variations in both the fortunes of the pre-nineteenth-century putting-out industries and the incidence of embezzlement control is sparse. Moreover, the evidence that does survive regarding variations in control is almost entirely confined to the use of the law. Legal remedies represented merely one set of alternatives, usually alternatives of last resort, among a number of control options. Employers could subject workers believed to have embezzled to wage abatements or informal fines. They could also dismiss them. Although the existence of these informal controls is well documented, there is little direct evidence about variations in their incidence. Nevertheless, in assessing the evidence regarding changes in the use of the law, it is always necessary to consider the changing relative attraction for employers of informal controls (or, indeed, of no controls) as compared with legal remedies.

The available evidence regarding the use of the law is itself limited. Statistical series are available only for those convictions under the summary statutes which were certified to Quarter Sessions or reported in the press. Neither certificates nor press reports – least of all the latter – can be regarded as wholly reliable guides to the number of convictions.[91] Although summary process was widely believed to facilitate convictions, by no means every prosecution ended in a conviction. Sometimes they were not intended to, an appearance before a magistrate representing an attempt by the employer to secure arbitration under duress rather than a deliberate act of prosecution.[92] Details of those legislative

---

91 Not only has the survival of summary conviction certificates in Quarter Sessions records been very sporadic (see P. B. Manche, 'The Game Laws in Wiltshire', in J. S. Cockburn [ed.], *Crime in England, 1550–1800* [London, 1977], pp. 224–5), but there were also complaints of failure on the part of magistrates to return them to sessions in the first place (see Bradford University Archives, WC/1/ii, Yorkshire, Lancashire and Cheshire Worsted Committee, Minute Book, 1786–1804, meeting of 20 June 1791). For press reporting see Apendix 1.

92 For a discharge on an embezzlement prosecution see Corporation of London Record Office, 204 B, Guildhall Justice Room Minutes, September and October 1781, entries for 22, 23 and 24 October. For an agreement before a magistrate see Corporation of London Record Office, 236 D, Mansion House Justice Room, Charge Book, 1728–33, entry for 4 February 1731.

initiatives that reached the statute book are, of course, available, although it is often difficult to determine their provenance. However, most of those that were never enacted are probably not recorded, irrespective of the reasons for their failure.

In order to come to terms with the manifold shortcomings of the available evidence this section offers a broad survey of the evidence regarding prosecution and legislation for a variety of industries. Its objective is to demonstrate that the range of observed relationships between the use of legal controls and industrial conditions was such that the adequacy of a number of the interpretations already discussed is called into question.

Most historical studies of criminal statistics have treated them as guides to fluctuations in the incidence of criminal behaviour. This study, by contrast, uses such statistics primarily as indices of changes in the propensity of employers to act against embezzlement. As Eric Monkkonen has pointed out, there is a powerful case for approaching any official records of offences as, *in the first instance*, records of changes in policing, rather than as records of changes in criminal behaviour.[93] There are particularly strong grounds for such an approach in the case of embezzlement. Although there was no unanimity among contemporaries about the manner in which the incidence of the offence fluctuated, they were generally of the opinion that it was endemic. Yet there are good reasons for believing that employers' responses to it were not consistent, the available serial conviction statistics suggesting an extremely erratic pattern of prosecution.

At Norwich between 1750 and 1779 half the reported convictions (62 out of 124) took place in three years, while ten of the thirty years saw no reported convictions (see Figure 8).[94] The overall pattern is one of several years of few or no convictions, interspersed with occasional years of intense activity. Even though the statistics are for convictions rather than for prosecutions, it is improbable that this pattern can be accounted for merely by shifts in the propensity of magistrates to convict. The fact that at Norwich the periods that saw large numbers of convictions were often those when the manufacturers advertised their determination to prosecute suggests that this pattern of convictions reflects a history of intense but intermittent campaigns to apply the law against embezzlers and receivers. There are strong indications that a similar pattern, or one of even more sporadic prosecution, was characteristic of the use of the summary embezzlement laws in other putting-out industries in the late seventeenth and eighteenth centuries. The major exception was false reeling prosecution in the late-eighteenth-century worsted industries. Here the establish-

---

93   E. H. Monkkonen, *Police in Urban America, 1860–1920* (Cambridge, 1981), pp. 22–3.
94   See Appendix 1.

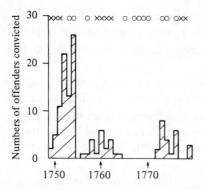

Key

⊞   Annual totals of those reported to have been convicted for embezzling and receiving work materials

× Relatively prosperous years

○ Relatively depressed years

Sources: convictions, see Appendix 1; industrial conditions, see note 96

Figure 8   Fluctuations in industrial prosperity and convictions for embezzlement and receiving in the city of Norwich worsted industry 1749–79

ment of statutory inspectorates resulted in sustained and systematic prosecution. Nevertheless, the most reliable available series of convictions for this offence reveals a pattern of fluctuations that primarily reflects changes in the character of policing, in this instance differences in effectiveness between inspectors.[95]

Precisely what occasioned employers' campaigns in those industries characterised by intermittent waves of prosecutions for embezzlement and receiving is more obscure. The available evidence (although in several respects deficient) suggests no consistent link between periods of intense prosecution and particular short-term fluctuations in industrial conditions. The Norwich worsted industry saw peaks in convictions during both good years, such as those around 1760, and bad years, such as 1773–4.[96] In the same way, there was no one set of industrial conditions that precipitated recourse to legislation. Acts providing for more severe penalties or enhanced facilities for detection were secured both during prosperous periods for the industries concerned (for example the 1777 worsted committee act for Yorkshire, Lancashire and Cheshire) and during difficult periods (for example the 1774 wool act, which emanated from Gloucestershire).

In order to understand the observed diversity of relationships between the pattern of convictions or legislation and fluctuations in industrial prosperity, it is necessary to bear in mind that employers' attitudes to these offences were not

95   Manchester Central Library Archives Department, MS 338.4 W 1, 'An account of frauds and offences committed by the spinners and others employed in the worsted manufactory'. This document is the inspectors' register book of convictions made and penalties paid in the South Lancashire and Cheshire district established by the Yorkshire, Lancashire and Cheshire Worsted Committee.

96   Information on the fortunes of the Norwich worsted industry during the second half of the eighteenth century is drawn from the *Norwich Mercury, passim*; J. K. Edwards, 'The Economic Development of Norwich 1750–1850', unpublished Ph.D. thesis (University of Leeds, 1963); P. J. Corfield, 'The Social and Economic History of Norwich, 1650–1850' unpublished Ph.D. thesis (University of London, 1976).

necessarily consistent and that the law was merely the control option of last resort. It has already been suggested that employers had strong reasons to attack embezzlement during periods of poor trade, when they were under extreme pressure to cut costs. Such periods were ones of unemployment and intermittent work, when informal controls over embezzlement, such as dismissals or wage abatements, were at their most effective. The employers' need to use the law to exercise control was therefore relatively slight. When the law was used to reinforce informal controls during such periods, it is likely that this was usually precipitated by special circumstances – for example the fierce, sustained resistance to all controls at Norwich during the depression between 1752 and 1754, and the existence of a particularly affluent and well-organised receiving network in the same city in the depressed year of 1776. In cases of this sort, the precise timing of prosecution or legislation depended on the circumstances which occasioned legal reinforcement, rather than on the timing of the trade depression itself.

During periods of industrial prosperity, when labour markets were tight, employers were often more tolerant of embezzlement. In 1776, a prosperous year, Yorkshire worsted manufacturers did not dare prosecute false reelers 'for fear of becoming unpopular among the spinners and losing their work', a justified fear in an industry with a 'great number of ... master manufacturers and the rivalship consequential thereon'.[97] The offence was believed to have become more widespread as a result. If employers could act in concert at such times, rigorous control of embezzlement offered a means of containing the costs of such depredations. Informal controls were weakened when labour markets were tight, so any attack on embezzlement had to be principally by means of the law. Whether or not prosecutions were undertaken during periods of industrial prosperity was therefore highly dependent on the degree of employer solidarity, which was itself strongly influenced by the structure of an industry. Indeed, in Yorkshire in 1776 the only way for concerned employers to enforce action against false reeling was to promote the worsted committee act of the subsequent year, which in effect forced solidarity on recalcitrant manufacturers.

Thus, although short-term fluctuations in industrial prosperity did have an influence on the use of the law, there was no single, direct connection between the two. Moreover, there were always instances where a spate of prosecutions bore no relationship, direct or indirect, to industrial conditions. For example, a small burst of prosecution at Coventry in 1764 was a spin-off from a magistrate's other activities.[98]

---

97 *Leeds Intelligencer*, 24 September and 26 November 1776.
98 John Hewitt, *Proceedings on the Silk Act from the Year 1756 to the Present Year 1791* (Birmingham, 1791), pp. 5–359 (pagination jumps).

If we turn from short-term to long-term changes in the use of the law, there are considerable evidential obstacles to a satisfactory evaluation of those interpretations of long-term changes in recourse to the law which emphasise a general eighteenth-century intensification in its use. There is little doubt that the second half of the eighteenth century saw a huge growth in the numbers of prosecutions for false reeling in the worsted industries of the north of England and East Anglia, relative to the numbers employed. Yet the admittedly limited evidence for the late-seventeenth-century Colchester worsted industry indicates a level of prosecution for embezzlement and receiving that may have been as high, relative to the town's population, as the equivalent level in the Norwich worsted industry during long periods in the late eighteenth century.[99] Unfortunately, the general paucity of evidence for the period before 1750 makes it unclear for most industries whether the embezzlement laws were used at all before the second half of the eighteenth century, let alone how intensively.

In so far as the use of the law in the later eighteenth century was more intense, there remain considerable doubts as to whether this can adequately be explained simply in terms either of growing pressures for the elimination of perquisites or of growing problems of industrial discipline. There is no doubt that several industries saw campaigns by employers to use the embezzlement laws to eliminate established and recognised perquisities. Yet it would be wrong to imagine that such attacks always brought about a once-and-for-all transformation of this component of a worker's income, or were intended to do so. In the Yorkshire worsted industry, for example, groups of manufacturers advertised penalties for the retention of waste by weavers in 1764, 1765, 1770, 1812 and 1819, but in 1837 many manufacturers were still 'in the habit of purchasing from their weavers worsted thrums or waste, the property of the said manufacturers'.[100] Irrespective of their short-term successes, such efforts were not sustained and clearly failed in the long run fundamentally to alter the pattern of perquisites in the industry. Indeed, most *employers* appear to have been decidedly unwilling to eradicate perquisites permanently, despite the insistence by some modern historians that this was one of the 'main tasks' of capitalist

99 Based on recorded convictions during the years 1667–87 at Colchester and the years 1759–79 at Norwich. Sources. for Colchester, Colchester Examination Book, *passim*; for Norwich, see Appendix 1. For population figures see C. W. Chalklin, *The Provincial Towns of Georgian England* (London, 1974), pp. 14 and 33. Both the Colchester and the Norwich sources for convictions probably record only a proportion of cases. Nevertheless, these findings remain strongly suggestive.

100 *Leeds Intelligencer*, 16 April 1765; *Leeds Mercury*, 31 July 1770; Bradford University Archives, WC/1/iii, Worsted Committee, Minute Book, 1804–40, entries for 23 March 1812, 5 April 1819 and 19 June 1837.

development.[101] Intermittent campaigns did not necessarily represent a project of long-term redefinition.

Nor is it at all clear that there was a consistent relationship between expansion in the industries concerned, resulting in greater problems of supervision, and an intensified recourse to the law. Admittedly an industry's initial adoption of summary procedure was usually associated with its transition to or early growth under the putting-out mode. Yet the later-eighteenth-century evidence suggests that thereafter increased recourse to the law was as likely to accompany long-term phases of stagnation or decline as phases of expansion.[102]

This study has repeatedly emphasised the complexity and ambiguities of the history of embezzlement in the putting-out industries. It has not, however, been its intention to deny changes in the embezzlement laws, in their implementation, or in attitudes to the offence. Rather it has set out to demonstrate that, before wide-ranging interpretations of these changes can be mounted, it is essential to specify the precise character and extent of change in context. Simply to interpret any spurt of prosecution or any ostensibly more severe piece of legislation as a manifestation of some long-term intensification of 'capitalist' disciplines within these industries is to do a gross injustice to the complexities of both legal and industrial history. This study has drawn attention to those complexities by means of a general survey. Future work on the subject must explore the same issues in the setting of particular industries and particular industrial regions.

101 Bradford University Archives, WC/1/iii, Worsted Committee, Minute Book, 1804–40, entry for 23 March 1812.
102 Thus the prosecution of false reeling intensified in the late eighteenth century both in Yorkshire, where worsted spinning was expanding, and in East Anglia and the East Midlands, where it was stagnant or in decline.

Appendix 1: Norwich embezzlement convictions in the eighteenth century: problems of evidence

Magistrates making convictions under the post-1749 embezzlement Acts were required to return certificates of conviction to Quarter Sessions for filing. Unfortunately the survival of Quarter Sessions files for the city of Norwich for the second half of the eighteenth century is incomplete. So is the survival of certificates within those files which do still exist. Some records of convictions were entered in the Norwich City Quarter Sessions Minute Books, but these too are deficient. By far the most complete available record of convictions for the city is provided by the continuous run of the *Norwich Mercury*, which regularly reported convictions in its local news column. All the data on Norwich convictions used in this essay are from the *Norwich Mercury*.

Although the manufacturers who undertook prosecutions tried to publicise convictions systematically in the press, especially during prosecution campaigns, some convictions were not reported. In order to use those convictions reported in the newspaper as a guide to the character and incidence of all convictions it is therefore necessary to establish by precisely how much they are deficient. It is possible to establish an approximate figure for this deficiency by comparing the convictions reported in the newspaper with those available from the city Quarter Sessions records. Between 1750 and 1779, 134 convictions for embezzlement and receiving were recorded in the *Norwich Mercury* and 76 in the Quarter Sessions records. Of that 76, 16% were not reported in the newspaper.

Assuming that this figure is indicative of the overall deficiency in the newspaper reporting of convictions, it does not pose a major obstacle to the use of the newspaper reports in aggregate as a guide to the character of convictions. However, more caution is necessary with regard to their use as a measure of fluctuations in the incidence of convictions. The reliability of reporting itself fluctuated, and appears to have been proportionately worse in non-campaign years, when the total numbers of convictions were probably small. It would therefore be wrong to assume that the newspaper figures can provide an accurate guide to year-by-year fluctuations in the numbers of convictions, though they do provide a broadly accurate indication of those periods that saw heavy convictions and those that saw few or none.

Sources: Norwich and Norfolk Record Office, Norwich City Records, 12. b. 117–31, 147–9, Norwich Quarter Sessions Files, 1749–79; 20. b. 21–23, Norwich Quarter Sessions Minute Books, 1732–86; *Norwich Mercury, passim*.

Appendix 2: Estimates of the size of the supplement to wages available through embezzlement in two eighteenth-century industries

The following computations are intended to provide no more than an indication of the supplement to wages (expressed as a percentage of money wages) that appears to have been available without much risk of detection in the Gloucestershire woollen industry and the Yorkshire worsted industry in the mid 1770s. The estimates are based on a conservative interpretation of the opinions of interested parties, and may considerably misrepresent the actual degree of appropriation undertaken by many workpeople. It should also be born in mind that money wages, especially for spinners, could fluctuate considerably from year to year and that they might also be subject to deductions (although the Yorkshire wage rate used here appears to be fairly accurate for the year concerned).

The Gloucestershire clothiers claimed in 1774 that a spinner of weft could embezzle one pound of yarn in twelve without fear of detection. A pound of weft was worth from 4s 6d to 5s 0d. From each pound of yarn the spinner could therefore appropriate materials worth (depending on whether or not they were worked) 4d to 5d on the legitimate market. Spinning piece-rates fluctuated considerably in the Gloucestershire woollen industry in the late eighteenth century and varied according to the type of yarn. However, even taking 11d per pound, a high rate for weft spinning, the spinner could supplement her earnings by over 20%, if it is assumed that embezzled materials generally fetched about half their market value. At a more realistic 9d per pound the supplement would amount to over 25% of her wages.

The Gloucestershire clothier also claimed that a weaver could embezzle five pounds of yarn (almost certainly weft) worth about 24 shillings at open market prices, out of a cloth weighing 60 pounds and 45 yards in length. Weaving rates in the Gloucestershire industry are not well documented for the later eighteenth century, but, even assuming a very high rate of 1s 4d per yard, the payment for such a cloth would have been 60 shillings. This represents the weaver's gross earnings, out of which he would have had to provide for expenses, in particular the second worker at the loom, who might be a journeyman, an apprentice, or a member of his family. Assuming that the embezzled yarn fetched half its market value, it represented a 20% supplement to these gross earnings, and considerably more to the weaver's net earnings.

In the Yorkshire worsted industry a 1776 commentator and the records of the post-1777 prosecutions suggest that yarn was reeled short by about 6.5% on average. One pound of yarn of 24 hanks to the pound quality was worth about 26d during the year concerned.

Assuming that the deficiency in length was entirely the result of embezzlement, the yarn so embezzled would be worth approximately 1s 7d on the legitimate market. During 1776 a spinner received 14d for spinning one pound of yarn. If the embezzled yarn sold at half its market value, the spinner could supplement her earnings by 0.84d, or 6%.

Sources: Gloucestershire: *C. J.*, 34 (1772–4), 451; Mann, *Cloth Industry*, pp. 316–24. Yorkshire: *Leeds Intelligencer*, 12 March 1776; West Yorkshire Record Office, QE 15/1–13, Memoranda of summary convictions, 1778–81, and QSF, Quarter Sessions Files, 1776–81, convictions before Joshua Horton, JP; James, *Worsted Manufacture*, pp. 280–1, 290.

Appendix 3: Statutes concerned with embezzlement in the putting-out industries, 1500–1800

Act	Date	Commodities/industries	Particular restricting provisions
3 Hen. VIII, c. 6	1512 (expired 1515)	woollen cloth manufacture	
7 Jac. I, c. 7	1610	manufacture of cloths and stuffs made of wool	
13 and 14 Car. II, c. 15	1662	silk throwing	
20 Car. II, c. 6	1668	silk throwing	
8 and 9 Wm. III, c. 36	1697	silk manufacture	
1 Anne, St. 2, c. 18	1703 (expired 1707, made perpetual 1711 by 9 Anne, c. 30)	woollen, linen, fustian cotton and iron manufactures	
9 Geo. 1, c. 27	1722	materials used in shoe making	restricted to the bills of mortality
13 Geo. I, c. 23	1726	woollen manufacture	concerned with gathering and receiving ends and waste only
13 Geo. II, c. 8	1740	as in 1 Anne St. 2, c. 18, plus leather manufactures	
22 Geo. II, c. 27	1749 (amended in 1750 with regard to certification by 23 Geo. II, c. 13)	as in 13 Geo. II, c. 8, plus hat, fur, mohair and silk manufactures	
27 Geo. II, c. 7	1754	clock and watch manufactures	

Appendix 3 *(cont.)*

Act	Date	Commodities/industries	Particular restricting provisions
24 Geo. III, c. 25	1774	woollen cloth manufacture as in 22 Geo. II, c. 27	
24 Geo. III, c. 44	1774 (amended in 1775 with regard to levying penalties and appeals by 25 Geo. III, c. 14)		concerned with false and short reeling only
17 Geo. III, c. 11	1777	worsted manufacture in Yorkshire, Lancashire and Cheshire as in 22 Geo. II, c. 27	manufacturers' committee
17 Geo. III, c. 56	1777	worsted manufacture in Suffolk	manufacturers' committee
24 Geo. III, St. 2, c. 3	1784	worsted manufacture in Bedford shire, Huntingdonshire, Northamptonshire, Leicestershire, Rutland, Lincolnshire and the Isle of Ely.	manufacturers' committee
25 Geo. III, c. 40	1785		
31 Geo. III, c. 56	1791	worsted manufacture in Norfolk and Norwich	manufacturers' committee
32 Geo. III, c. 44	1792	silk manufacture	concerned with receiving and selling only.

Except where specific limitations are indicated, all the acts listed are concerned with the general terms of summary jurisdiction over embezzlement by workpeople in the industries mentioned. Many also include provisions regarding receiving, unexplained possession, etc., and the scope of several extends far beyond embezzlement and associated matters.

Index